Anyone who thinks apologetics is no longer important doesn't know the world students live in and the questions they ask—and are being asked. But Jonathan Morrow knows students. He knows what they need to know, and that's why this book is so helpful. In it, you will find clear, concise answers that Christians need when the truthfulness of their faith is challenged.

JOHN STONESTREET,
Senior Fellow of Worldview and Culture for the
Colson Center for Christian Worldview

This is simply a fabulous book. It asks the skeptical questions people are asking about the Bible and then gives solid answers. Morrow is aware of where the real discussion is and what the good options are. In a world that is becoming more skeptical and in a church where many have no idea how to answer such questions, here is a resource that can give real aid and comfort.

DARRELL BOCK
Senior Research Professor of New Testament
and Executive Director of Cultural Engagement
at Dallas Theological Seminary

The Bible is under more scrutiny than ever before. *Questioning the Bible* offers insightful and well-researched responses to the top objections. It is ideal for the person who genuinely wants to know whether the Bible can be trusted. I highly recommend it for individuals and group study.

SEAN MCDOWELL
Assistant Professor at Biola University and
the author of *Apologetics for a New Generation*

Jonathan Morrow charts the erosion of confidence in the Bible and addresses the waves that are causing this erosion. No other book so thoroughly addresses the contemporary challenges to the authority of God's Word. *Questioning the Bible* should be read and studied by any Christian attempting to be faithful to Scripture.

GARRETT J. DEWEESE
Research Professor, Talbot School of Theology

The Bible is a big target for the skeptic, who raises serious questions about alleged errors, apparent contradictions, canonicity, authorship, and textual corruption. Tragically, most believers have no adequate response and retreat into an anti-intellectual privatized "faith" or worse, lose all confidence in the Bible's authority. That's why Jonathan's book is so important. He answers the most pressing objections to the Bible in a way that is intelligent, relevant and accessible.

BRETT KUNKLE
Student Impact Director at Stand to Reason:
www.str.org

QUESTIONING *the* BIBLE

11 MAJOR CHALLENGES *to the* BIBLE'S AUTHORITY

JONATHAN MORROW

MOODY PUBLISHERS
Chicago

© 2014 by
JONATHAN MORROW

All rights reserved. No part of this book may be reproduced in any form without permission in writing from the publisher, except in the case of brief quotations embodied in critical articles or reviews.

All Scripture quotations, unless otherwise indicated, are taken from *The Holy Bible, English Standard Version.* Copyright © 2000; 2001 by Crossway Bibles, a division of Good News Publishers. Used by permission. All rights reserved.

Scripture quotations marked NIV are taken from the *Holy Bible, New International Version®, NIV®.* Copyright © 1973, 1978, 1984, 2011 by Biblica, Inc.™ Used by permission of Zondervan. All rights reserved worldwide. www.zondervan.com. The "NIV" and "New International Version" are trademarks registered in the United States Patent and Trademark Office by Biblica, Inc.™

Scripture quotations marked NASB are taken from the *New American Standard Bible®*, Copyright © 1960, 1962, 1963, 1968, 1971, 1972, 1973, 1975, 1977, 1995 by The Lockman Foundation. Used by permission. (www.Lockman.org)

Scripture quotations marked NLT are taken from the *Holy Bible, New Living Translation*, copyright © 1996, 2004. Used by permission of Tyndale House Publishers, Inc., Wheaton Illinois 60189, U.S.A. All rights reserved.

All websites and phone numbers listed herein are accurate at the time of publication, but may change in the future or cease to exist. The listing of website references and resources does not imply publisher endorsement of the site's entire contents. Groups and organizations are listed for informational purposes, and listing does not imply publisher endorsement of their activities.

Edited by Jim Vincent
Interior design: Design Corps
Cover design: Kent Jensen, Knail LLC

Library of Congress Cataloging-in-Publication Data
Morrow, Jonathan, 1978-
    Questioning the Bible : 11 major challenges to the Bible's authority / Jonathan Morrow.
        pages cm
    Includes bibliographical references.
    ISBN 978-0-8024-1178-5
    1. Bible--Evidences, authority, etc.--Miscellanea. I. Title.
    BS480.M6727 2014
    220.1--dc23

                                                                    2014016912

We hope you enjoy this book from Moody Publishers. Our goal is to provide high-quality, thought-provoking books and products that connect truth to your real needs and challenges. For more information on other books and products written and produced from a biblical perspective, go to www.moodypublishers.com or write to:

Moody Publishers
820 N. LaSalle Boulevard
Chicago, IL 60610

1 3 5 7 9 10 8 6 4 2

Printed in the United States of America

To our children,
Austin, Sarah Beth, and Madison

May your confidence that God has spoken in His Word grow as each of you grow. Whether in days filled with light and laughter or through dark nights of the soul, always seek the ancient paths. Never doubt that my love for you always will remain and your heavenly Father can be trusted at all times. You are a delight to me.

I'm excited to see the adventures God has in store for each of you. Walk with courage, wisdom, and in the truth.

Thus says the Lord: "Stand by the roads, and look, and ask for the ancient paths, where the good way is; and walk in it, and find rest for your souls."

Jeremiah 6:16

And we also thank God constantly for this, that when you received the word of God, which you heard from us, you accepted it not as the word of men but as what it really is, the word of God, which is at work in you believers.

1 Thessalonians 2:13

CONTENTS

Foreword 9

Introduction:
    What You May Not Have Learned in Church about the Bible 11

1. Is the Bible Anti-intellectual? 17

2. What Can We Really Know about Jesus? 31

3. How Do We Know What the Earliest Christians Believed? 45

4. Why Were Some Gospels Banned from the Bible? 57

5. Did the Biblical Writers Lie about Their Identity? 77

6. Has the Biblical Text Been Corrupted over the Centuries? 93

7. Are the Gospels Full of Contradictions? 107

8. Is the Bible Unscientific? 123

9. Is the Bible Sexist, Racist, Homophobic, and Genocidal? 139

10. What Do Christians Believe about the Bible? 159

11. Which Interpretation of the Bible Is Correct? 173

Conclusion:
    What If a New Generation Took the Bible Seriously? 189

Notes 193

Acknowledgments 213

Appendix 1:
    A Noncircular Argument for the Bible as God's Word 215

Appendix 2:
    Archaeology and the Historical Reliability of the Bible 225

Appendix 3:
    Why a New Generation Doesn't Take the Bible Seriously 229

FOREWORD

As I write this, I am the proud grandfather of five: two girls (six and three years old) and three boys (six and three years old—and three weeks old). Everything people say about grandparenting is true—the joys of watching your grandchildren play, develop, and receive and give love to others. Oh, I almost forgot: You do, indeed, get to send them home at the end of the day. It doesn't get any better than that.

Unfortunately, there is another aspect of being a grandparent that is not very pleasant. And this aspect is made worse by being a philosopher (which I am). I am speaking of the job of watching the movements and changes of culture and wondering—no, worrying—about the sort of world they will live in when they go to college. The reason this part of grandparenting is made worse by being a philosopher is that philosophers are trained to see ideas and their implications in ways that the average person cannot. And from my perspective, I agree with those who see culture—education, government, values, the family, art and entertainment, technology, and so forth—getting worse and not better. In fact, things are changing so rapidly, that it is hard for us to keep tabs on the unconscious impact that change is having on us and on those we love.

As Christians, what can we do about this? I am not qualified nor do I have the space to give anything approximating a full answer to this question. But I think it is wise for us to recall that ideas are at the bottom of all this change. Ideas are the prime movers of culture. So no matter whatever else we Christians do to provide solutions to these issues, we must become more comfortable and competent in working with the central ideas at issue.

In regard to Christian involvement in these ideas, I have good news and bad news. The good news is that there has never in my lifetime been better resources defending the existence of God, the resurrection of Jesus, moral absolutism, and a host of ethical issues of importance to the Christian faith. The bad news is that most have overlooked the

Bible; there are very, very few, if any, books that attempt to address the question: Can a thoughtful person today seriously believe that the Bible is the very speech of God Himself?

The book you hold in your hands, *Questioning the Bible*, changes all that. In this one book, Jonathan Morrow deftly addresses eleven major challenges to the Bible's authority. I have known Jonathan for over fifteen years. He is a personal friend of mine and a former student. He is extremely well educated, he writes with great clarity and readability, he has a passion for God and His kingdom, and he knows how to put his finger on the issues that really matter.

In my opinion, there will be more and more attacks on the Bible as culture turns more secular. Thus, Morrow's book is very timely. It needs to be read and studied in groups or individually. And it must be given to friends and relatives, especially college students, who need to consider the wisdom in its pages. *Questioning the Bible* is for such a time as this.

J. P. MORELAND
Distinguished Professor of Philosophy,
Talbot School of Theology, California
Author of *The Soul: How We Know It's
Real and Why It Matters*

WHAT YOU MAY NOT HAVE LEARNED IN CHURCH ABOUT THE BIBLE

When students are first introduced to the historical, as opposed to a devotional, study of the Bible, one of the first things they are forced to grapple with is that the biblical text, whether Old Testament or New Testament, is chock-full of discrepancies, many of them irreconcilable.[1]
Bart Ehrman

We don't have the originals of any of the books of the New Testament . . .

Scribes along the way deliberately changed the New Testament manuscripts so that we can no longer know what the original authors of Scripture wrote . . .

The Bible's authors are not who we think they are and at least nineteen of the twenty-seven books in the New Testament are forgeries . . .

The Bible is anti-intellectual and unscientific . . .

The Bible is full of contradictions and historical inaccuracies . . .

The Bible can't be authoritative because so many people disagree how to interpret it.

Those are just a handful of the controversial claims being made about the Bible these days. Odds are that if you grew up in church, attended Sunday school and youth group, then you've never heard about most of this. But if you take a religious studies class at a typical university, watch some recent documentaries exploring how we "really" got the Bible, do any Internet searches on the Bible, or read any of the books by Christian fundamentalist-turned-skeptic Bart Ehrman, then these are the kinds of claims you will run into. But are they true? And if they are true, can you still maintain your confidence in the Bible? More importantly, can you still trust the Author of the Bible? After all, the Bible is supposed to be God's book, right? These are vitally important questions, and there is more at stake in this discussion than you may realize. But before we explore the merits of these provocative claims, we need to make a quick stop in New Haven, Connecticut.

QUESTIONS THAT MATTER

Eager to commence the next season of their life journey, the incoming class of 2011 took their seats awaiting the freshman address by Yale University President Richard C. Levin. As they listened, his objective for this occasion became abundantly clear—during their time here at Yale, they need to be about asking questions that matter:

- What constitutes a good life?

- What kind of life do you want to lead?

- What values do you hope to live by?

- What kind of community or society do you want to live in?

- How should you reconcile the claims of family and community with your individual desires?

- How was the physical universe created?

- How long will it endure?

- What is the place of humanity in the order of the universe?

"An important component of your undergraduate experience," Levin told the freshmen, "should be seeking answers to the questions that matter: questions about what has meaning in life. . . . The four years ahead of you offer a once-in-a-lifetime opportunity to pursue your intellectual interests wherever they may lead, and, wherever they may lead, you will find something to reflect upon that is pertinent to your quest for meaning in life. It is true that your professors are unlikely to give you the answers to questions about what you should value and how you should live. *We leave the answers up to you.*"[2]

Read that last bit again. Really? These are the questions that matter in life. But even a world-class Ivy League institution like Yale doesn't have answers for you. Levin's admission is telling. Of course, the elements of the periodic table or how one determines the velocity of an object ($v = d/t$) are not left up to you. Why? Because Levin assumes these two questions are actually subjects of knowledge, whereas questions of meaning, morality, value, and purpose are not.

I am all for good questions, but how does one find good answers? And more importantly, what constitutes a good answer? The tragedy is that this generation is longing for answers to these kinds of questions. While summarizing the most extensive sociological study to date of the religious and spiritual lives of emerging adults, Christian Smith, director of the Center for the Study of Religion and Society, pointedly describes the crisis of knowledge facing this generation:

> Very many emerging adults simply don't know how to think about things, what is right, what is deserving for them to devote their lives to. On such matters, they are often simply paralyzed, wishing they could be more definite, wanting to move forward, but simply not knowing how they might possibly know anything worthy of conviction and dedication. Instead, very many emerging adults exist in a state of basic indecision, confusion, and fuzziness. *The world they have inherited, as best they can make sense of it, has told them that real knowledge is impossible and genuine values are illusions* [emphasis mine].[3]

Have you ever felt like that?

My goal is not to be overly critical of President Levin. He certainly deserves credit for attempting to bring the important questions of life to the surface for his students to consider. But the most important questions were left unspoken that day. Who has the *authority* to answer such questions? And can we actually come to *know* what the meaning of life is? At the end of the day, big questions without the hope of big answers will lead to despair.

WHEN QUESTIONS AND DOUBTS GO UNADDRESSED

If you are breathing, then you have questions. But what do we do with them? And what happens when questions about God, the Bible, or Christianity turn into doubts? Real Christians aren't supposed to doubt, are they? Unfortunately this is a common misunderstanding in many churches, and tragically many young Christians are growing up without a safe place to ask the tough questions and wrestle with their doubts. Here was what one young Christian admitted, "I kept my doubts to myself, because I didn't think my leaders would want to know that I really didn't believe. Maybe they could have helped me more, but I never believed they would be able to."[4] A Barna Group survey found that a stunning 36 percent of young Christians agree with the statement, "I don't feel that I can ask my most pressing life questions in church."[5] What a heartbreaking admission.

If you come out of a "toxic environment" where questions are discouraged, I want you to know that what you encountered was not biblical Christianity. Tim Keller, who pastors a church full of young professionals and seekers in New York City, offers some sage advice:

> A faith without some doubts is like a human body without any antibodies in it. People who blithely go through life too busy or indifferent to ask hard questions about why they believe as they do will find themselves defenseless against either the experience of tragedy or the probing questions of a smart skeptic. A person's faith can collapse almost overnight if she has failed over the years to listen patiently to her own doubts, which should only be discarded after long reflection.[6]

We will explore this dynamic more as we go along, but you need to know that having questions and doubts doesn't make you a bad person or a bad Christian, and God is certainly not disappointed with you. In fact, he is the God who says, "Come now, let us reason together" (Isaiah 1:18). But you also don't want to let those doubts just sit there, because when doubts go unaddressed they inevitably steal the vitality of our faith; one's faith begins to shrivel up. The end result is usually not a dramatic crisis-of-faith moment but a subtle drifting from life with God. Just like when you are swimming in the ocean and you don't realize just how far you have drifted down the beach. That wasn't what you set out to do, but that is where you find yourself nonetheless.

If that is you, let me encourage you to keep fighting the tide and keep seeking God in the midst of your doubts. Too much is at stake. The God of the universe may really have spoken. Your life could really have eternal significance and purpose. After years of study and investigation I have become convinced that Christianity is not a hopelessly outdated superstition that only the uneducated and gullible believe. It is entirely reasonable to believe that God has spoken in the Bible. Christianity is not a fairy tale for grown-ups.

Drifting is easy, but seeking is hard work. The journey of faith will require courage, effort, and diligence. But I also need to warn you that some of the truths we encounter in the pages ahead may make you a little uncomfortable. But that shouldn't surprise us, for as C. S. Lewis put it, "If you look for truth, you may find comfort in the end: if you look for comfort you will not get either comfort or truth—only soft soap and wishful thinking to begin with and, in the end, despair."[7] At the end of the day, we all know that truth is the only sure foundation on which to build a life.

THE JOURNEY BEGINS

This book is about questions that matter. Our journey to answer them will take us to some fascinating places in history and introduce you to some unfamiliar concepts and ideas (usually only talked about in dusty academic journals). We need to remember that our goal is a deeper understanding of the Bible's origins so that we can decide if it can be trusted. It is impossible to accomplish this if we stay at the surface level. But going deeper also means that you may need to reread some paragraphs to fully understand the evidence or argument we are exploring. (I have to do this all the time!) You have my word that where we talk about new ideas I will do my best to clearly explain them and then connect the dots so you know why they matter. Lastly, I have intentionally tried to introduce you to leading Christian thinkers and scholars throughout this book. You need to know that Christianity is a thoughtful faith and there are many intelligent people who believe the Bible is God's Word.

That about covers it. Let's get going. So, is the Bible anti-intellectual?

IS THE BIBLE
ANTI-INTELLECTUAL?

*Remember that God is a rational God, who has made us
in His own image. God invites and expects us to explore
His double revelation, in nature and Scripture, with the
minds He has given us, and to go on in the development
of a Christian mind to apply His marvelous revealed truth
to every aspect of the modern and post-modern world.*[1]
John Stott

Culture has been compared to a river that we are all floating in. The only
real question is if we are aware of where we are drifting and are going to do
something about it. One of the prevailing currents today is an overemphasis on
emotion and a devaluing of reason. Our culture worships at the altar of sound
bites, slogans, and quick updates. This makes sustained thought and critical
reflection challenging, to say the least.

Couple this with the fact that our lives are overscheduled and hurried, and
that is a recipe for superficiality. I don't say this to be mean or with a holier-
than-thou attitude; I fight these tendencies as well. What has happened, however, is that both the broader culture and the American church have become
shallow. We exalt the trivial and dismiss the meaningful.

This has consequences in many areas of life, but especially when it comes to religion and spirituality. How does the Bible—if it really is the Word of God—speak within such a culture? What cultural assumptions keep us from hearing and considering its message?

Claims are never made or heard in a cultural vacuum. The conversation about the Bible today is heard in a cultural backdrop that includes a lot of misunderstanding of religion in general and Christianity in particular. The goal in this chapter is modest but important. We need to expose some of these misperceptions about how to find spiritual truth, and then allow the Bible itself to inform our understanding of key words like *faith*, *truth*, and *reason*.

THREE SPIRITUAL DEAD ENDS TO AVOID

As I talk to people in the local church or the students I teach, I run into three common misunderstandings about God and spirituality. Whether or not you are ultimately convinced that Christianity is true, these are three dead ends you will surely want to avoid in your quest for truth.

"People are free to believe whatever they want about God"

Yes and no. If all that is meant here is that people should not be coerced or forced to believe something or follow a certain religion—then I wholeheartedly agree. Religious liberty and freedom of conscience are extremely important principles to defend. The Manhattan Declaration captures this well: "No one should be compelled to embrace any religion against his will, nor should persons of faith be forbidden to worship God according to the dictates of conscience or to express freely and publicly their deeply held religious convictions."[2] In his excellent book *The Case for Civility*, Os Guinness articulates a vision of what we should be after in public discourse about our various religious beliefs:

> The vision of a civic public square is one in which everyone—people of all faiths, whether religious or naturalistic—are equally free to enter and engage public life on the basis of their faiths, as a matter of "free exercise" and as dictated by their own reason and conscience; but always within the

double framework, first, of the Constitution, and second, of a freely and
mutually agreed covenant, or common vision for the common good, of what
each person understands to be just and free for everyone else, and therefore
of the duties involved in living with the deep differences of others.[3]

This is an example of what true tolerance is. True tolerance is where we
extend to each other the right to be wrong.[4] False tolerance, on the other hand,
naïvely asserts that all ideas are created equal and this must be rejected. Not
only is this obviously false, it's unlivable. Unfortunately, "The ideal of religious
tolerance has morphed into the straitjacket of religious agreement."[5] Contrary
to what is commonly believed, the height of intolerance is not disagreement,
but rather removing the public space and opportunity for people to disagree.

However, true tolerance is usually not what people have in mind when they
say people should be free to believe in whatever God (or no god at all) they
want to. Here is the simple, but profound point to grasp—*merely believing
something doesn't make it true*. Put differently, people are entitled to their own
beliefs, but not their own truth. Belief is not what ultimately matters—truth is.
Our *believing* something is true doesn't *make* it true. The Bible isn't true simply
because I have faith. Truth is what corresponds to reality—telling it like it is.

The bottom line is that we discover truth; we don't create it. Reality is what
we bump (or slam!) into when we act on false beliefs. Spending a few minutes
fondly reflecting on your junior high, high school, and college years will bring
this principle vividly and painfully to life.

"All religions basically teach the same thing"

Let's be honest . . . we don't like to offend people and we want people to
like us. Because of this, we let some pretty silly ideas go unchallenged in our
culture today. One perennial offender is the notion that all religions basically
teach the same thing. If anyone is to find the truth about God or ultimate
reality, then this myth has to be dispensed with quickly. *New York Times*
columnist Ross Douthat hits the nail on the head:

> The differences between religions are worth debating. Theology has con-
> sequences: It shapes lives, families, nations, cultures, wars; it can change

people, save them from themselves, and sometimes warp or even destroy them. If we tiptoe politely around this reality, then we betray every teacher, guru and philosopher—including Jesus of Nazareth and the Buddha both—who ever sought to resolve the most human of all problems: How then should we live?[6]

It is out of a sense of false tolerance that we think we are actually loving one another if we never challenge ideas that we believe to be false. In addition to this liability, we often lack the courage to (respectfully) say what needs to be said.

With that in mind, the first thing to do when encountering this claim is simply ask a question—"That's interesting; in what specific ways are all religions basically the same?" And then wait for a response. Fight the temptation to answer for them. Often, this will be enough to expose the superficial slogan so that you can have a more productive spiritual conversation. In his book *God Is Not One*, Boston University professor Stephen Prothero observes, "No one argues that different economic systems or political regimes are one and the same. Capitalism and socialism are so obviously at odds that their differences hardly bear mentioning. The same goes for democracy and monarchy. Yet scholars continue to claim that religious rivals such as Hinduism and Islam, Judaism and Christianity are, by some miracle of the imagination, essentially the same, and this view resounds in the echo chamber of popular culture."[7] Chart 1 points out key differences among the four major religions.

Chart 1

HOW FOUR MAJOR RELIGIONS DIFFER IN CORE BELIEFS

Buddhism	Hinduism	Christianity	Judaism
no God	thousands of gods	one God, triune in nature	one God
—	(impersonal)	(personal)	(personal)
different teachings on God, reality, sin, salvation, heaven, hell			
similar teachings on ethics			

Many imagine God to be waiting at the top of a mountain and eventually, all paths will get to the top. But who's waiting for you at the top?[8] Which God? The Christian God—the one true God who is a trinity? No God at all? Thousands of gods? Those are very different peaks! Admittedly, you will find similarities in the foothills in terms of basic ethics, but the farther you go up the mountain, the more pronounced the differences become because you are dealing with the nature of God, eternity, redemption, heaven, and hell.

A simple thought experiment makes this clear. Imagine you were at a table about to eat dinner and you have two bowls of white powder in front of you. Do you put them on your food? After all, they look pretty similar. But what if I told you that one was ordinary table salt and the other was cyanide? The differences matter far more than the similarities! So it is with religion and its path for your eternal future.

Finally, the fact that the religions of the world make exclusive and mutually contradictory claims means they can't be the same. Take Jesus of Nazareth as an example: either Jesus was not the Messiah (Judaism), was the Messiah (Christianity), or was a great prophet (Islam)—but not all three (cf. John 14:6).

"God is a psychological crutch humans invent to feel better"

In *The Future of an Illusion*, Sigmund Freud wrote that religious beliefs are "illusions, fulfillments of the oldest, strongest, and most urgent wishes of mankind. . . . As we already know, the terrifying impression of helplessness in childhood aroused the need for protection—for protection through love—which was provided by the father; and the recognition that this helplessness lasts throughout life made it necessary to cling to the existence of a father, but this time a more powerful one. Thus the benevolent rule of a divine Providence allays our fear of the dangers of life."[9] In short, we project the existence of God based on a human need for Him.

Sean McDowell and I spent a whole book (*Is God Just a Human Invention?*) addressing various angles of this issue, but let me highlight just two reasons this is not a helpful way to think about the God question. First, it begs the question against God. Freud's argument is, essentially, since we know that God doesn't exist, what are the most compelling psychological explanations of this belief? His

I don't put my trust in God for soley psychologic reasons, though I receive psych. benefits. my trust in God is based on truth/evidence.

argument assumes from the outset that no object of belief—namely God—exists.[10]

And second, the projection theory logic cuts both ways. If it can be argued that humans created God out of a need for security or a father figure, then it can just as easily be argued that atheism is a response to the human desire for the freedom to do whatever one wants without moral constraints or obligations. Perhaps atheists don't want a God to exist because they would then be morally accountable to a deity. Or maybe atheists had particularly tragic relationships with their own fathers growing up, projected that on God, and then spent most of their adult lives trying to kill a "Divine Father Figure"?

New York University psychologist Paul Vitz helps us prioritize the right question: "Since both believers and nonbelievers in God have psychological reasons for their positions, one important conclusion is that in any debate as to the truth of the existence of God, psychology should be irrelevant. A genuine search for evidence supporting or opposing the existence of God should be based on the evidence and arguments found in philosophy, theology, science, history, and other relevant disciplines."[11]

THREE THINGS ABOUT CHRISTIANITY THAT MAY SURPRISE YOU

Whenever people use the word *Christian* in a conversation, I don't assume they are using the term correctly (i.e., something that the founder of Christianity, Jesus of Nazareth, would recognize). Again, I'm not being critical here; we just live in a postChristian culture today. There's simply too much misinformation out there. Moreover, people tend to repeat commonly used slogans or embrace a vision of Christianity that sounds curiously like twenty-first-century American values. In light of that, I have found that when I share what the New Testament actually teaches, people are genuinely surprised. In fact, many Christians I encounter also are surprised (and even resist) what I am about to share.

1. Christianity Rises to the Level of True or False

It's always best to begin at the beginning. If Christianity does not rise to the level of being true or false, then it has been completely removed from the cognitive realm. If something can't be false, then it can't be true either. And rational investigation becomes impossible. Please don't mishear me, I think there are very good reasons to believe Christianity is actually true and best explains reality. But Christianity is the kind of thing that could be false. It's at this point in my talk when people tend to get nervous (along with those who invited me in to speak!). My point is simply this: In a culture that relativizes (everybody has their own truth) and then privatizes (my spiritual truth is personal and therefore off-limits) religious belief, we must reintroduce Christianity to our culture with its very public truth claims and let the best ideas win. To use a football analogy, we have to take the red practice jersey off of Christianity so it can take some hits.

Nancy Pearcey puts her finger on the problem: "When Christians are willing to reduce religion to non-cognitive categories, unconnected to questions of truth or evidence, then we have already lost the battle."[12] When it comes to Christianity, the most important question we need to help people ask is not will it work for them or help them feel better, but rather is it true?

And that leads us to another important but often misunderstood concept—truth. As we hinted at above, truth is simply telling it like it is. A more philosophically precise definition is that truth is what corresponds to or matches up with reality.[13] For example, if you have the belief that it is raining outside and it actually is raining outside, then that belief is true. This is the classical and commonsense view of truth we all use every day. However, at this point it will be helpful to make a distinction between objective and subjective truth claims. For something to be *objective* simply means that it is not dependent on what anyone believes, thinks, or agrees on. (Objective claims refer to reality as it is "out there," is fixed, and discoverable.) On the other hand, to say something is *subjective* is to affirm that it is dependent on what someone believes, thinks, or agrees on. (Subjective claims are not fixed, i.e., can change, and refer to the beliefs and opinions of the person.) Greg Koukl offers a helpful illustration on the differences between ice cream and insulin:

> Forgive me for stating something so obvious, but there is a difference between choosing an ice cream flavor and choosing a medicine. When choosing ice cream, you choose what you like. When choosing medicine, you have to choose what heals.

objective - mind independent
subjective - mind dependent

Many people think of God like they think of ice cream, not like they think of insulin. In other words, they choose religious views according to their tastes, not according to what is true. The question of truth hardly even comes up in the conversation.[14]

In this illustration, the ice cream claims are *subjective* and insulin claims are *objective*. While many think religious claims are ice cream kinds of claims, this is incorrect. Biblical Christianity is making an insulin kind of claim, as we will see below.

Before concluding this section, we need to briefly say a word about why truth even matters anymore. To put it simply, truth matters because ideas have consequences for people. What you think is true is the map you will use to try to navigate reality—spiritually, morally, relationally, and intellectually. Wasting a few minutes because Google Maps led you down yet another dead end is one thing, wasting your life because you have sincerely believed a lie is another. God's position as stated in the New Testament is clear, "This is good, and it is pleasing in the sight of God our Savior, who desires all people to be saved and to come to the knowledge of the truth" (1 Timothy 2:3–4).

2. Biblical Faith Is Not Blind Faith

When it comes to the word *faith* there is mass confusion both inside and outside the church. Faith has come to mean anything and everything. Unfortunately, the most common assumption is that faith is a blind leap in the dark and opposed to reason and evidence. Former *Newsweek* religion editor Lisa Miller put it this way: "Reason defines one kind of reality (what we know); faith defines another (what we don't know)."[15] Prominent Harvard cognitive psychologist Steven Pinker says essentially the same thing but mixes in some disdain for effect. "Universities are about reason, pure and simple. Faith—believing something without good reasons to do so—has no place in anything but a religious institution, and our society has no shortage of these."[16] Is that true? Does the Bible encourage blind faith? The short answer is no, it does not. And to make my case I will call three biblical witnesses to the stand—Moses, Jesus, and Paul.

First, God (through Moses) did not require "blind faith" of the Israelites in Egypt.

> But the Lord said to Moses, "Put out your hand and catch it by the tail"—so
> he put out his hand and caught it, and it became a staff in his hand—"*that
> they may believe* that the Lord . . . has appeared to you." . . . Israel *saw* the
> great power that the Lord used against the Egyptians, so the people feared
> the Lord, and they *believed* in the Lord and in his servant Moses. (Exodus
> 4:4–5; 14:31, *italics added*)

Notice that God knew the Israelites would need some evidence and he graciously provided it. As humanity's creator, God has perfect insight into how he created us to function and relates accordingly.

Next, Jesus did not demand "blind faith" of those who questioned if he was the Messiah.

> Now when John heard in prison about the deeds of the Christ, he sent word
> by his disciples and said to him, "Are you the one who is to come, or shall
> we look for another?" And Jesus answered them, "Go and tell John what
> you *hear* and *see*: the blind receive their sight and the lame walk, lepers are
> cleansed and the deaf hear, and the dead are raised up, and the poor have
> good news preached to them." (Matthew 11:2–5, *italics added*)

In this passage, Jesus does not scold John the Baptist for his inability to believe without evidence. Rather Jesus tailors evidence that would be helpful to him because John knew the prophecies concerning the Messiah in the Hebrew Scriptures.

Finally, Paul did not appeal to "blind faith" when discussing the resurrection of Jesus. "If Christ has not been raised, *your faith is worthless*; you are still in your sins. . . . If we have hoped in Christ in this life only, we are of all men most to be pitied". (1 Corinthians 15:17–19 NASB, *italics added*)

In this passage, Paul clearly established the historical nature of Christianity. This distinguishes Christianity from every other world religion by making its central claim testable. Pearcey observes, "Biblical Christianity refuses to separate historical fact from spiritual meaning. Its core claim is that the living God has acted in history, especially in the life, death, and resurrection of Jesus."[17] As a historical claim, the resurrection can be investigated with eyes wide open.

In summary, if you can get Moses, Jesus, and Paul saying essentially the same thing, then I think you can consider this question settled: biblical faith is not opposed to reason and evidence. As Gordon Lewis put it, "Spirituality without understanding is not faith; it is superstition."[18]

What is faith then? There is the general kind of faith we all use in our daily lives. For example, we use faith when we take a prescription from the doctor, hop on a plane, hire an employee, or get married. In this sense, faith is active trust in what you have good reason to believe is true. Sincerity is not enough; faith is only as good as the object in which it is placed. Biblical faith just narrows the focus. In the everyday circumstances of life, biblical faith is active trust that God is who he says he is and will do all that he has promised to do (see Psalm 9:10; cf. Hebrews 10:19–23; 11:1). In the Bible, faith is always pointing toward a future reality (i.e., things that have not yet happened). The contrast is with sight, not with reason (cf. 2 Corinthians 5:7). God's past and present faithfulness is the basis for our faith in an unseen future. This insight also helps us understand how faith relates to knowledge—faith acts on knowledge; it's not a substitute for knowledge. The more we know of and about God, the more faith we will be able to exercise. And it is this kind of faith with which God is pleased (cf. Hebrews 11:6).

3. Christians Are Commanded to Defend the Faith

Defending the faith is not optional. The Bible makes this clear: "In your hearts honor Christ the Lord as holy, always being prepared to make a defense [apologia] to anyone who asks you for a reason for the hope that is in you; yet do it with gentleness and respect" (1 Peter 3:15; cf. Philippians 1:7). From this passage we learn that apologetics involves responding to objections (defense), making a case (offense), and giving hope (Christ-centered). In addition to Peter, the book of Acts repeatedly records Paul reasoning with people about Christianity (Acts 14:15–17; 17:2, 4, 17–31; 18:4). Luke records that Paul "entered the synagogue and for three months spoke boldly, reasoning and persuading them about the kingdom of God. But when some became stubborn and continued in unbelief, speaking evil of the Way before the congregation, he withdrew from them and took the disciples with him, reasoning daily in the hall of Tyrannus. This continued for two years, so that all the residents of Asia heard the word of the Lord, both Jews and Greeks" (Acts 19:8–10). For hours each day, Paul sought to persuade the intellectuals of his day that Christianity was true!

When discussing the importance of apologetics, three common objections are often raised. *First, people claim that apologetics is not practical.* Isn't apologetics only for academics and intellectuals? The short answer is no. Here's why. Everyone has questions—you do, your kids do, your friends and neighbors do, your family does, and our culture certainly does. It's that simple. We will either think carefully or poorly about these questions, but the questions themselves cannot be avoided. By the way, Christianity welcomes tough questions!

Next, people say you should just preach the simple gospel and not worry about all of that intellectual stuff. Pearcey's observation is critical here: "The ultimate goal is to preach the gospel. But the gospel is not simple to those whose background prevents them from understanding it. Today's global secular culture has erected a maze of mental barriers against even considering the biblical message."[19] Apologetics serves evangelism and the Great Commission (Matthew 28:19–20).

Finally, some Christians object that too much knowledge leads to arrogance. I would suggest that the remedy for arrogance is not ignorance, but humility. John Stott is right on target: "I am not pleading for a dry, humorless, academic Christianity, but for a warm devotion set on fire by truth."[20] Dallas Willard observed that part of what it means to be a follower of Jesus Christ and love others well is to think clearly. "Bluntly, to serve God well we must think straight; and crooked thinking, unintentional or not, always favors evil. And when the crooked thinking gets elevated into group orthodoxy, whether religious or secular, there is always, quite literally, hell to pay."[21] Engaging our minds as Christians is an act of worship and part of loving God with all of our minds (Matthew 22:37).

CHRISTIANITY IS NOT A FAIRY TALE FOR GROWN-UPS

If Christianity is relegated to the realm of fairy tales, which may provide personal significance or meaning but not knowledge, then people will continue not taking the claims of Jesus or the Christian worldview very seriously. If, however, people are invited to rationally consider the claims of Christianity as a knowledge tradition, then chances are good that they might come to know the living God and live life according to the knowledge provided in His Word.

I hope this chapter has cleared away some of the cultural debris so that we can better explore tough questions about the Bible and in doing so, discover the truth.

Three Big Ideas

1. We called three witnesses (Moses, Jesus, and Paul) to demonstrate that biblical faith is not blind faith. Faith is active trust in what you have good reason to believe is true. Moreover, while people are entitled to their own beliefs, they are not entitled to their own truth. Simply believing something doesn't make it true.

2. True tolerance occurs when we extend to each other the right to be wrong. False tolerance, on the other hand, happens when we naïvely assert that all ideas are created equal; and this must be rejected. Not only is this obviously false, it's unlivable.

3. Defending the faith is not optional. Apologetics—based on 1 Peter 3:15—involves responding to objections (defense), making a case (offense), and giving hope (being Christ-centered). This gives Christians confidence and offers nonbelievers something to think about.

Conversation Tips

Since there is such a widespread assumption that the Bible (and Christianity by extension) is anti-intellectual, you will need to work hard at showing people this is not the case.

- The best way to show that the Bible is not anti-intellectual is to talk about reality and not religion. In today's culture, religion is understood as a personal and private feeling that is not accessible by everyone else. You can't question, challenge, or investigate it; you must simply be tolerant of it (false tolerance). That's why having a conversation about Christianity as a religion is a dead end. It's a nonstarter. We need to talk about Christianity in the context of reality where terms like truth, knowledge, reason, and evidence apply.

- The key here is to use rational language (i.e., I think) rather than emotional language (i.e., I feel).

- When you have the opportunity, define faith the way Moses, Jesus, and Paul did in the Bible.

Digging Deeper

• J. P. Moreland. *Love Your God with All Your Mind: The Role of Reason in the Life of the Soul.* Updated edition. Colorado Springs: NavPress, 2012.

• Sean McDowell and Jonathan Morrow. *Is God Just a Human Invention? And Seventeen Other Questions Raised by the New Atheists.* Grand Rapids: Kregel, 2010.

WHAT CAN WE REALLY KNOW ABOUT JESUS?

Biblical Christianity refuses to separate historical fact from spiritual meaning. Its core claim is that the living God has acted in history, especially in the life, death, and resurrection of Jesus.[1]

Nancy Pearcey

Everywhere Jesus went there was controversy. Mark, one of the earliest biographers of Jesus, recounts a crowd's response to an exorcism Jesus performed. "And they were all amazed, so that they questioned among themselves, saying, 'What is this? A new teaching with authority! He commands even the unclean spirits, and they obey him.' And at once his fame spread everywhere throughout all the surrounding region of Galilee" (Mark 1:27–28). Two thousand years later, Jesus is still drawing a crowd.

Loved by some and hated by others, Jesus could always be counted on to stir things up. That is, of course, if he ever actually existed. Maybe you were one of the millions of kids who sang "Jesus Loves Me" growing up. But have you ever stopped and asked yourself how you really know that Jesus ever existed? And if he did, can you be confident about what he said and did? Is it more reasonable to believe that gullible people invented the idea of Jesus or that there really was a Jewish miracle worker from Nazareth who claimed to

be the long-awaited Messiah? Especially if you can't assume the Bible is historically accurate. To answer these questions, we need to go back to the sources.

THREE QUESTS FOR JESUS

This idea may be new to you but historians have been looking for "the real"
Jesus for quite a while.[2] Their various searches over the past three hundred
years can be divided into three quests, each quest being characterized by a
distinctive approach. This backstory is important because you won't be able to
understand current "historical" discussions about Jesus without being aware
of some of the key players and approaches.

The First Quest (Late 1600s–1953)

The first quest can best be characterized by a memorable observation of
the German enlightenment scholar Gotthold Ephraim Lessing (1729–1781).
Lessing argued that there is a gap separating the Jesus of history and the Christ
of faith. The image that he famously used to separate the historical from the
religious was a ditch—"That, then, is the ugly, broad ditch which I cannot get
across, however often and however earnestly I have tried to make the leap."[3]
One of the main aims of this quest was to get back to the historical Jesus of
Nazareth by peeling away the theological layers that later Christians (i.e., the
early church) allegedly read onto the lips of the real Jesus.

What was a ditch for Lessing had grown into a canyon for influential scholar
Rudolf Bultmann (1884–1976). "I do indeed think," concluded Bultmann,
"that we can know almost nothing concerning the life and personality of Jesus,
since the early Christian sources show no interest in either, are moreover
fragmentary and often legendary; and other sources do not exist."[4] Bultmann
wrote after the first quest began to lose steam during what has been called
the "no quest" period simply because getting back to Jesus seemingly was
not possible.

Significantly, the cultural backdrop for this quest was the Enlightenment.
During this time a strong anti-supernaturalistic or naturalistic sentiment per-
meated the whole discussion about Jesus. Consequently, critical scholars

began with the assumption that the miracle accounts recorded in the four Gospels were invented along with many of the more remarkable words and works of Jesus. As Beilby and Eddy observe:

> As the nineteenth century drew to a close, the critical quest had left in its wake a wonderfully "liberal" Jesus—a Jesus stripped of the more unenlightened entanglements associated with the Gospels and Christian orthodoxy such as miracles and divine status. This Jesus was a moral reformer to be sure a teacher who revealed the fatherhood of God, the brotherhood of humankind, and the simple tenets of a reasonable, love-based religion.[5]

If that description of Jesus sounds familiar, it is because many in the media and the university hold that view today. Before moving to the second quest for Jesus, there are three other major ideas you need to know about.

First, the controversial scholar David Strauss at the University of Tubingen in Germany introduced the concept of myth when interpreting the miracle accounts of Jesus contained in the Gospels. It wasn't just that it was irrational to believe Jesus could walk on water, but that these miracle stories were legends created much later by the Gospel writers and a community that did not have access to eyewitnesses. The effect this perception had on the historical value of the Gospels was devastating. Jesus was now in the category of Paul Bunyan and Babe the blue ox. In essence, the real Jesus cannot be recovered because of the layers of myth that had been piled up in the Gospels.[6]

The attack on the historical credibility of the Gospels was not complete, however. Writing at the turn of the twentieth century, William Wrede introduced the concept of theological propaganda to the Gospels conversation. Not only did the layers of myth obscure Jesus, but also the Gospel writers were not motivated to write accurate history. Wrede argued their purposes were theologically motivated and thus fell into the category of propaganda.

If the overall confidence in the historical reliability of the Gospels wasn't shaken enough, the early twentieth century saw the advent of the history-of-religions school. Wilhelm Bousset and his book *Kyrios Christos* in 1913 highlighted the trend that understood religions to evolve over time from simple to complex. For example, how might you get a Jewish peasant named Jesus to be eventually worshiped as a god? Enter the hypothesis that pagan mythological influences found in the Hellenistic religions turned the historical Jesus into someone he never claimed to be, namely, God (we will revisit this claim below).[7]

Before moving further, it is worth noting that these were claims and stories that explained Jesus and the early Christian movement *if you assumed* the impossibility of miracles and dismissed the Gospels as early eyewitness testimony. But what if these presuppositions are without merit? As we move throughout this book, I hope you will see how the historical evidence continues to challenge both of these assumptions.

In summary then, the first quest was the most skeptical and the portraits of Jesus that emerged from this period illustrate this point.

The Second Quest (1953–1970s)

During the second quest the goal was to separate the Greek Jesus from the Jewish Jesus. One of the ways this came about was to try to analyze the forms (i.e., form criticism) of the stories as they were developed. One unfortunate consequence of this period was that the focus on the literary dimension began to diminish the possibility of the historical. While not as skeptical as the first quest, it was also during this time that the burden of proof rested on anyone who wanted to show anything to be historical in the Gospels. When it came to history, the Gospels were seen as guilty until shown to be innocent by various critical tools (i.e., form, source, and redaction criticism).[8]

The Third Quest (1980s–today)

However, things began to change with the discovery of the Dead Sea Scrolls in 1945. As they were eventually translated, published, and made accessible to scholars, it became increasingly clear that the Jewish context would be essential in understanding Jesus of Nazareth (a time period known as second-temple-period Judaism). Bock explains, "Unlike the second questers, they did not start by trying to peel away at texts of the gospels, but by trying to understand the historical setting in which Jesus lived" and "how Jesus' actions and teachings would be understood and whether they could fit together well in such a setting."[9] This has been the main thrust of the third quest, and it has been (generally) helpful in filling out a more accurate portrait of the world in which Jesus lived and taught.

PLAYING BY THE RULES

At this point you might be wondering why this more technical discussion matters. Why not just take the Gospels by faith? That is a fair question, but as we have seen, biblical faith is not blind faith. Faith is only as good as the object in which it's placed. Faith is active trust in what you have good reason to believe is true. But now we are right back to the issue that prompted Lessing to create a wide ditch in between the Jesus of history and the Christ of faith.

As a result of the three quests for the historical Jesus, mainline scholarship has concluded one can cross the ditch with varying degrees of success and has developed some generally agreed upon rules to use.[10] (The technical name for these are "Criteria of Authenticity.") These rules sound very strange to many in the church today, but if we are going to engage the public conversation about Jesus (and not merely assert our opinion), we need to be conversant with the rules of the historical Jesus studies game. And the heart of this game is corroboration.

A key indicator in corroboration is a rule known as "multiple attestation." We use this principle in a court of law when the jury is looking to see consistency across several witnesses when they discuss the evidence. In historical Jesus studies, this takes place when a saying, teaching, or event concerning Jesus shows up in multiple sources. New Testament scholar Darrell Bock explains:

> Multiple attestation argues that if a saying, teaching, or theme is attested in multiple sources, then it has a better chance of being authentic, that is, of going back to authentic events in the life of Jesus. . . . The rationale here is that the more widely distributed an idea is across the independent levels of tradition, the more likely it is to be old and reflective of actual events. The independence of the sources from one another means that no one of them created this event, but rather the event stands attested across distinct pieces of the tradition and is older than a given source.[11]

In short, this means that the events were not invented because several independent sources are referring back to this event.

WHAT ARE THE SOURCES FOR THE GAME?

When it comes to playing the game, the general consensus is that there are four key sources. If you grew up in church you might be tempted to think this one is easy to answer, Matthew, Mark, Luke, and John—the four canonical gospels found in the Bible. To quote ESPN's Lee Corso, "Not so fast, my friend!" This is where it gets a bit more complicated. The four sources historical Jesus scholars use for corroboration are Mark, Q, L, and M. As you begin to look more closely at the Gospels and compare them, you will find that they depended on one another in specific kinds of ways. This is known as the Synoptic Problem. Whole books have been devoted to this discussion, but here is a brief summary by Stein:

Chart 2

TWO-SOURCE HYPOTHESIS

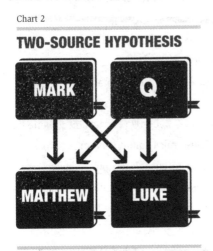

> In reading the four Gospels it is apparent that three of them resemble one another and one does not. A brief time spent in any synopsis of the Gospels will indicate that Matthew, Mark and Luke share a number of striking similarities. The "Synoptic Problem" is the name that has been given to the problem of why the Gospels of Matthew, Mark and Luke look so much alike. Why are they so similar in content, in wording and in the order of events found within them?[12]

Mark is thought to have been written first because both Matthew and Luke (independently) use a lot of material found in Mark. But there is also unique material in Matthew (M) that did not originate from Mark and there is unique material in Luke (L) that did not originate in Mark. And there seems to be a common (written/oral) source used by both Matthew and Luke that has been hypothetically called "Q" (which means source). As of now, this "two-source" hypothesis [see chart 2] is the dominant view of the academy. Now that you have your source scorecard you will be able to understand the categories that are being used to "reconstruct" the historical Jesus.

MULTIPLE ATTESTATION IN ACTION

Today, virtually all professional New Testament scholars agree that Jesus *claimed* that the kingdom of God had arrived in his ministry. The primary reason is the Criterion of Multiple Attestation. Here are at least six independent lines of corroboration: Mark (2:21–22); "Q" (Luke 11:20); "M" (Matthew 5:17); "L" (Luke 17:20–21); John (4:23); Paul (1 Corinthians 10:11; Colossians 1:13; 1 Thessalonians 2:12). Let's look at those verses:

> "No one sews a piece of unshrunk cloth on an old garment. If he does, the patch tears away from it, the new from the old, and a worse tear is made. And no one puts new wine into old wineskins. If he does, the wine will burst the skins—and the wine is destroyed, and so are the skins. But new wine is for fresh wineskins." (Mark 2:21–22)

> "But if it is by the finger of God that I cast out demons, then the kingdom of God has come upon you." (Luke 11:20)

> "Do not think that I have come to abolish the Law or the Prophets; I have not come to abolish them but to fulfill them." (Matthew 5:17)

> Being asked by the Pharisees when the kingdom of God would come, he answered them, "The kingdom of God is not coming in ways that can be observed, nor will they say, 'Look, here it is!' or 'There!' for behold, the kingdom of God is in the midst of you." (Luke 17:20–21)

> "But the hour is coming, and is now here, when the true worshipers will worship the Father in spirit and truth, for the Father is seeking such people to worship him." (John 4:23)

> Now these things happened to them as an example, but they were written down

for our instruction, on whom the end of the ages has come. (1 Corinthians 10:11)

He has delivered us from the domain of darkness and transferred us to the kingdom of his beloved Son. (Colossians 1:13)

We exhorted each one of you and encouraged you and charged you to walk in a manner worthy of God, who calls you into his own kingdom and glory. (1 Thessalonians 2:12)

At this point you might wonder why John has been minimized (receiving just one verse) in this discussion. Wasn't his Gospel a source? According to the rules that most critical scholars are playing by, a singly attested event cannot be corroborated and is set aside in the "may have happened but can't be historically demonstrated" category. So the vast majority of the gospel of John is immediately set aside because it contains 92 percent unique material. This is one of the legacies of the second historical quest for Jesus.

EVEN A MINIMAL JESUS CANNOT BE IGNORED

So what happens if we play by the rules set by people outside the church and unsympathetic to the reality of God or the Christian faith? Unlike the hyper-skeptical Jesus Seminar, an international group of Jesus scholars met over the course of a decade (1998–2008) and investigated this very question using mainstream rules. Their conclusion was that there were at least twelve significant events in the life of Jesus of Nazareth that can be positively established by these criteria.[13] What that means—if true—is that even without accepting the Bible as the Word of God and limiting the material you can use, you can still arrive at a robust portrait of the life and teachings of Jesus that takes you far beyond merely a prophet or religious leader. What would this minimal historical portrait look like? Here are the twelve significant events:

1. **Jesus affirmed the ministry of John the Baptist.** John was announcing that a new era of God (i.e., the kingdom of God) was approaching. Included in this message was that people were accountable to God and that a response was required.

2. Jesus collected twelve key followers. This was symbolic of the work that God had done in the past with Israel and was now doing with this new community.

3. Jesus publicly associated with sinners. This highlighted that forgiveness was available and that Jesus was in the middle of this process.

4. Jesus claimed to be Lord of the Sabbath. This was an authoritative claim that connected mercy to the mission of the Messiah.

5. Jesus cast out demons. This also demonstrated his authority and that the scope of his mission was far bigger than Rome and politics. He was dealing with spiritual realities as well.

6. Jesus accepted Peter's declaration that he was the Christ (i.e., Messiah). This is a pivotal identity event. Jesus begins to reshape expectations concerning what his being the Messiah would mean.

7. Jesus rode into Jerusalem on a donkey. Jesus' kingly entrance presented people with a choice to follow or reject—he would not dominate and force people into his kingdom.

8. Jesus claimed to have authority over the sacred space of the temple. Jesus' invitation should not be confused with timidity. God takes things very seriously.

9. Jesus connects the Passover meal with his disciples to his claim to be the deliverer of God's people. Jesus' messianic identity as a sacrifice to provide salvation is made explicit.

10. Jesus claimed unique divine authority when examined by Jewish leadership. Jesus, drawing from Daniel's prophecy concerning the Son of Man, makes clear the divine authority he is claiming.

11. The Roman ruler Pontius Pilate publicly executed Jesus for sedition. This indicates the very public need to do something about who Jesus was and what he was claiming.

12. Following Jesus' crucifixion and burial, his tomb was found empty by a group of women followers. Jesus made good on his promises. He was who he claimed to be.[14]

These twelve events have been summarized this way: "What Jesus offered was new and challenged the way things were being done. Jesus was more than a prophet or religious teacher. His claims went beyond simply pointing the way to God. His claims involved a personal level of authority through which God was revealing himself."[15] And then when you tie these claims to the resurrection event, the significance is seen in full bloom:

> Risen and alive, the one who stood at the center of God's kingdom was vindicated. His claims of kingship, heavenly rooted authority, and God's kingdom stood firm. Life triumphed over death. The disciples' grief became conviction. The offer of life had found in him a fresh focal point—forever. The disciples taught what Jesus had preached. They proclaimed the new promise of God. They shared that life had come in the message and person of Jesus. Resurrection not only meant new life for Jesus, but the offer of new life to the world.[16]

JESUS OUTSIDE THE NEW TESTAMENT DOCUMENTS

But what if we didn't rely on any of the accounts or source material that eventually are found in the Bible? A fair question. Without a single Bible verse, we know from history that:

> There was a Jewish man who lived early in the 1st century by the name of Jesus who was born out of wedlock, whose life intersected with that of John the Baptist, who as an adult became a very popular teacher in Israel who worked wondrous feats—apparently miraculous signs of different kinds, who gathered a closer group of followers together that he called disciples—5 of them are named—who consistently challenged conventional Jewish teaching on key topics of the Law and because of that was eventually arrested, was crucified (a Roman form of execution) as ordered by the Roman governor

Pontius Pilate (which narrows the time period down to his reign in Judea between AD 26–36) and that despite this horrible and shameful death his followers believed he was the Jewish Messiah, or Christ, and they claimed to have seen resurrected from the dead and within a couple of generations (at the latest) were singing hymns to him; worshipping him as if he were a god.[17]

That is pretty remarkable! Amazingly, some people still claim that Jesus never existed. To which Ben Witherington replies, "There is more historical evidence for the existence of Jesus than there is for the historical existence of Julius Caesar for example. . . . The only persons who doubt the existence of Jesus of Nazareth are those who either hate Christianity and so want it to disappear, or those who have not bothered to do the proper historical homework."[18] Even the skeptical Bart Ehrman admits, "Whether we like it or not, Jesus certainly existed."[19]

THREE REASONS THE STORY OF JESUS WAS NOT BORROWED FROM PAGAN MYSTERY RELIGIONS

During the first quest, the history of religions school was very popular among scholars. The idea was simply that Christianity was a copycat religion that had borrowed from other popular myths and created the Jesus myth. This claim was soundly refuted and scholars (whether liberal, moderate, or conservative) have abandoned it. However, it is a favorite of Internet skeptics and it makes the rounds on YouTube. So I do want to offer three reasons the copycat myth is false.

First, Christianity emerged out of first-century Judaism that was monotheistic and exclusive. The Jewish people had learned their lesson about worshiping other gods (cf. being judged by Assyria and Babylon). They were committed to one and only one God. The Shema in Deuteronomy 6:4 makes this clear, declaring, "Hear, O Israel: The Lord our God, the Lord is one." The New Testament teachings were clear as well: "For they themselves report concerning us the kind of reception we had among you, and how you turned to God from idols to serve the living and true God" (1 Thessalonians 1:9).

Second, the alleged parallels disappear once the specifics of each myth are examined. A dying and rising Jesus is not a meaningful parallel with crops coming to life in the spring dying off again in the winter. As Mary Jo Sharp notes, "The suggested 'parallels'—such as themes of virgin birth, sacrificial death, and resurrection—are not paralleled in the content of the texts. There is no sound evidence of overlap within the details of these two types of texts. The biblical account of Jesus cannot be grouped into the genre of mythological literature based on either story details or structure."[20]

Lastly, if any borrowing was going on, it was the pagan mystery religions copying from Christianity. Gregory Boyd and Paul Eddy observe, "With the exception of Osiris, all the written accounts of these myths date *after* the birth of Christianity."[21] If anything, mystery religions were copying from and being influenced by Christianity in the first two centuries because they had to compete to gain new converts and survive. And when you add all of the positive historical evidence for Jesus we have already discussed, it's easy to see why professional New Testament historians and scholars have abandoned this theory.

A COMPELLING JESUS

My point in sharing this minimal Jesus is not to diminish him. If you are seeking to believe, I hope this gives you confidence that at the very least you still get a pretty compelling Jesus. And for my friends who are reading this from the more skeptical side of the spectrum, everyone must come to terms with the radical claims and life of Jesus of Nazareth. He cannot simply be dismissed as a mythic moral teacher. I think we can know far more than just this minimal Jesus...but even if not, we still have preserved the core of Jesus without begging the question in the public conversation. And the significance of this should not be understated. Now, we turn our attention to discovering what the earliest Christians really believed.

Three Big Ideas

1. In order to engage the public conversation about Jesus today, we need to be familiar with the various quests for the historical Jesus and the methods that critical scholars are using to try to "recover" him. Even by playing by these rules, we still see a portrait of Jesus emerge who was claiming the authority of God and to be the Messiah. History reveals that Jesus cannot be simply dismissed as a good moral teacher.

2. The Gospels (and their sources: Mark, M, L, and Q) should not automatically be dismissed as unhistorical, because this begs the question of their reliability and historicity. But even without appealing to the New Testament writings, we see the broad strokes of Jesus' life and teachings attested by sources outside of the New Testament (e.g., Pliny, Josephus, and Tacitus). You still must do something with Jesus.

3. If we cannot know that Jesus of Nazareth existed, then we can know virtually nothing from history—that's how strong the evidence is. Moreover, the story of Jesus was not borrowed and then invented from copying mystery religions. We saw, among other things, that the context of first-century Jewish monotheism from which early Christianity would emerge was exclusive in nature and would not have tolerated this form of idolatry.

Conversation Tips

When it comes to Jesus, everyone wants to claim him. The main thing you want to try to do as you talk to people is make sure they are not inventing a Jesus they are comfortable with rather than investigating the real Jesus.

- One of the ways to do this is simply to ask them. So ask, "Who do you think Jesus claimed to be?"

- Then be ready to follow up with another question that tries to get at how they arrived at their position.

- Finally, do not get distracted by secondary issues when it comes to Jesus; stay on task and let Jesus' words and actions speak for themselves. As we have seen in this chapter, you have a lot to talk about even if someone doesn't already accept the Bible as the Word of God.

Digging Deeper

- Darrell Bock. *Who is Jesus?: Linking the Historical Jesus with the Christ of Faith*. New York: Howard Books, 2012.

- Mark Strauss. *Four Portraits, One Jesus: An Introduction to Jesus and the Gospels*. Grand Rapids: Zondervan, 2007.

HOW DO WE KNOW WHAT THE EARLIEST CHRISTIANS BELIEVED?

*There never was a time when the message of Jesus'
resurrection was not an integral part of the earliest
apostolic proclamation.*[1]
Gary Habermas

Was Christianity invented? Bart Ehrman pulls no punches when he declares:

Christianity as we have come to know it did not, in any event, spring into
being overnight. It emerged over a long period of time, through a period of
struggles, debates, and conflicts over competing views, doctrines, perspectives, canons, and rules. The ultimate emergence of the Christian religion
represents a human invention . . . arguably the greatest invention in the
history of Western civilization.[2]

There is a lot going on here and it will be our task, in this chapter and
the next, to sort out some of these shocking claims. But the core objection
is straightforward—do Christians believe today and does the New Testament
contain what the earliest Christians really believed from the beginning? Or
have Christians for centuries been basing their lives on creative storytelling,
myth making, and power plays?

Did you know that the first list containing all twenty-seven books in our New Testament doesn't show up until Athanasius writes an Easter letter to the churches in AD 367? (In case you are wondering, that is technically true.) In the next chapter we will explore the question of how we know the New Testament contains the right books, but as I began investigating this question I noticed that AD 30—the date of Jesus' crucifixion—is 337 years earlier than that letter from Athanasius. After all, the United States of America hasn't even been a country that long! How can we be confident that the core message of Christianity wasn't changed, misremembered, or deliberately distorted along the way?

What I found was surprising. Here are two lines of evidence that mutually reinforce one another, and as I will argue, demonstrate that we can be confident that the message Christians proclaim today is the very same message that the earliest Christians proclaimed within months of the crucifixion.[3]

A TIMELINE OF THE RESURRECTION MESSAGE

An Early Proclamation

It is no overstatement to say that the resurrection of Jesus of Nazareth is the central claim of the Christian faith.[4] You simply can't have Christianity without it. But how early was the proclamation of the message that Jesus was raised from the dead? This is a historical question about what happened in the first century, and as such, first-century eyewitness testimony will give us the best chance at a reasonable conclusion.

The four (canonical) Gospels are the earliest biographies of the life of Jesus dating from the first century.[5] According to a more liberal dating, the Gospels were written between AD 70 and 100 (Mark about AD 70; Matthew and Luke about AD 85; and John about AD 95).[6] Considering that Jesus of Nazareth was publically crucified in Rome in AD 30 (or 33), writings from thirty to seventy years after this event are still early when it comes to ancient history. For example, did you know that the earliest biography of Alexander the Great—included by Plutarch in his *Lives*—wasn't composed until about four hundred years after Alexander's death?

Interestingly, critical scholars love the apostle Paul and generally accept at least six of the thirteen letters attributed to him in the New Testament as authentic (cf. Romans, 1 and 2 Corinthians, Galatians, Philippians, and 1 Thessalonians). The reason for this is they have a named person as the author and historical setting to attach a date to; whereas the Gospels (they argue) are anonymous and the setting is uncertain. (We'll pick up the authorship of the Gospels in chapter 5.)

This is relevant to our discussion because one of the main texts concerning the proclamation of the resurrection message occurs in 1 Corinthians 15. This letter was *written* around AD 55 but the message that Paul *preached* to the Corinthians likely took place around AD 50 (cf. 1 Corinthians 15:1-2). If you are following the argument so far, the Gospels only get us to a maximum of seventy years from the crucifixion (which is still very early). However, Paul gives us a written text twenty-five years after the crucifixion and a preached message twenty years after the resurrection. We're getting closer.

Paul Gets His Message from the Eyewitnesses

Further examination of the message that Paul preached to the Corinthians reveals that this message did not originate with him:

> Now I make known to you, brethren, the gospel which I preached to you, which also you received, in which also you stand, by which also you are saved, if you hold fast the word which I preached to you, unless you believed in vain. For I *delivered* to you as of first importance what *I also received*, that Christ died for our sins according to the Scriptures, and that He was buried, and that He was raised on the third day according to the Scriptures, and that He appeared to Cephas, then to the twelve. After that He appeared to more than five hundred brethren at one time, most of whom remain until now, but some have fallen asleep; then He appeared to James, then to all the apostles; and last of all, as to one untimely born, He appeared to me also. (1 Corinthians 15:1-8 NASB, *italics added*)

Paul clearly admits that he is simply passing on to them what he had received. It is no small point that Paul places himself in the "chain of transmission."[7] But when and from whom did he get this material? The book of

Galatians—which critical scholars accept as being written by Paul—fills in some of the missing pieces:

> But when God, who had set me apart even from my mother's womb and called me through His grace, was pleased to reveal His Son in me so that I might preach Him among the Gentiles, *I did not immediately consult with flesh and blood*, nor did I go up to Jerusalem to those who were apostles before me; but I went away to Arabia, and returned once more to Damascus. Then three years later I went up to Jerusalem *to become acquainted* with Cephas, and stayed with him fifteen days. But I did not see any other of the apostles except James, the Lord's brother. (Now in what I am writing to you, I assure you before God that I am not lying.) (Galatians 1:15–20 NASB, *italics added*)

The literary context of Galatians 1 makes clear that the topic under discussion is the content of the gospel message. Here is a summary of what we learn. First, after Paul's conversion he did not consult with anyone. However, after three years, Paul traveled to Jerusalem to investigate and check out (the Greek term in 1:18 is *historesai* which is related to our word *history*) Peter and James's (the brother of Jesus) understanding of the gospel. The critical scholarly consensus is that Paul "received" the message, which he would later deliver to the Corinthians at this time. "Based on the usual date for Paul's conversion of between one and three years after Jesus' crucifixion, Paul's reception of this material in Jerusalem would be dated from approximately four to six years later, or from AD 34–36."[8] Given a crucifixion date of AD 30, we now have the message that was being proclaimed within four to six years.

Before we see if we can push this date any earlier, we need to mention one of the more amazing passages in the New Testament. Just to make sure he had the message right, Paul went back fourteen years later:

> Then after fourteen years, I went up again to Jerusalem, this time with Barnabas. I took Titus along also. I went in response to a revelation and, meeting privately with those esteemed as leaders, I presented to them the gospel that I preach among the Gentiles. *I wanted to be sure I was not running and had not been running my race in vain* . . . *they added*

nothing to my message. On the contrary, they recognized that I had been entrusted with the task of preaching the gospel to the uncircumcised, just as Peter had been to the circumcised. For God, who was at work in Peter as an apostle to the circumcised, was also at work in me as an apostle to the Gentiles. James, Cephas and John, those esteemed as pillars, gave me and Barnabas the right hand of fellowship when they recognized the grace given to me. (Galatians 2:1–2, 6–9 NIV, *italics added*)

Paul's academic pedigree is as impressive as it gets in the ancient world. He knew the law and was a "Hebrew of Hebrews" (Philippians 3:4–6). Yet, he went and submitted his gospel message to the earliest eyewitnesses—Peter, James the brother of Jesus, and John. The verdict? "They added nothing to my message." Regardless of a Jewish audience or a Gentile audience, they are all preaching the same gospel. The apostolic preaching of the gospel consisted of three elements: the deity, death, and resurrection of Jesus.[9] Paul would later recount, "Whether, then, it is I or they [i.e., Peter, James, or John] this is what we preach, and this is what you believed" (1 Corinthians 15:11 NIV).

A Resurrection Message

If Paul received the message from Peter and James, then where did they get the message? *From the beginning.* You will remember in 1 Corinthians 15:5–7 Peter and James are listed as eyewitnesses to the risen Jesus. Bauckham sums up the evidence by concluding, "There can be no doubt that . . . Paul is citing the *eyewitness testimony* of those who were recipients of resurrection appearances."[10] "There never was a time," concludes Habermas, "when the message of Jesus' resurrection was not an integral part of the earliest apostolic proclamation."[11]

The impact of the resurrection cannot be overstated, "The widespread belief and practice of the early Christians is only explicable if we assume that they all believed that Jesus was bodily raised, in an Easter event something like the stories the gospels tell: the reason they believed that he was bodily raised is because the tomb was empty and, over a short period thereafter, they encountered Jesus himself, giving every appearance of being bodily alive once more."[12]

Before moving on to the second argument, I want to sound a note of caution. You may be tempted to think that this is a case of the Bible proving the Bible—which is circular reasoning and a logical fallacy. However, in this argument, we have not been appealing to the Bible "as the inspired Word of God." (We'll have more to say about inspiration in a later chapter.) We have taken what critical scholars will give us—namely a handful of Paul's letters—and then worked with that material as historical first-century documents to see what we can learn about the origin of the resurrection message concerning Jesus of Nazareth. It's really important to make this distinction in your own mind and in your conversations with others.

THE FOUR S'S OF ORTHODOXY, FROM JESUS TO IRENAEUS (AD 30–AD 180)

The question before us is, How do we know what the earliest Christians really believed and how were they able to reliably pass core theology down *before* there was a functional canon of Scripture? In other words, how was the early message of Jesus' resurrection and other core doctrines that Paul received protected and transmitted among early Christians?

It is crucial to recognize that the ancient world was predominantly an oral culture. That is, societies were used to functioning without books. We, however, live in a post-Guttenberg world, so many of us have a hard time imagining how an oral culture could produce reliable history. Oral tradition is often caricatured as crude storytelling along the lines of the telephone game we all played as kids. This is an inaccurate picture to say the least.

Richard Bauckham, professor of New Testament studies at the University of St. Andrews, has done extensive research on oral tradition and eyewitness testimony in the first-century Jewish context. He writes, "Trusting testimony is not an irrational act of faith that leaves critical rationality aside; it is, on the contrary, the rationally appropriate way of responding to authentic testimony. Gospels understood as testimony are the entirely appropriate means of access to the historical Jesus."[13] He further notes that modern skeptics of testimony find themselves in an awkward position because "it is also a rather neglected fact that all history . . . relies on testimony."[14] In other words, you can dispense with testimony as a legitimate source of knowledge *only* if you are willing to dispense with the ability to discover *anything* about the past.

With the importance of testimony in mind, New Testament scholar Darrell Bock uses four S's to describe the organic process by which orthodoxy was maintained until there was a functioning canon of Scripture.[15]

1. Scriptures

As noted in our discussion of the historical Jesus in chapter 1, the earliest Christians were Jewish. Consequently, they took as their starting point the worldview of Jewish monotheism. (We will return to this when we discuss Gnosticism and the Lost Gospels in the next chapter.) This group saw continuity in what God had done in the Old Testament (i.e., the Hebrew Scriptures) and what God was doing now through Jesus the Messiah. Therefore it was natural and common for them to read the Hebrew Scriptures at public worship services. Notice Paul's words in light of this reality: "For everything that was written in the past was written to teach us so that through the endurance taught in the Scriptures and the encouragement they provide we might have hope" (Romans 15:4 NIV). The foundational documents of the earliest Christians were the Hebrew Scriptures. They were the theological baseline.

2. Summaries

Early Christians memorized and recited doctrinal summaries alongside the Hebrew Scriptures when they gathered for worship in house churches as they spread out across the Greco-Roman world. These oral texts were later *embedded* in written texts. It is important to highlight that these summaries often included the technical language of "delivered" and "received," language that related to how Jewish rabbis passed on formal tradition to their disciples. As Bauckham notes that, "We have unequivocal evidence, in Paul's letters, that the early Christian movement did practice the formal transmission of tradition."[16] In the previous section we looked at the most famous of these doctrinal summaries above—1 Corinthians 15:3–5. (Others include Romans 1:2–4; 1 Corinthians 8:4–6; 11:23–24.) But notice the core theology embedded here:

Jesus died as a substitute for sin, was buried, and raised again to new life just as the Hebrew Scriptures anticipated. And remember, that creedal statement goes all the way back to months following the crucifixion around AD 30.

3. Singing

How did you learn the words to "Amazing Grace"? Did you sit down and memorize it or did you absorb it over time? The same was true for the earliest Christians. When they gathered, early Christians sang their theology in hymns to show their devotion to the Lord Jesus Christ (Philippians 2:5–11 and Colossians 1:15–20 are two of the most famous in the NT). And just like catchy songs you can't get out of your head, the theologically rich lyrics stuck with them. Here is a classic passage concerning Yahweh (YHWH) in the Old Testament: "Turn to me and be saved, all the ends of the earth! For I am God, and there is no other. . . . To me every knee shall bow, every tongue shall swear allegiance" (Isaiah 45:22–23). Now look at the hymn the earliest Christians were singing to Jesus: "Therefore God has highly exalted him and bestowed on him the name that is above every name, so that at the name of Jesus every knee should bow, in heaven and on earth and under the earth, and every tongue confess that Jesus Christ is Lord, to the glory of God the Father" (Philippians 2:9–11).[17] The very same exaltation due to YHWH in Isaiah 45:23 is now due to Jesus Christ as well. And this essential belief is in place from the very beginning.

4. Sacraments

Baptism and the Lord's Supper were practiced on a regular basis in the local church context and they both pictured the basic elements of the salvation story as core theology (cf. Matthew 28:19–20; 1 Corinthians 11:23–26; Ephesians 4:4–6). Essentially you have a theological object lesson going on every time each of these ordinances is practiced in early Christianity.

These creeds, hymns, and practices *predated* the writing of the New Testament documents. (Remember that this was an oral culture and most people in the ancient world could not read.) Think of these last three S's as "oral texts" that the earliest Christian community recited and practiced *before* a completed New Testament existed. These foundational beliefs (sometimes called the "rule of faith") established the nonnegotiable core of orthodoxy from the very beginning.

HOW EARLY WAS JESUS BEING WORSHIPED AS GOD?

As we wrap up our discussion about the beliefs of earliest Christianity, let's revisit the question of how early Jesus was being worshiped as God. We have already learned from Paul's letter to the Philippians (which critical scholars accept as authentic) that Jesus was being worshiped as God within twenty-five years of his crucifixion. We have also seen that belief within early Christian singing (hymns). But it also can be found in early Christian summaries. The earliest occurs in the apostle Paul's words to the Corinthians:

> Therefore, as to the eating of food offered to idols, we know that "an idol has no real existence," and that "there is no God but one." For although there may be so-called gods in heaven or on earth—as indeed there are many "gods" and many "lords"—*yet for us there is one God, the Father,* from whom are all things and for whom we exist, and one Lord, Jesus Christ, through whom are all things and through whom we exist. (1 Corinthians 8:4–6, *italics added*)

Paul has done something unthinkable; he has taken the Shema of Deuteronomy 6:4—the most sacred Jewish expression of exclusive allegiance to the one God—and included Jesus "in the unique divine identity."[18] The belief that Jesus was God was very early, and the most natural explanation for this core belief was that he had been in fact raised from the dead.

And to show how public the worship of Jesus had become in earliest Christianity, see the comments of the Roman governor, Pliny the younger, as he wrestles with what to do about the Christians: "They [the Christians] were in the habit of meeting on a certain fixed day before it was light, when they sang in alternate verses a hymn to Christ, as to a god, and bound themselves by a solemn oath, not to any wicked deeds, but never to commit any fraud, theft or adultery, never to falsify their word."[19]

REJECTING EHRMAN'S WISHFUL THINKING

In his magisterial (and massive!) work, *Lord Jesus Christ: Devotion to Jesus in Earliest Christianity*, Larry Hurtado directly challenges Ehrman's claim that exalted beliefs, proclamation, and even worship of Jesus emerged gradually over time:

> Devotion to Jesus as divine erupted suddenly and quickly, not gradually and late, among first-century followers. More specifically, the origins lie in Jewish Christian circles of the earliest years. Only a certain wishful thinking continues to attribute the reverence of Jesus as divine decisively to the influence of pagan religion and the influx of Gentile converts, characterizing it as developing late and incrementally.[20]

We have established what the earliest Christians believed about Jesus. But why think any of this should be written down and collected in a predominantly oral culture and have the title "scripture" attached to it? In other words, why do we have a New Testament at all? And what about all of those so-called lost gospels that have been found in the scorched sands of Nag Hammadi, Egypt? We will answer these questions in the next chapter.

Three Big Ideas

1. The timeline for proclaiming Jesus' resurrection allows us to establish the core of what the earliest Christians believed without appealing to the Bible as God's Word to settle the matter. Since critical scholars will grant you certain books of Paul, you can establish a chain of testimony that gets you back to within months of the resurrection event itself.

2. During the time between the resurrection event and when Gospels began being recognized and received as Scripture, the four S's of orthodoxy—scripture, summaries, singing, and sacraments—provided the vehicle to maintain orthodoxy that originated with the apostolic teachings.

3. Jesus was worshiped remarkably early—within twenty-five years of his death. Something very unusual and significant must have happened to cause the earliest Christians, who were monotheists, to begin worshiping Christ as if he were God. This must be explained.

Conversation Tips

When it comes to the origins of Christianity, you want to frame the conversation in a proactive way. Here's what I mean.

- State positively why you think that we can be confident about what the earliest Christians believed. This tactic will help you avoid all of the "possibilities" that people can throw at you.

- Conversely, avoid the hypothetical argument and evidence. If you have presented positive evidence, then that beats a hypothetical every time.

Digging Deeper

- Robert M. Bowman and J. Ed Komoszewski. *Putting Jesus in His Place: The Case for the Deity of Christ*. Grand Rapids: Kregel, 2007.

- Andreas Kostenberger and Michael Kruger. *The Heresy of Orthodoxy: How Contemporary Culture's Fascination with Diversity Has Reshaped Our Understanding of Early Christianity*. Wheaton, IL: Crossway, 2010.

WHY WERE SOME GOSPELS BANNED FROM THE BIBLE?

The question "Why did you choose these Gospels?" would not have made sense to many Christians in the second century, for the question assumes that the church, or someone in it, had the authority to make the choice. To many, it would be like the question, 'Why did you choose your parents?'"[1]
Charles Hill

If you pick up a copy of Bart Ehrman's *Lost Scriptures: Books That Did Not Make It into the New Testament* and read the back cover, here is what you will find: "While most people think that the twenty-seven books of the New Testament are the only sacred writings of the early Christians, this is not at all the case."[2] Ehrman explains in the opening pages why the traditional view—that the twenty-seven books in our New Testament are the ones we are supposed to have and that the earliest Christians believed in the death, deity, and resurrection of Jesus—seems so obvious today, but is nonetheless incorrect:

> Only one set of early Christian beliefs emerged as victorious in the heated disputes over what to believe and how to live that were raging in the early centuries of the Christian movement. These beliefs, and the group who promoted them, came to be thought of as "orthodox" (literally meaning, "the right belief"), and alternative views—such as the view that there are two gods, or that the true God did not create the world, or that Jesus was

not actually divine, etc.—came to be labeled "heresy" (= false belief) and were then ruled out of court. Moreover, the victors in the struggles to establish Christian orthodoxy not only won their theological battles, they also rewrote the history of the conflict; later readers, then, naturally assumed that the victorious views had been embraced by the vast majority of Christians from the beginning, all the way back to Jesus and his closest followers, the apostles.[3]

Every Easter a new conspiracy theory about Christianity shows up on the History Channel or is published highlighting one or more of the elements from Ehrman's aforementioned narrative. The year 2013 was no exception, with Hal Taussig publishing *The New, New Testament* with thirty-seven instead of the traditional twenty-seven books in his New Testament—"Although the western branch of Christianity has implied that the Bible is eternally stable, this has really never been the case."[4]

WERE SOME GOSPELS LOST?

In 1945, fifty-two papyri were discovered at Nag Hammadi in Lower Egypt and some of these texts had the word "gospel" in the title. Scholars have known about these and other second- through fourth-century documents for a long time, but only recently has the general public been introduced to them, which has caused quite a bit of controversy and speculation.

This is due to the fact that our culture is generally skeptical of authority and enjoys a good conspiracy theory; sprinkle in some high-definition documentaries around Easter and Christmas with titles like *Banned Books of the Bible* or *Bible Secrets Revealed* and the recipe for confusion is complete. People began to wonder—was there a cover-up by the church? Were we lied to about Jesus?

These so-called "lost gospels" fall into two categories: (1) New Testament Apocrypha and (2) Gnostic writings. *Apocrypha* means "hidden things." These writings tried to fill in the gaps about two periods of Jesus' life—his childhood and the three days between his death and resurrection. The motivations for these works range from entertainment to the comprehensive redefinition of the Jesus revealed in the first-century writings of the New Testament.

In case this is news to you, here are some of the titles: *Gospel of Thomas*, *Gospel of Judas*, *Apocryphon of James*, *Apocryphon of John*, *Hypostasis of the Archons*, *Gospel of Mary*, *Gospel of Philip*, *Gospel of Peter*, *Gospel of Truth*, and my personal favorite *The Second Treatise of the Great Seth* (and no, these are not the lost writings of Darth Maul of *Star Wars* fame).

So, are these writings Scripture? Should they be included in our New Testament? Do we need to revise our understanding of "orthodox" Christianity?

WHY DO WE HAVE A NEW TESTAMENT AT ALL?

The prevailing view among critical scholars is that the canon (i.e., those books that are supposed to be in our New Testament and read as Scripture) is (1) a late development and (2) was artificially imposed by people who had the power to do so. Whether the canonized listing came through the books selected by the Emperor Constantine in the fourth century for political reasons or through the creativity and influence of bishops like Irenaeus in the second century, this is just another example of history being written by the winners, these scholars argue. This approach is known as an *extrinsic* model of canon.[5]

I think the best way to respond is by asking which of these documents tells us the truth about the faith that was preached and received in the early church (cf. Jude 3). This is both a theological and historical question—what did the early church believe and preach from the very beginning?

In the last chapter, we established from history the core of what the earliest Christians preached and believed concerning Jesus. Of course believing something doesn't make it true (see the summary of the argument for the resurrection in appendix 1), but there can be little doubt that they preached Jesus risen from the dead and worshiped him as God shortly after his humiliating and very public crucifixion. But why think any of this should be written down, collected, and authoritatively read? In other words, why do we have a New Testament at all?

It probably seems strange for you to even read those words; after all, the reason why we have a New Testament is because it's part of the Bible. The problem with this response is that it does not address the fundamental challenges being made by Ehrman and others as to how we know the Bible has the right books or even would have been looking to have books in the first place.

AN INTRINSIC MODEL OF THE NT CANON

In this section I will offer three good reasons to believe that the texts of the New Testament canon would have emerged naturally on its own—the *intrinsic* model.[6] I think the critical view (i.e., the extrinsic only model) is mistaken because it is starting from faulty assumptions; it starts late and moves backward rather than starting early and moving later.

Reason 1: The Beliefs of First-Century Jews and the Earliest Christians

The intrinsic model of the NT canon recognizes that *first-century Jews were waiting for God to finish the story of the Old Testament, and the earliest Christians believed that God was completing the story through Jesus of Nazareth.*

As we have already noted, the cultural context for the life, teachings, and death of Jesus as well as the earliest Christians was Jewish monotheism (specifically the second-temple-period Judaism). New Testament scholar N. T. Wright draws out one of the key implications of this concerning our question of New Testament origins:

> The great story of the Hebrew scriptures was therefore inevitably read in the Second Temple period as a story in search of a conclusion. This ending would have to incorporate the full liberation and redemption of Israel, an event which had not happened as long as Israel was being oppressed, a prisoner in her own land. And this ending would have to be *appropriate*: It should correspond to the rest of it in obvious continuity and conformity.[7]

The Hebrew Scriptures (what we refer to today as the Old Testament) were looking for God to break into history in a redemptive way. In short, the people of God were waiting on God to do something, to send a Messiah, to finish the story. The words of the prophet Amos fueled this hopeful expectation:

"In that day I will raise up the booth of David that is fallen and repair its breaches, and raise up its ruins and rebuild it as in the days of old, that they may possess the remnant of Edom and all the nations who are called by my name," declares the Lord who does this. "Behold, the days are coming," declares the Lord, "when the plowman shall overtake the reaper and the treader of grapes him who sows the seed; the mountains shall drip sweet wine, and all the hills shall flow with it. I will restore the fortunes of my people Israel, and they shall rebuild the ruined cities and inhabit them; they shall plant vineyards and drink their wine, and they shall make gardens and eat their fruit. I will plant them on their land, and they shall never again be uprooted out of the land that I have given them," says the Lord your God. (Amos 9:11–15)

Understanding this background illuminates why the disciples ask the risen Jesus, "Lord, will you at this time restore the kingdom to Israel?" (Acts 1:6).

What is significant for our purposes here is that these first-century Jewish people believed that God had acted redemptively through Jesus of Nazareth. They understood the kingdom of God to be arriving through him as the long-awaited Messiah. Mark recounts, "Now after John was arrested, Jesus came into Galilee, proclaiming the gospel of God, and saying, 'The time is fulfilled, and the kingdom of God is at hand; repent and believe in the gospel'" (1:14–15; cf. Jesus in Luke 4:18–19 as fulfillment of Isaiah 61:1–2). They also believed Jesus was the long-awaited prophet whom Moses spoke of in Deuteronomy 18:18: "I will raise up for them a prophet like you from among their brothers. And I will put my words in his mouth, and he shall speak to them all that I command him." The silence was broken, the messianic age had dawned, and God was speaking again.

Before moving on to the next reason for an intrinsic model, it is important to highlight the pattern in the Old Testament; after God acted in a redemptive way, he usually gave his people new revelation. The clearest example of this was the exodus where they were rescued from Egyptian captivity. After God had delivered them, he gave them new revelation (i.e., Genesis through Deuteronomy). The idea is that if God gave new revelation following the physical redemption of Israel from Egypt, then how much more so following the ultimate redemption of Israel (and all the peoples of the world) through Jesus the Messiah?

Reason 2: The Earliest Christians Believed Jesus Had Established a New Covenant

The intrinsic model of the NT canon recognizes that *the earliest Christians understood that covenants in the ancient world were written documents and believed Jesus the Messiah had inaugurated the New Covenant.*

The New Covenant was the lens through which Jesus' ministry was viewed. Given their Jewish heritage, the earliest Christians "naturally understood the activity of Jesus and the inaugurated kingdom of God through the category of God's covenantal promises. The Last Supper was interpreted as a covenantal meal as Jesus declared, 'This cup that is poured out for you is the new covenant in my blood' (Luke 22:20; cf. Matthew 26:28; Mark 14:24)—a vivid echo of Jeremiah 31:31."[8] It is noteworthy that Paul understood himself and the other apostles as "ministers of a new covenant" (2 Corinthians 3:6). At this point, you might be thinking, *OK, but why does this matter for why we have a New Testament?* (By the way, *Testament* is a synonym for *Covenant*.)

Here's the connection: Covenants in the ancient Near Eastern/Jewish context were essentially written documents that specified the terms of the agreement between the two parties—usually a ruling king and an under-king. In Israel's case, the other party was Yahweh himself—the High King. Here are just two examples:

Then he took the Book of the Covenant and read it in the hearing of the people. (Exodus 24:7)

And the Lord will single him out from all the tribes of Israel for calamity, in accordance with all the curses of the covenant written in this Book of the Law. (Deuteronomy 29:21)

Kruger summarizes the major takeaway: "Since the Old Testament witness suggests a tight relationship between covenants and written texts, it would be natural for the earliest Christians (who were Jews) to anticipate new covenant documents."[9]

Reason 3: The Earliest Christians Believed the Apostles Were Authorized to Communicate the New Covenant Message

If the earliest Christians anticipated new covenant documents, who would have the authority to write such documents? The answer is the apostles. *The earliest Christians believed that the apostles were uniquely authorized by Jesus to communicate the message of the New Covenant to the world.* They were— and understood themselves to be—authorized by Jesus to preach the gospel of the New Covenant and would have carried Christ's authority. "And he [Jesus] appointed twelve (whom he also named apostles) so that they might be with him and he might send them out to preach and have authority" (Mark 3:14–15; cf. John 14:26 and 2 Corinthians 3:6). Writing at the end of the first century, Clement of Rome expresses the logic of this derived authority: "The Apostles received the Gospel for us from the Lord Jesus Christ, Jesus the Christ was sent from God. The Christ therefore is from God and the Apostles from the Christ" (1 Clement 42:1–2).[10]

This brings us to a second key point. With this understanding of apostolic authority in mind and given the Jewish heritage of earliest Christianity, it would be only natural and even expected that the apostles write down the New Covenant teachings from God through Jesus the Messiah. The Hebrew Scriptures reveal many examples[11] of God's revealed redemptive activity needing to be written down for future generations to learn from or be reminded of:

> Write this as a memorial *in a book.* (Exodus 17:14 [God to Moses], *all italics added*)

> And now, go, *write* it before them *on a tablet* and inscribe it in a book, that it may be for the time to come as a witness forever. (Isaiah 30:8 [God to Isaiah])

So it should come as no surprise when the apostle John declares, "These are *written* so that you may believe that Jesus is the Christ, the Son of God, and that by believing you may have life in his name" (John 20:31). Furthermore, as Richard Bauckham reminds us, the Gospels were written, "to give permanence to eyewitness testimony beyond the lifetime of the eyewitnesses."[12] The apostles were unquestionably seen as the authoritative eyewitnesses and founders of the Christian movement resting on the cornerstone of Jesus Christ (cf. Ephesians 2:20).

Lastly, they were authorized eyewitnesses on a mission to the world. As Luke the historian reminds us, "But you [the apostles] will receive power when the Holy Spirit has come upon you, and you will be my witnesses in Jerusalem and in all Judea and Samaria, and to the end of the earth" (Acts 1:8). Theirs was a global mission. But if they couldn't be in more than one place at once, then how would they ensure the message could reach—and remain consistent—throughout the world? They had to write it down. In his massive two-volume work, *Early Christian Mission*, Eckhard Schnabel writes, "There is no doubt, however, that the missionary work of the early believers in Jesus the Messiah in the first century led to the establishment of Christian communities in dozens of cities of the Roman Empire."[13] This is powerful evidence that the apostles were successful in getting the word out about Jesus the Messiah and then entrusted these apostolic writings to the elders and leaders of these New Covenant communities as they grew.

Were the New Testament Authors Aware They Were Writing Scripture?

One of the questions that usually comes up while teaching students on the origins of the Bible is, Were the New Testament authors aware they were writing *Scripture*? A fascinating question, to be sure. But it kind of depends on what you mean by *Scripture*. If by that you mean, Did they envision the current state of our Bible post printing press? Well, no. However, I would suggest that a better question would be whether they thought of themselves as writing with the authority of the risen Christ. If that is the question, then yes, there are numerous occasions in the New Testament documents where we see evidence of this. Here are some of them:

> Paul, an apostle—not from men nor through man, but through Jesus Christ and God the Father, who raised him from the dead. (Galatians 1:1)

> And we also thank God constantly for this, that when you received the word of God, which you heard from us, you accepted it not as the word

of men but as what it really is, the word of God, which is at work in you believers. (1 Thessalonians 2:13)

In the name of the Lord Jesus Christ, we command you, brothers and sisters, to keep away from every believer who is idle and disruptive and does not live according to the teaching you received from us. . . . Take special note of anyone who does not obey our instruction in this letter. Do not associate with them, in order that they may feel ashamed. (2 Thessalonians 3:6, 14 NIV)

The beginning of the good news about Jesus the Messiah, the Son of God. (Mark 1:1 NIV)

This is the disciple who is bearing witness about these things, and who has written these things. (John 21:24)

This is now the second letter that I am writing to you, beloved. In both of them I am stirring up your sincere mind by way of reminder, that you should remember the predictions of the holy prophets and the commandment of the Lord and Savior through your apostles. (2 Peter 3:1–2)

A careful study of these and other passages has led NT scholar Michael Kruger to conclude that the

New Testament authors are quite aware of their own authority . . . they were consciously passing down the authoritative apostolic message. Given the authoritative role of the apostles in early Christianity, and the manner in which they were commissioned to speak for Christ, an apostolic writing would bear the highest possible authority. Indeed it would bear Christ's authority. Thus, it matters not whether the New Testament authors specifically used the term "Scripture" when speaking of their own books . . . it would have functionally been the same as Scripture.[14]

SETTING THE RECORD STRAIGHT ON DIVERSITY IN EARLY CHRISTIANITY

When thinking about the diversity of beliefs in early Christianity, we need to remember three things. First, the fact of diversity and disagreement—by itself—proves nothing. This is simply a logical issue. Just because people give different answers to a question, it does not follow that there is no answer to that question. Furthermore, why think that everyone must have agreed immediately? Lastly, certainty is not possible regarding history, but a high degree of probability is—and that should be our goal.

Second, we must avoid two extremes in our thinking. When we think about disagreements and diversity in early Christianity, it's important to avoid both the overly sanitized version and the exaggerated version. As evangelicals, we're more often guilty of the sanitized version. This is the version where there's no disagreement whatsoever about any of the books and certainty is achieved. It's pristine, perfect, everybody agrees, and all is well. That's not quite how it happened. The other extreme is when you see disagreement about everything. Everything was up for grabs. It was the wild, wild West of Scripture formation. And that's not the case either.

We need to remember the Bible was inspired through a fully divine process *and* a fully human process. We sometimes forget the fully human part. If things were going to be written down, that would be a normal historical process. Naturally you would have geographical considerations where communication would take time and people would disagree sometimes. That is all part of the messiness of human life. And all sorts of normal conventions go along with the history writing that we need to recognize as part of the process.

Third, we need to draw a distinction between the core of canonical books and the boundaries of the canonical books, "We should not use lack of *agreement* over the edges of the canon as evidence for the *existence* of a canon."[15] In other words, the core was established very early, but the boundaries took some time to sort out. As we established with the resurrection proclamation timeline and the four S's of orthodoxy in the previous chapter, the core theological trajectory was established from the beginning.

EARLY WITNESSES TO THE CORE OF THE CANON

One approach to the canon is that it only really began to take shape at the instigation of Irenaeus around the turn of the second century (ca. 180). However, I think there are good reasons to see a core group of authoritative books established well before then. But since he tends to be a lightning rod for critics when we approach the formation of the canon, let's begin with Irenaeus, who was the bishop of Lyons. Significantly, he was a disciple of Polycarp, and Polycarp knew the apostle of John personally. Irenaeus's most famous statement indicated that there are and can only be four Gospels: "It is not possible that the Gospels can be either more or fewer in number than they are. For, since there are four zones of the world in which we live, and four principal winds, while the Church is scattered throughout all the world, and the "pillar and ground" of the Church is the Gospel and the spirit of life; it is fitting that she should have four pillars."[16] In addition to the four Gospels, he also affirmed as Scripture all of Paul's writings (except Philemon), Acts, Hebrews, James, 1 Peter, 1 and 2 John, and Revelation. He affirmed twenty-three of the twenty-seven books of the New Testament.

Irenaeus' statement is usually critiqued on the basis of modern (post-enlightenment) history writing that typically does not employ artful language nor seek scientific precision. But it's illegitimate to hold him to that standard. The goal should be to understand him in light of the conventions of that day. The argument he is making is not one of logical necessity (i.e., that it's not logically possible for there to be more than four Gospels) but rather one of beauty or proportion. Rather than arbitrarily establishing four Gospels in AD 180, he "is simply offering a retrospective theological explanation for a longstanding church tradition,"[17] notes Kruger.

Now let's turn our attention to some of the writings of earlier apostolic fathers that indicate the Gospels were not somehow magically established as authoritative at the end of the second century.

- **The Muratorian Canon/Fragment (ca. 180).** As our earliest canonical list, the Muratorian Canon "confirms the scriptural status of twenty-two of the twenty-seven New Testament books, including all four Gospels, Acts, the thirteen epistles of Paul, Jude, 1 and 2 John . . . and Revelation."[18] Even though this list is technically anonymous, it is very similar to Irenaeus' list and is an independent line of evidence indicating agreement around a core of New Testament writings.

- **Theophilus of Antioch (ca. 177).** As bishop of Antioch, Theophilus put the Gospels on the same level of authority as the Old Testament prophets because they both originated from the same source, the Spirit of God: "Moreover, concerning the righteousness which the law enjoined, confirmatory utterances are found both with the prophets and in the Gospels, because they all spoke inspired by one Spirit of God."[19] His collection of scriptural writings includes the four Gospels, the (thirteen) Pauline letters, and probably a few more (also very similar to Irenaeus).[20]

- **Clement of Alexandria (ca. 198).** Clement was the brilliant head of the catechetical school in Alexandria.[21] He affirmed as scriptural the four Gospels, all thirteen of Paul's letters, Hebrews, Acts, 1 Peter, 1 and 2 John, Jude, and Revelation. One point sometimes brought up is that he also quoted from extrabiblical literature such as the *Gospel of the Egyptians* and the *Gospel of the Hebrews*. But given his interaction with a wide variety of literature, this should not be surprising. Just because someone refers to a book does not mean it should be regarded as being on par with Scripture. The textual evidence bears this out as Clement referenced the canonical Gospels significantly more: Matthew 757 times, Luke 402 times, John 331 times, and Mark 182 times; the apocryphal gospels a meager sixteen times.[22]

- **Tatian (ca. 150–60).** Tatian famously composed a harmony of the four Gospels called the Diatessaron. This is highly significant; as Bruce Metzger notes, "The Diatessaron supplies proof that all four Gospels were regarded as authoritative, otherwise it is unlikely that Tatian would have dared to combine them into one gospel account."[23] It is also important to note that as we have discovered so far, no one bound together in a codex anything other than the four canonical Gospels.

- **Justin Martyr (ca. 150–160).** Justin was an apologist and philosopher in the early church and also the teacher and mentor of Tatian (who you will recall wrote the first harmony of the four canonical gospels). He described the worship practices of the early Christians this way: "And on the day called Sunday, all who live in cities or in the country gather together to one place, and the memoirs of the apostles or the writings of the prophets are read, as long as time permits; then, when the reader has ceased, the president verbally instructs, and exhorts to the imitation of these good things" (1 Apology 67).[24]

Notice again the pattern of reading the works of the apostles alongside the prophets. Justin uses the term *memoir* instead of *Gospel* due to his audience, and these "were drawn up by His apostles and those who followed them.[25] The writings were authoritative because of their source—Christ's apostles.

- **Tertullian (ca. 160–230).** Writing from Carthage in Africa against the Marcionite heresy of a version of Gnosticism (in Marcionem 4.2.2), he acknowledges "all four canonical Gospels and indicates they were written either by apostles or by associates of the apostles."[26] Bruce Metzger summarizes Tertullian's views on authoritative Scripture: "Tertullian cites all the writings of the New Testament except 2 Peter, James, and 2 and 3 John" and that he "regarded the Scriptures of the Old Testament as divinely given, and he attributed to the four Gospels and the apostolic Epistles an authority equal to that of the Law and the Prophets. The orally transmitted 'rule of faith' and the written Scriptures were mutually appealed to, and any writing that did not conform to the rule of faith could not be accepted as Scripture."[27]

- **Papias (ca. 125).** As the bishop Hierapolis, Papias was the friend of Polycarp and had heard the apostle John preach (i.e., "the hearer of John, and a companion of Polycarp").[28] So Papias would have received John's testimony around the end of the first century—and that is very early. Concerning the canonical Gospels, he writes, "This also the presbyter said: Mark, having become the interpreter of Peter, wrote down accurately, though not in order, whatsoever he remembered of the things said or done by Christ. . . . For he was careful of one thing, not to omit any of the things which he had heard, and not to state any of them falsely. . . . But concerning Matthew he writes as follows: 'So then Matthew wrote the oracles in the Hebrew language, and every one interpreted them as he was able.'"[29] This clearly affirms Matthew and Mark as *written* documents (i.e., not just oral tradition). In addition, Kruger notes, "As for the other New Testament writings, it appears that Papias also knew 1 John, 1 Peter, Revelation, and also some Pauline epistles. Given that Papias knew Johannine writings and also sat under John's preaching, we have good grounds for thinking that he would have known John's Gospel."[30] Papias is a very important witness.

- **Ignatius (ca. 110).** As the bishop of Antioch, Ignatius was martyred early in the second century. Regarding apostolic authority, he says, "I do not, as Peter and Paul, issue commandments unto you. They were apostles; I am but a condemned man."[31] Furthermore, Ignatius knew several of Paul's writings including 1 Corinthians, Ephesians, Romans, Philippians, Galatians, and 1 and 2 Timothy.[32]

- **Polycarp (ca. 110).** As the bishop of Smyrna, Polycarp knew both Papias and the apostle John and was martyred around AD 155. He affirms the apostleship of Paul in contrast with himself. "For neither I, nor any other such one, can come up to the wisdom of the blessed and glorified Paul."[33] Polycarp also cites several of Paul's letters (Romans, 1 Corinthians, Galatians, Ephesians, Philippians, 1 and 2 Timothy). Finally, he probably cites Ephesians 4:26 as Scripture.[34]

- **Clement of Rome (ca. 95).** Clement writes very early and affirms the authority of the apostles: "The Apostles received the Gospel for us from the Lord Jesus Christ, Jesus the Christ was sent from God. The Christ therefore is from God and the Apostles from the Christ." Recognizing Paul's unique authority, he says, "Take up the epistle of the blessed Apostle Paul. What did he write to you at the time when the Gospel first began to be preached? Truly, under the inspiration of the Spirit, he wrote to you concerning himself, and Cephas, and Apollos, because even then parties had been formed among you."[35]

More could be said, but enough has been documented to clearly indicate that a core of Scripture existed from very early on and was most certainly not the creative invention of Irenaeus at the end of the second century or Constantine in the fourth century.[36] Because the core was established so early, this would also mean that certain books simply could not be accepted as Scripture.

WHY WERE CERTAIN BOOKS *ULTIMATELY REJECTED* FROM THE CANON?

By now it should be clear that books were not just arbitrarily rejected for no good reason. "Eventually, three kinds of literature were decisively rejected as noncanonical: (1) those that were obvious forgeries (2) those that were late productions (second century or later) and (3) those that did not conform to the orthodoxy of the core books *already known* to be authentic."[37]

The twenty-seven books we have were included in the New Testament Canon because they fit with the authoritative, apostolic teaching that can be traced back to Jesus himself. "Recognized books" formed the canonical core and were firmly established by mid–second century; "disputed books," while also orthodox, did not gain immediate acceptance by all. Meanwhile, "rejected books" were rejected from the canon, although they were orthodox and regarded as useful—much as C. S. Lewis might be quoted in church today, but not as Scripture. Finally, "heretical books" were forgeries, both nonorthodox and not to be read. Chart 3 lists the books in each of the categories of acceptance and rejection.[38]

Chart 3

BOOKS CONSIDERED FOR THE NEW TESTAMENT CANON

Recognized Books	Disputed Books	Rejected Books	Heretical Books
The four Gospels, Acts, Epistles of Paul, Hebrews, 1 John, 1 Peter, and Revelation	James, Jude, 2 Peter, 2 and 3 John	Shepherd of Hermes, the Epistle of Barnabas, and 1 Clement	Gospel of Thomas, Gospel of Peter, and the Acts of John
The canonical core of orthodox books was firmly established by the middle of the second century.	While these orthodox books did not gain immediate and universal acceptance, "they were known to most."	These are generally orthodox books that were rejected from the Canon, but still regarded as useful (e.g., C. S. Lewis might be quoted in church today, but not as Scripture). Early Christians made careful distinctions.	These forgeries are not to be read and are not orthodox.

Reading the Lost Gospels for Yourself

The first time I heard about these "lost gospels," it honestly made me nervous . . . *until I read them.* The juiciest of the apocryphal writings is probably the Infancy Gospel of Thomas. Here are some things I discovered about Jesus' childhood: he called a child an "unrighteous, irreverent idiot" (3:1–3). Another child bumped into Jesus, which aggravated Him so much that Jesus struck him dead (4:1–2). Evidently those who provoked *childhood Jesus* fell dead a lot (14:3). No, I'm not making this up.

Then there are the Gnostic writings. Gnosticism can get kind of complicated, so chart 4 contrasts it with the worldview of the earliest Christians who were Jewish monotheists (the Greek word *gnosis* means "knowledge"). Think oil and water.

Chart 4

ORTHODOX CHRISTIANITY VERSUS GNOSTICISM

Orthodox Christianity	Gnosticism
There is only one God and Creator.	There are multiple creators.
The world, body, soul, and spirit are good.	The world and body are evil. *Only* spirit and soul are good.
Jesus is fully human and fully divine.	Jesus only *appeared* human; he was only a spirit being.
Jesus came to restore relationships broken by sin.	Ignorance, not sin, is the ultimate problem.
Faith in Christ brings salvation (available to all).	"Special knowledge" brings salvation (available to only a few).

The most popular example of Gnostic writings is the *Gospel of Thomas*. It certainly wins the most scandalous passage award: "Simon Peter said to them, 'Let Mary leave us, for women are not worthy of life.' Jesus said, 'I myself shall lead her in order to make her male, so that she too may become a living spirit resembling you males. For every woman who will make herself male will enter the kingdom of heaven'" (Saying 114). Both of these documents were written long after the time of Jesus and his earliest followers.[39]

The bottom line is that these gospels were not lost to the early church; early Christians knew about them and rejected them for good reasons (cf. Irenaeus in AD 180). While historically interesting, these so-called "lost gospels" offer us nothing significant about the historical Jesus. The canonical writings in the New Testament are still the earliest and most reliable witnesses to the words and works of Jesus.

History Written by the Winners?

In response to the belief that history is written by the winners, I think the evidence we have set forth in this and the previous chapter show that sometimes the winners deserved to win.[40] Moreover, writes Kruger, "the idea of canon was built into the DNA of the Christian religion and thus emerged quite naturally. In this sense, the canon was like a seedling sprouting from the soil of early Christianity—although it was not fully a tree until the fourth century, it was there, in nuce, from the beginning."[41]

Therefore, it is perfectly reasonable for the twenty-first-century Christ-follower to have confidence that the chain of testimony from the first century until now remains strong. As the apostle John wrote:

> That which was *from the beginning*, which we have heard, which we have seen with our eyes, which we looked upon and have touched with our hands, concerning the word of life—the life was made manifest, and we have seen it, and testify to it and proclaim to you the eternal life, which was with the Father and was made manifest to us—that which we have seen and heard we proclaim also to you, so that you too may have fellowship with us; and indeed our fellowship is with the Father and with his Son Jesus Christ. And we are writing these things so that our joy may be complete. *This is the message we have heard from him and proclaim to you.* (1 John 1:1–5, italics added)

Three Big Ideas

1. Rather than an external collection of books being forced on Christians by the church in the fourth century (extrinsic model), we have seen at least three good reasons to think that a collection of New Testament documents would have emerged on their own (intrinsic model): (1) First-century Jews were waiting for God to finish the story of the Old Testament and the earliest Christians believed that God was completing the story through Jesus of Nazareth; (2) the earliest Christians understood that covenants in the ancient world were written documents and believed that Jesus the Messiah had inaugurated the New Covenant; and (3) the earliest Christians believed that the apostles were uniquely authorized by Jesus to communicate the message of the New Covenant to the world.

2. The fact of diversity and disagreement—by itself—proves nothing. Just because people give different answers to a question, it does not follow that there is no answer to that question. Also, when we think about disagreements and diversity in early Christianity, it's important to avoid both the overly sanitized version and the exaggerated version. We can affirm that there were some disagreements around the edges of canon while also affirming with confidence that a core set of books was already functioning as canon by the middle of the second century. We should expect this from a fully human (as well as fully divine) process.

3. The lost gospels were banned because they were late (not written during the time of the apostles) and were at odds with the four S's of orthodoxy (the teaching of the apostles). Further, the theology contained in Judaism and that of Gnosticism are like oil and water. This was not an arbitrary decision or power play made by the early church.

Conversation Tips

When talking with others about canon, the disagreement and diversity challenges typically are where you need to concentrate. The reason for this is that a version of this objection when talking about the diversity of beliefs already gets a lot of play in our culture—it's the "there can't possibly be just one way" objection.

* Help people see the flaw in this way of thinking.

* Then introduce them to the idea that rather than a set of books being imposed on the church by the "winners," there are actually good reasons to think that a collection of New Testament writings would have naturally emerged.

* The time before the "finalized" list of books of the Bible is like a black box to people—help them understand the resurrection timeline and the four S's arguments of chapter 3.

Digging Deeper

* Michael J. Kruger. *The Question of Canon: Challenging the Status Quo in the New Testament Debate.* Downers Grove, IL: InterVarsity, 2013.

* Darrell Bock. *The Missing Gospels: Unearthing the Truth Behind Alternative Christianities.* Nashville: Thomas Nelson, 2007.

DID THE BIBLICAL WRITERS LIE ABOUT THEIR IDENTITY?

*Those who say that forgeries exist in the Bible really
need to take a closer look at the evidence. The
onus of proof weighs heavily upon them . . . any
objections to the authenticity of biblical books can
be plausibly answered. The evidence we possess
points to the trustworthiness of Scripture.*[1]

Terry Wilder

You might be surprised to learn that of the twenty-seven New Testament
books, "only eight almost certainly go back to the author whose name they
bear."[2] That means nineteen books in our New Testament were forged—or at
least that's what Bart Ehrman is arguing. He goes on further to say that:

> Even now many scholars are loath to call the forged documents of the New
> Testament forgeries—this is, after all, the Bible we're talking about. But the
> reality is that by any definition of the term, that's what they are. A large
> number of books in the early church were written by authors who falsely
> claimed to be apostles in order to deceive their readers into accepting their
> books and the views they represented.[3]

Basically, since everyday people still revere the Bible, scholars do not
want to spoil that by letting the rest of us in on this dirty little secret of NT
studies. After all, who wants to burst our bubble? Ehrman does not share

those reservations and is only too happy to slip some added skepticism into your Sunday morning service.

Did you ever hear any of this growing up in church? I certainly didn't. It wasn't until graduate school that I encountered the idea that many scholars at places like Princeton and Harvard think there are forgeries in the New Testament. We will come to some specific disputed books below, but my entry point into this conversation concerned Paul and the authenticity of the Pastoral Epistles. I discovered that many critical scholars often argue that Paul really didn't write 1 and 2 Timothy, and Titus—even though they bear his name in the opening lines. So I investigated the evidence and wrote a paper defending Paul as the author of the Pastoral Epistles. In this chapter I will share some of the things that I learned along the way. But before we dive in, we need to put this issue in context, clarify some assumptions, and define some important terms. If you have never heard about any of these claims before, then the word *pseudepigrapha* alone is probably enough to scare you off.

DEFINING OUR TERMS

We need to define some terms (and it's OK if you have to reread this section a few times to get it straight!). *The Dictionary of New Testament Background* offers these two related words: "Pseudonymity and pseudepigraphy denote the practice of ascribing written works to someone other than the author—that is, the works in question are falsely (*pseud-*) named (*onoma*, 'name') or [falsely] attributed (*epigraphos*, 'superscription')."[4] This is what Ehrman refers to as a forgery. Next, while these forged books are also considered *apocryphal* (used as an adjective), which just means "any text or saying of doubtful authority or truthfulness," they are not to be confused with the books of the Apocrypha (used as a proper noun), which refer to the additional Old Testament books the Roman Catholic church includes in their canon (e.g., 1 and 2 Maccabees).[5] In addition, there are the apocryphal Gospels, which are "letters and apocalyptic literature written between the second and sixth centuries AD, and are not part of any Christian canon" (e.g., The Gospel of Thomas, The Gospel of Peter, and The Gospel of Judas).[6] And just to make sure you were paying attention, most if not all of these so-called apocryphal Gospels are pseudepigraphic or forged.

Finally, a work that is *anonymous* simply contains no formal (internal) claim to authorship (e.g., Matthew, Mark, Luke, John, and Hebrews are all technically anonymous works).

ARE WE ALL STARTING IN THE SAME PLACE?

There may be no topic in this book that is more deeply affected by one's starting points than the alleged forged writings. New Testament scholar D. A. Carson makes this clear when he writes, "The entire complex apparatus of technical scholarship and historical criticism, not to say theology and worldview, impinge on a complex string of judgments that bear on the question of whether or not there are pseudepigrapha among the NT documents."[7] In other words, the headwaters of multiple disciplines and worldview assumptions converge when seeking to sort out this question. In the court of critical opinion, are the claims of the New Testament authors innocent until proven guilty or guilty until proven innocent?

When coming to this question, it is important not to forget the arguments we have been making in chapters 4 and 5 about the origins of orthodoxy and the core of the canon. We have been making the case that the trajectory for orthodoxy (the four S's) was already set very early and is guarded by the apostle's eyewitness testimony. Unless skeptics like Ehrman are able to produce some major new evidence that refutes this trajectory, then I think the most reasonable starting point is accepting the authors as whom they claim to be unless we discover a compelling reason otherwise.

One last thing. Is certainty necessary in order for us to determine authorship? As we noted in the introduction, 100 percent absolute certainty is not necessary for us to reasonably say we know something. That standard is far too high. And history relies on probabilities, not repeatability. Is it possible that we are mistaken? Yes, but again, this does not mean that we throw up our hands in exasperation and despair of all knowledge. The reality of an error does not logically follow from the mere possibility of error. We examine claims on a case-by-case basis and come to a reasonable conclusion.

Authorship is usually determined by several factors. First there are external factors that come from outside the document (other writers or historical corroboration). Then there are internal factors that are contained within the documents themselves (claims of the author, style, and theology). Finally, it's significant whether a particular document was disputed by those closest to its composition. In other words, historical proximity matters. As we begin, it's important to note that the twenty-seven documents contained in the New Testament are the earliest Christian writings in existence and therefore the closest to the resurrection event.

LITERACY AND CHRISTIAN LITERARY PRODUCTION IN THE FIRST CENTURY

One modern assumption that needs to be challenged is the belief that because the first-century culture was an oral culture and most people couldn't read or write, Christians were not all that interested in or proficient at writing. Kruger's summary is instructive:

> Early Christianity was quite a "bookish" religion from the very start. Christians found their identity in books (the Old Testament), they quickly produced their own books, they preached and taught from these books, and were keen to copy and reproduce these books for generations to come.... Oral and written modes of communications were not mutually exclusive; neither were they hostile to one another.... When we examine the remnants of the earliest Christian literary culture, we see that Christians not only wrote at a very early point but also exhibited a rather developed and sophisticated book technology, as evidenced by scribal handwriting, the use of the *nomina sacra*, and the widespread adoption of the codex.[8]

The earliest Christians were Jewish and highly valued reading, writing, and explaining the Hebrew Scriptures. Young males in first-century Palestine would have received at least some educational training in their local synagogues when the Law was explained. The earliest Christians would have had a level of literary sophistication that needs to be factored into the discussion concerning pseudepigraphic texts.

Jesus never wrote a book (at least that we know of), but was he literate? Noted scholar Paul Meier provides a helpful summary of the available evidence:

If we take into account that Jesus' adult life became fiercely focused on the Jewish religion, that he is presented by almost all the Gospel traditions as engaging in learned disputes and halaka [the body of Jewish regulations passed down by scribes and rabbis] with students of the Law, that he was accorded the respectful—but at the time vague—title of rabbi or teacher, that more than one Gospel tradition presents him as preaching or teaching in the synagogues (presumably after and on Scripture readings), and that, even apart from formal disputes, his teaching was strongly imbued with the outlook and language of the sacred texts of Israel, it is reasonable to suppose that Jesus' religious formation in his family was intense and profound, and included reading biblical Hebrew.[9]

Everyone recognizes that Jesus' native tongue was Aramaic, but did Jesus know Greek as well? While we can't be certain, a reasonable case can be made that he spoke Greek. For example, on at least two occasions that Jesus is reported to have conversed with people, the words were likely in Greek: a Roman centurion (Matthew 8:5–13) and a Roman governor, Pontius Pilate (Matthew 27:11–14; John 18:33–38). New Testament scholar Mark Roberts asks,

If Jesus knew enough Greek to converse with a Roman centurion and a Roman governor, where did he learn it? Some have suggested that he might have learned it during his early years in Egypt. A more likely explanation points to his location in Galilee. Though Aramaic was the first language of Nazareth, Jesus' hometown was a short walk from Sepphoris, which was a major city and one in which Greek was spoken. Jesus quite probably had clients in Sepphoris who utilized his carpentry services, and he would have spoken with them in Greek. But given the multi-lingual context in which Jesus lived, it's not surprising that he would have been reasonably fluent in Greek and Hebrew, in addition to Aramaic.[10]

But what about the disciples; could they read and write? First, they would have grown up in the same general environment that Jesus did. It is often claimed that Peter and John were just ignorant fishermen and did not possess the literacy or literary sophistication necessary to write the things they did—Acts 4:13 is the passage commonly appealed to: "Now when they saw the boldness of Peter and John, and perceived that they were uneducated, common men, they were astonished. And they recognized that they had been with Jesus." However, it has been documented that even as fishermen they would have had at least a tradesman's knowledge of Greek.[11] Moreover, this verse only means they did not have a *formal* rabbinic education, not that they were illiterate peasants. Actually, it reveals that they were quite impressive in their understanding because of the education they had received from Jesus.

More recently, it has even been suggested that Matthew was the official note taker during the ministry of Jesus.[12] In summary, the earliest Christians were not merely ignorant peasants unaware of the literary practices of the day.

FORGERIES IN THE ANCIENT WORLD AND THE EARLY CHURCH

When it comes to forged documents in the ancient world and the early church, there are three things Christians should know:

1. Forgeries existed in the ancient world, but they were rejected when discovered.

2. Forgeries occurred among some early Christian writings, but Christians rejected them when they were discovered.

3. We have no reason to think that a known forgery made it into the New Testament canon.

Let's consider each of these truths. **First, forgeries existed in the ancient world, but they were rejected when discovered.** It was no small matter in the ancient world to forge a document. Ehrman convincingly argues and rightly concludes, "Ancient sources took forgery seriously. They almost universally condemn it, often in strong terms."[13] Moreover, "if a text that claimed philosophical or religious authority was recognized by Greek or Roman critics as a literary forgery, that is, as a text with a pseudonymous author, it was rejected."[14] Writing in the first century BC, the Roman author Vitruvius is characteristic of the ancient attitude toward pseudonymous writings:

It was a wise and useful provision of the ancients to transmit their thoughts to posterity by recording them in treatises, so that they should not be lost. . . . So, while they deserve our thanks, those, on the contrary, deserve our reproaches, who steal the writings of such men and publish them as their own; and those also, who depend in their writings, not on their own ideas, but who enviously do wrong to the works of others and boast of it, deserve not merely to be blamed, but to be sentenced to actual punishment for their wicked course of life. With the ancients, however, it is said that such things did not pass without pretty strict chastisement. What the results of their judgments were, it may not be out of place to set forth as they are transmitted to us. (Introduction 1, 3)[15]

Clearly such spurious documents were seen as deceptive and were met with a swift and public rejection. As we will see, the earliest Christians shared that sentiment.

Second, forgeries occurred among some early Christian writings, but Christians rejected them when they were discovered. Right out of the gates we need to clearly state that the earliest Christians held to the thoroughly Jewish conviction (rooted in the Hebrew Scriptures) that God does not lie and he hates deception. As the Scriptures declare, "Lying lips are an abomination to the Lord, but those who act faithfully are his delight" (Proverbs 12:22); "You shall not steal; you shall not deal falsely; you shall not lie to one another" (Leviticus 19:11). Lying—even in the name of an apostle, done in love and for the greater good—would not be tolerated.

Also, we need to recognize that there were plenty of forgeries being circulated in the early Christian literature. (Ehrman is correct about this point as well.) However, once discovered, each forgery was immediately dealt with. Here are two notable examples. Carson observes, "When Asian elders examined the author of an *Acts of Paul*, which included the pseudonymous *3 Corinthians*, they condemned him for presuming to write in Paul's name."[16] Then there was an instance concerning the *Gospel of Peter* that was initially allowed to be read until it was more carefully investigated. When about AD 200 Serapion, bishop of Antioch, first read Gospel of Peter, he thought it might be genuine.

When further investigation led him to conclude it was not, he rejected it and provided a rationale for the church of Rhossus in Cilicia: "For we, brothers, receive both Peter and the other apostles as Christ. But pseudepigrapha in their name we reject, as men of experience, knowing that we did not receive such [from the tradition]" (Eusebius *Hist. Eccl.* 6.12.3; cf. 2.25.4-7—widely cited in the literature).[17]

Lastly, the New Testament writings include an instructive example. The author of 2 Thessalonians 2 is aware that certain forgeries and false teachings are circulating and seeks to address it: "Now concerning the coming of our Lord Jesus Christ and our being gathered together to him, we ask you, brothers, not to be quickly shaken in mind or alarmed, either by a spirit or a spoken word, or a letter seeming to be from us, to the effect that the day of the Lord has come" (vv.1-2). To further authenticate this instruction, he writes, "I, Paul, write this greeting with my own hand. This is the sign of genuineness in every letter of mine; it is the way I write" (2 Thessalonians 3:17). But this leads to an interesting choice. "If the author was not Paul, as many scholars think, then our pseudonymous author is in the odd position of condemning pseudonymous authors; a literary forgery damns literary forgeries. If the author was Paul, then the apostle himself makes it clear that he is aware of pseudonymity and condemns the practice, at least when people are using his name."[18] Whether from hypocrisy or integrity, pseudonymity is being condemned here as well. (By the way, there is good evidence to support Pauline authorship of 2 Thessalonians.)[19]

Third, given what we have already seen concerning the establishment of the core of the canon, we have no reason to think that a known forgery made it into the New Testament canon. Eckhard Schnabel categorically states, "The early church rejected writings as noncanonical [whose] authorship was pseudonymous."[20] Carson is equally strong on this point. "But so far as the evidence of the fathers goes, when they explicitly evaluated a work for its authenticity, canonicity and pseudonymity proved mutually exclusive."[21] The reason for this is that the church fathers understood that the apostles were the authorized agents of the new covenant message and documents. Therefore, if the writings were not apostolic in origin, they were not regarded as authoritative. Period.

DO FORGERIES NOW EXIST IN
THE NEW TESTAMENT CANON?

Do we have good reason to believe that forgeries slipped past the earliest Christians and made it into the New Testament canon? That is essentially what Ehrman and others are claiming. These forgeries slipped past the earliest Christians, but today, however, we are able to tell that they were forged.

The books commonly categorized as forged are *Ephesians, Colossians, 2 Thessalonians*, the Pastoral Epistles (*1* and *2 Timothy, Titus*), *1* and *2 Peter, James*, and *Jude*. There are basically three lines of evidence offered: (1) stylistic/literary, (2) historical, and (3) theological. It is beyond the scope of this chapter to interact with all the technical issues involved, but I do want to introduce the contours of this discussion. To narrow the scope, we will generally examine some of the stylistic/literary arguments concerning Paul and the Pastoral Epistles.[22] I will state the general argument and then suggest why other scholars don't think it is compelling or conclusive enough to overturn traditional (and internal) claims to authorship.

First, it is argued that the style, vocabulary, and grammar of the Pastoral Epistles are significantly different from those of the accepted letters of Paul. Here are a few responses that have been offered. First, an accurate statistical analysis on the Greek text of the Pastoral Epistles requires a bigger sample. Linguistic experts say that you need at least 10,000 words to work with, whereas the Pastoral Epistles only contain 3,488.[23]

Second, stylistic arguments are highly subjective and depend on what kind of assumptions you are using. For example, the authenticity of each book should be weighed separately. The way current studies are being employed treats 1 and 2 Timothy and Titus as a literary unit and then the undisputed letters of Paul as a literary unit. Interestingly, statistical tests using the same methods were applied comparing the vocabulary, style, and grammar of 1 Timothy to a comparably sized passage in Romans (1:1–9:17), which yielded favorable results.[24]

Third, the purpose of writing is what determines the style used; this can vary along with the vocabulary that Paul wanted to use on that occasion. Also, the style could have been affected by the amanuensis (a hired scribe) that Paul may have used. We know that Paul used Tertius in the writing of Romans (cf. Romans 16:22: "I Tertius, who wrote this letter, greet you in the Lord." We also know that Silvanus (Silas) was involved in the composition of 1 and 2 Thessalonians (1:1). After a detailed study of these issues, Schnabel concludes, "The degree of difference between the style of the Pastoral Epistles and the Pauline letters generally accepted as authentic is a matter of judgment. The language of the Pastoral Epistles, despite some distinctive characteristics, renders Pauline authorship neither impossible nor implausible."[25]

While a full defense of Pauline authorship is not possible here, it is not insignificant that the early church fathers did not doubt that Paul authored these books and that "Pauline authorship of the Pastorals was not seriously questioned until the nineteenth century" during the height of enlightenment rationalistic scholarship.[26]

WHO WROTE THE FOUR "ANONYMOUS" GOSPELS?

Earlier we mentioned that the four Gospels—Matthew, Mark, Luke, and John—are technically anonymous. There are no definitive statements, such as "Paul, an apostle—not from men nor through man, but through Jesus Christ and God the Father, who raised him from the dead" (Galatians 1:1). Not surprisingly, many within modern scholarship take this as a launching point to cast doubt on the identity and credibility of these documents. For example, Ehrman states, "The Gospels are probably misattributed. John the disciple did not write John, and Matthew did not write Matthew."[27] In light of this challenge, what does the fact of technical anonymity mean for our confidence in the Gospel accounts?

First, our goal is to say (and defend) what the Bible says—no more and no less. In the case of Paul writing a letter that bears his name, we are compelled to defend his authorship as a matter of biblical integrity. However, when it comes to the four Gospels, there is no one specifically to defend. As a thought experiment, let's say it was somehow discovered that Andrew wrote what we now know as the Gospel of Matthew. Would that mean that there is an error in the Bible? Actually, no, because no claim of authorship was technically made in this document (the same logic would hold for the book of Hebrews). However, all of this doesn't mean we can't be confident in who wrote them. As you might imagine, these "added titles" have received considerable attention by scholars over the years. But rather than shake our confidence, I think they strengthen it.

First of all, the grammar of the titles themselves is telling. "The Gospel according to . . ." is probably best translated, "The Gospel—the one and only gospel message—according to Mark's account."[28] The very fact that you have titles means that it became necessary to distinguish between early Gospel accounts because "a Christian community that knew only one Gospel writing would not have needed to entitle it in this way. Even a Gospel writer who knew other Gospels to be circulating around the churches could have given this form of title to his work."[29] Therefore, the "unusual form of the titles and the universal use of them as soon as we have any evidence suggest that they originated at an early stage. Once the Gospels were widely known it would have been much more difficult for a standard form of the title for all four Gospels to have come into universal use."[30] If titles were added very late because no one knew who wrote them, then how do you achieve such uniformity? Lastly, the existing manuscripts and codices that have been unearthed demonstrate the authority given only these four Gospels. "The manner in which early Christian manuscripts regularly connect the four canonical Gospels is borne out by the telling fact that we possess no instance where an apocryphal gospel is joined with canonical Gospels within a single manuscript."[31]

In addition to this evidence, New Testament scholar Michael Wilkins notes that, "the true identities of the authors of the four Gospels were never in question historically. From the very earliest witnesses we find the author's names associated with each Gospel."[32] Regarding the question of technical anonymity, he explains, "The anonymity of the Gospels themselves is not surprising since the Evangelists were not writing letters to far-off church communities . . . most likely the Evangelists were compiling Gospel stories for churches in which they were active participants and leaders. . . . To attach their names as authors would have been unnecessary because their audiences obviously knew their identity."[33]

In a way, all but John seem like unlikely candidates. So we will briefly examine the Synoptics (Matthew, Mark, and Luke) and then the Gospel of John.

Matthew

Regarding Matthew, "there is no patristic evidence that anyone else was ever proposed as the author." (Papias, Irenaeus, Clement of Alexandria, Eusebius, and Origen all affirm Matthean authorship.)[34] The literary evidence reveals that Matthew was the most popular Gospel in the earliest period of the church and it was circulated widely.[35]

There are two common objections to his authorship. First, it is argued that Matthew, an apostle himself, would not have relied so heavily upon Mark, who was not an apostle, when composing his Gospel. But as we will see, since we have very good evidence that Peter stands behind Mark's Gospel, Matthew would have had no issue utilizing the recorded testimony of Peter. The other common objection is that the Greek is too good to have been written by Matthew. However, as we have noted above, Matthew was likely trilingual (Aramaic, Greek, and Latin) by growing up as a Jew in the region of Galilee, and as a tax collector he would have been required to know Greek well.[36]

Mark

Concerning Mark, "there is no external evidence for any other author."[37] Papias describes Mark as Peter's interpreter: "Mark, having become the interpreter of Peter, wrote down accurately, though not in order, whatsoever he remembered of the things said or done by Christ. . . . For he was careful of one thing, not to omit any of the things which he had heard, and not to state any of them falsely."[38] Furthermore, "the Anti-Marcionite Prologue (ca. AD 180), Irenaeus (*Against Heresies* 3.1.1–2), and Clement of Alexandria (as reported in Eusebius, *Eccl. Hist.* 6.14) confirm this identification."[39]

Luke

There is very good evidence for Luke as well. Lukan expert Darrell Bock summarizes that the external evidence is consistent in

> naming Luke as the author (Justin [*Trypho* 103.19] notes that "this memoir of Jesus" was written by a follower of the apostles). Allusions to Luke's Gospel appear as early as 1–2 Clement (ca. AD 95 and 100). The Muratorian Canon

also attributes the Gospel to Luke, a doctor. Irenaeus (*Against Heresies* 3.1.1; 3.14.1) also ties the Gospel to Luke, a follower of Paul, and notes the evidence of the "we" sections of Acts as pointing to one who knew Paul. Tertullian (*Against Marcion* 4.2.2; 4.5.3) calls Luke's Gospel a "digest of Paul's Gospel." Eusebius (*Eccl. Hist.* 3.4.7) notes that Luke is a native of Antioch. What makes this evidence impressive is the large list of possible companions of Paul who might have filled in the blank of the "we" sections had the author not been known. The unanimity of the tradition on authorship is important."[40]

Concerning the Synoptics then, "All of the evidence uniformly supports the belief that Matthew (the tax collector turned disciple), Mark (the companion of Peter and Paul), and Luke (Paul's "beloved physician") were the authors of the Gospels attributed to them. It is difficult to conceive why Christians as early as the second century would ascribe these otherwise anonymous Gospels to three such unlikely candidates unless they knew with certainty that they were the authors."[41] If someone wanted to successfully forge documents, one would surely pick better-known apostles like Peter and Thomas instead of Mark and Luke—unless you were constrained by the facts.

John

Last and certainly not least, is John. In *The Historical Reliability of John's Gospel*, Craig Blomberg notes, "Every piece of ancient, external evidence, save one, agrees that the author was the Apostle John, the son of Zebedee. . . . No orthodox writer ever proposes any other alternative for the author of the fourth Gospel and the book is accepted in all of the early canonical lists, which is all the more significant given the frequent heterodox misinterpretation of it. It is not until the early fourth century with the writings of Eusebius that any ambiguity appears."[42]

As Bock summarizes,

The well-known argument from internal evidence seeks to identify the author, working into increasingly narrow points of identification. The author was (1) a Jew, (2) of Palestine, (3) an eyewitness of what he describes, (4) an apostle, and (5) John. The linking of the argument with the "beloved disciple" (13:23; 19:26; 20:2; 21:7, 20) is key and shows up in Irenaeus's remark about the one who leaned on Jesus's breast. The best candidate for this identification is John the son of Zebedee, especially given the frequent pairing of John and Peter in the Synoptics and the beloved disciple and Peter in the Fourth Gospel.[43]

While some recent scholars have suggested other possibilities for the identity of the beloved disciple, I think the best case is made for John, the son of Zebedee.[44]

To claim that many of the writings of the New Testament have been forged is a very serious charge. However, even the brief survey of evidence here has shown that it is reasonable to believe that the authors of the New Testament are who they claim to be.

Three Big Ideas

1. Even though the first-century literacy rate would have been around 10 percent, we have seen that Christianity—because of its emergence from Judaism—enjoyed "above-average" literary sophistication and had utilized advanced scribal practices like *nomina sacra* and widely used the codex. Moreover, we have good reason to believe that both Jesus and the disciples would have been literate.

2. The three realities Christians should know about forgeries in the ancient world and the early church are:

   1) Forgeries existed in the ancient world, but they were rejected when discovered.

   2) Forgeries occurred among some early Christian writings, but Christians rejected them when they were discovered.

   3) We have no reason to think that a known forgery made it into the New Testament canon.

3. While the four canonical Gospels we know as Matthew, Mark, Luke, and John, are *technically* anonymous, there are good reasons to think that these men wrote them. As noted earlier, "The true identities of the authors of the four Gospels were never in question historically. From the very earliest witnesses we find the author's names associated with each Gospel" (the only possible exception to this is a late issue pertaining to John).

Conversation Tips

- When talking with someone about the possibilities of forgeries in the New Testament, the best place to start is asking them for specific reasons why you should take this claim seriously. What evidence can they point to that indicates a forgery made it into the New Testament?

- If they don't provide you with evidence, then you are not obligated to defend anything. However, you can make a positive case by pointing out that Christians were aware of forgeries and rejected them when discovered.

Digging Deeper

- D. A. Carson and Douglas J. Moo. *An Introduction to the New Testament*, 2nd ed. Grand Rapids: Zondervan, 2005.

- Charles Hill. *Who Chose the Gospels?: Probing the Great Gospel Conspiracy.* Oxford: Oxford University Press, 2010.

HAS THE BIBLICAL TEXT BEEN CORRUPTED OVER THE CENTURIES?

The impression sometimes given in discussions of the text of the New Testament is that the text itself is entirely fluid and unstable, and that it was subject to so much variation and change through especially the first two centuries that its very stability is threatened. This simply is not true.[1]
Stanley Porter

Have you ever been reading the Bible and come across a passage set off in brackets and then followed by a footnote? Next, you follow the footnote and discover that this particular passage is not found in the earliest manuscripts (e.g., John 8:1–13; Mark 16:9–20). You ask yourself, *How can the Bible be the Word of God if we aren't sure which texts should be included?*

Is the biblical text accurate? To put it bluntly, how do we know that what was written in the first century is what we have today in the twenty-first century?

Evangelical turned skeptic Bart Ehrman admits in frustration, "I kept reverting to my basic question: how does it help us to say that the Bible is the inerrant word of God if in fact we don't have the words that God inerrantly inspired, but only the words copied by the scribes—sometimes correctly and sometimes (many times!) incorrectly? What good is it to say that the auto-graphs (i.e., the originals) were inspired? We don't *have* the originals!"[2]

Big questions about the Bible like this have gone mainstream. Questioning the Bible has become big business. Just ask bestselling author Ehrman or TV's Discovery and History channels as they continue to roll out shows challenging what people have been traditionally taught about Jesus, the Bible, and Christianity. Conversations that used to occur only in dusty academic journals are now taking place in prime time on shows like Comedy Central's *The Colbert Report* and on the big screen in films like *The Da Vinci Code* (based on the runaway bestselling book by Dan Brown). The bottom line is that the church can no longer ignore these questions.

THE PROBLEM WITH ANCIENT DOCUMENTS

To begin, you need to know that *none* of the original manuscripts of either the Old or New Testaments is still in existence—all that remains are imperfect copies. But this is exactly the same situation for every other ancient work of literature; e.g., Plato, Livy, Herodotus, Thucydides. No one has the originals. (There are several natural explanations for this; manuscripts could be lost, worn out through copying, damaged by insects or rodents, rot or decay due to the climate, or even be destroyed by foreign armies.) This may come as a surprise, but this fact should not turn us into skeptics regarding ancient texts. Scholars use the copies we have discovered to reconstruct the original classical writings and the Old and New Testaments.

Generally speaking, the more copies we have to examine and the closer they are to when they were written, the better. This practice of reconstruction is known as textual criticism.

IS THE "TELEPHONE GAME" A HELPFUL ANALOGY?

Before we explore textual criticism further, we need to discuss the telephone game. Many of us grew up playing the telephone game with friends or at birthday parties. Basically one person sitting in a circle whispers a message to the player on his right, who then turns to the next person and repeats the message. That person turns and restates the message; finally the last player announces the message to the entire group. "Errors typically accumulate in the retellings, so the statement announced by the last player differs significantly, and often amusingly, from the one uttered by the first."[3] However, this analogy is often applied to the transmission of the New Testament. If the copying process was this unstable and error filled, then we should be skeptical of the biblical text.

Nevertheless, this is not a good analogy of how the text of the New Testament has come down to us. Here are just a few reasons why. First, the telephone game is linear (person A to B to C to D . . .), whereas the copying process was not one-to-one, like individual links in a chain. When it comes to the text of the New Testament, there are multiple lines of transmission, and the original documents were very probably copied several times and as we will see below, we have access to earlier copies to compare with later copies (think branches spreading out and descending from a tree). Next, the telephone game is verbal, while the text was written, and so the words and phrases can be examined along the way. In the telephone game, the person only has the last person in line to interrogate; with Scripture text, earlier texts are often available to inspect.

Finally, life, death, and eternity usually do not hang in the balance at a birthday party! In other words, if Jesus really was who he claimed to be and the offer of eternal life was legitimate, then there would have been a high degree of motivation among the copiers to get this message right.

TEXTUAL CRITICISM 101: ASKING THE RIGHT QUESTIONS

In order to get at the truth, we need to ask and answer three fundamental questions when it comes to reconstructing the New Testament: (1) How many manuscripts do we have to work with? (2) How early are the manuscripts we have to work with? (3) How important are the textual variants among these manuscripts?

1. How Many Manuscripts Do We Have?

Do scholars have enough copies of the New Testament to work with in order to reconstruct? And how does that compare with other classical authors? Regarding the number of copies, Dan Wallace, a leading New Testament textual critic and the founder of The Center for the Study of New Testament Manuscripts (see its website, CSNTM.org), says:

> The wealth of material that is available for determining the wording of the original New Testament is staggering: more than fifty-seven hundred Greek New Testament manuscripts, as many as twenty thousand versions, and more than one million quotations by patristic writers. In comparison with the average ancient Greek author, the New Testament copies are well over a thousand times more plentiful. If the average-sized manuscript were two and one-half inches thick, all the copies of the works of an average Greek author would stack up four feet high, while the copies of the New Testament would stack up to over a mile high! This is indeed an embarrassment of riches.[4]

Chart 5 shows how other ancient writers like the Greek historian Herodotus or the Roman historian Tacitus compare. The New Testament is by far the best-attested work of Greek or Latin literature in the ancient world—it's not even close! You can consider the first question sufficiently answered.

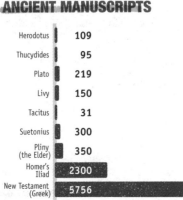

Chart 5

COMPARING COPIES OF ANCIENT MANUSCRIPTS

Herodotus	109
Thucydides	95
Plato	219
Livy	150
Tacitus	31
Suetonius	300
Pliny (the Elder)	350
Homer's Iliad	2300
New Testament (Greek)	5756

At this point, I need to offer a brief caveat about counting and comparing ancient manuscripts. The moment this book hits the stores, the numbers will be outdated.[5] But there is still value in the bibliographic test for textual reliability. The bottom line is that texts in the ancient world like Homer's *The Iliad* were carefully copied, and you can trust their accuracy. We don't compare to cast doubt on "secular" classical texts; rather, Christians are grateful for this insight because the New Testament documents are even better attested and numerous than are *The Iliad* and other historical writings. And that means we can have a high degree of confidence in the accuracy of the text.

By the way, new discoveries are being made all the time! They just have not been made public yet and haven't been published in academic journals. So stay tuned for even more exciting news concerning biblical texts.[6]

2. *How Early Are the Manuscripts We Have?*

The significance of this question is that it will allow us to limit the amount of intentional/unintentional corruption that might have crept in through the copying process. The principle at work here is the closer the gap, the better. Looking at some of the most prominent classical authors in chart 6, we find that there is a 1,350-year gap between the time when the ancient Greek historian Herodotus wrote and our earliest manuscript. The Roman historian Tacitus fairs a little better with a manuscript dating to eight hundred years after the fact (see chart for more comparisons). What is the time gap between the composition of a New Testament document and the first existing copies? Thirty-five years!

The earliest fragment of the New Testament is the John Rylands papyrus that was found in Egypt. It contains a portion of John 18 and dates to AD 117–134. If John wrote his gospel around AD 95 in Ephesus—allowing for the time to be translated and circulated down to Egypt—you will find this date getting us fairly close to the time when John actually wrote it. Moreover, manuscripts of almost the entire New Testament were already established by AD 250 (e.g., Bodmer papyri and Chester Beatty papyri).[7] Dan Wallace summarizes, "There are three times more New Testament manuscripts within the first 200 years than the average Greco-Roman author has in 2000

Chart 6

TIME OF COMPOSITION VS. FIRST EXISTING COPIES

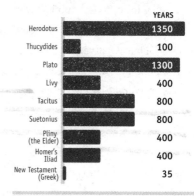

	YEARS
Herodotus	1350
Thucydides	100
Plato	1300
Livy	400
Tacitus	800
Suetonius	800
Pliny (the Elder)	400
Homer's Iliad	400
New Testament (Greek)	35

years."[8] Scholars Andreas Kostenberger and Michael Kruger highlight the importance of the evidence we have just considered: "The brief span of time between the production of the New Testament and our earliest copies gives us access to the New Testament text at a remarkably early stage, making it very unlikely that the textual tradition could have been radically altered prior to this time period *without evidence for those alterations still being visible within the manuscript tradition*" (emphasis mine).[9]

3. How Important Are the Textual Variants among These Manuscripts?

"We could go on nearly forever," Ehrman claims, "talking about specific places in which the texts of the New Testament came to be changed, either accidentally or intentionally. . . . The examples are not just in the hundreds but in the thousands."[10] Even more shocking is his statement that "there are more variations among our manuscripts than there are words in the New Testament."[11] He uses the number of 400,000 textual variants. Keep in mind the entire Greek New Testament contains only 138,162 words. While his account of textual variants is technically accurate, these statistics are very misleading to those not familiar with how textual criticism works.

What do we make of the "400,000" variants claim? For starters, we need to be clear about what variants are and how they are counted. A *variant* is any place among the existing New Testament manuscripts where there is not uniformity of wording. For example, a misspelled word in a single manuscript that is different from 2,000 other manuscripts would be counted as 2,000 variants. Moreover, the reason we have so many variants is because we have so many manuscripts to work with (far more than any other classical work)!

Secondly, we need to cut the ancient scribes some slack. Remember, ancient scribes didn't have spell-check, the lightbulb, or the printing press! Sometimes we forget this, but the printing press was not invented until 1439. *Everything* before that time had to be copied by hand and not always in the best of lighting. Lest you feel too good about yourself living in the modern age, even with spell-check and auto-correct we still have typos! (I've lost track of the number of textual errors I've sent out because of my iPhone's auto-correct feature.)

Given what they had to work with, ancient copyists did an extraordinary job preserving the text. In order to gain an appreciation of the ancient setting for composing and copying a book, Stanley Porter paints for us this picture of one of the NT writers committing words to papyrus, which was the paper of the ancient world:

> Perhaps this scene took place in a small room in Rome. Some people think that the apostle Peter, having made it to Rome on his lesser-known missionary endeavors, and nearing the end of his life, decided to leave a written record of his remembrances of being with Jesus the Christ. Tradition says that he recounted his remembrances to John Mark, who wrote them down and formed them into a Gospel, quite possibly our first Gospel (Eusebius, Hist. eccl. 2.15.1; 3.39.14–15). In this room is Peter, perhaps with some other Christians, and Mark is positioned at a bench with a papyrus scroll spread before him, or he is sitting, Egyptian style, crossed-legged with a scroll on his lap. He sharpens a stick into a nib, dips it into a container of ink made from charcoal and other ingredients, and presses the nib to the papyrus. The fibers of the papyrus scroll, made up of a number of sheets, run lengthwise along the papyrus, and Mark begins to write carefully as Peter speaks. . . . Moving forward a number of years, we enter what looks to be a scriptorium. This is a room where manuscripts are regularly copied, usually located in a monastery. There are two monks in a small room, and one is about to start reading from the biblical book that the scribes are working on. As they are ready, the reader begins to read slowly, giving the other scribe time to write out each word as he goes. In another place in the monastery is another monk [with] his own papyrus book beside him on his desk, and he is copying this text into his own parchment book made of prepared dry skins. He carefully keeps one hand on the complete manuscript and then attempts to copy what he sees into the blank one. He is careful not to skip a line, or even a letter, as he moves his eyes back and forth between the two.[12]

Porter notes that once the monk completes his taking of dictation, the other monk "who did the reading comes down to check the work that the scribe has been doing. Similarly, the scribe who is working on his own manuscript carefully counts the number of rows, and letters in a row, so that he can check the work that he has been doing to ensure fidelity to the original."

THE QUALITY OF VARIANTS

Now that we better understand the number of variants, let's take a closer look at the variants themselves. I'll end the suspense and give you the big idea right up front: 99 percent of the "variants" (i.e., 396,000!) have no bearing on our ability to reconstruct the original New Testament text. Curiously, Ehrman agrees, "Most of the changes found in our early Christian manuscripts have nothing to do with theology or ideology. Far and away the most changes are the result of mistakes, pure and simple—slips of the pen, accidental omissions, inadvertent additions, misspelled words, blunders of one sort of another."[13] New Testament textual critic Dan Wallace breaks down the kinds of variants into four categories:[14]

1. **Spelling differences.** The great majority of variants (70 to 80 percent, or 320,000) are spelling errors and easily correctable upon manuscript comparison.

2. **Minor differences that involve synonyms or do not affect translation.** These differences include whether definite articles are used with proper names (e.g., "The Joseph or The Mary" in Luke 2:16) or words are transposed (word order is very important in English, but in an inflected language like Greek, word order is not nearly as important). Another cause of differences is the flexibility of the language, evident in the fact that you can say something like "Jesus loves John" in at least sixteen different ways in the Greek language.

3. **Meaningful but not viable differences.** Sometimes a single manuscript will differ from the rest of the manuscripts that contain the same alternate reading (e.g., 1 Thessalonians 2:9 either reads "gospel of God" or "gospel of Christ"). This does affect the meaning of the passage, but the textual evidence supporting it is not very good.

4. **Meaningful and viable differences.** These meaningful and viable differences

are not things like "Jesus often told lies" or "Jesus was a thief." One of the most famous differences is Romans 5:1, which either reads "let us have peace with God" or "we have peace with God." The manuscripts are pretty evenly divided. The Greek letters omicron and omega look very similar and would have likely been pronounced the same. The difference is merely a grammatical one, but both readings are supported by other passages in the New Testament, which means we don't have a theologically novel point being made here. [15]

Chart 7

COMMON COPYING ERRORS

1. Confusion of common letters
2. Substitution of similar sounding words
3. Omission of letter or word
4. Letters/words written twice
5. Incorrect word division
6. Scribe attempts to clean up spelling or grammar
7. Scribe attempts to harmonize passage or remove difficulties

Wallace summarizes, "Less than 1 percent of all textual variants are both meaningful and viable, and by 'meaningful' we don't mean to imply earth-shattering significance but rather, almost always, minor alterations to the meaning of the text."[16] That comes out to less than 4,000 of the original 400,000 variants *having any real significance at all for the meaning of a verse.* And regarding the verses where questions remain, "significant textual variants that alter core doctrines of the New Testament have not been produced."

WHAT ABOUT THE OLD TESTAMENT?

The New Testament gets a lot of attention because Christianity rises or falls with Jesus. But you need to know you can trust the Old Testament as well. Perhaps the strongest evidence for the reliability of the Old Testament is the discovery of the Dead Sea Scrolls in 1947 at Qumran. The significance of this discovery cannot be overstated. Up until the time of the discovery, we had known how carefully scribes had passed down the text. But critics of the Bible continually claimed that if we ever found earlier documents, proof could be shown for how much the text had been changed and corrupted. So when a shepherd boy who was tending his goats stumbled upon pottery in a cave containing ancient texts, it sent shock waves through the biblical world. Eight hundred scrolls, containing fragments from every book of the Old Testament except Esther, were discovered dating from 250 BC to AD 50.

The most significant was that an entire manuscript of Isaiah was found dating to circa 75 BC. Old Testament scholars were then able to compare this text of Isaiah with the earliest existing copy of Isaiah in the Masoretic text (Hebrew text of the Jewish Bible) dating to AD 1008–1009. Their conclusion? Ninety-five percent word-for-word copying accuracy over almost 1,100 years! And the 5 percent of variations consisted of nothing more significant than omitted letters or misspelled words—slips of the pen.[17] In light of the discovery of the Dead Sea Scrolls at Qumran, it is fair to say that the burden of proof is on the critic who claims that the Old Testament has not been reliably preserved.

The oldest Old Testament manuscript discovered so far is a fragment of the priestly blessing from Numbers 6:24–27 found in a silver amulet near Jerusalem dating to the seventh century BC (2,600 years old!). If you are wondering why we don't have more Old Testament documents, here are three key reasons: (1) old manuscripts written on papyrus or leather would age and deteriorate over time; (2) much of Israel's history is marked by war; Jerusalem was destroyed and burned at least twice during the time the Old Testament was written; and (3) "When manuscripts began to show signs of wear, the Jewish scribes reverently disposed of them because they bore the sacred name of God. Disposing of the manuscripts avoided defilement from pagans. Since scribes were meticulous in copying biblical manuscripts, there was little reason to keep old manuscripts."[18] Once all of these factors are considered, we shouldn't be surprised that we have not found more.

After a lifetime of studying the text of the Old Testament, Bruce Waltke concludes that "95 percent of the Old Testament is . . . textually sound."[19] The remaining 5 percent does not affect any key Christian doctrine and as more texts are discovered and existing ones translated, that percentage should continue to decrease.

Summarizing the textual accuracy of the Bible, Douglas Stuart writes,

> 99 percent of the original words in the New Testament are recoverable with a very high degree of certainty. In the case of the Old Testament the figure might be more like 95 percent. When the words that are recoverable with a fairly high degree of certainty are added, we may be confident that we are able to read, reflect upon, and act upon what is practically equivalent to the original itself. There is no area of Christian faith or practice that actually stands or falls on textual studies.[20]

BEYOND REASONABLE DOUBT: A FAITH WELL PLACED

While studying at Princeton, Bart Ehrman studied under arguably the leading textual critic of the late twentieth century, Bruce Metzger. If the New Testament text had skeletons in the closet and dirty little secrets, he knew all about them. Here is the conclusion of an interview that journalist and author Lee Strobel had with Metzger:

> All the decades of scholarship, of study, of writing textbooks, of delving into the minutiae of the New Testament text—what has all that done to your personal faith? "It has increased the basis of my personal faith to see the firmness with which these materials have come down to us, with a multiplicity of copies, some of which are very, very ancient," Metzger responded. So, scholarship has not diluted your faith—. He jumped in before I could finish my sentence. "On the contrary, it has built it. I've asked questions all my life, I've dug into the text, I've studied this thoroughly, and today I know with confidence that my trust in Jesus has been well placed . . . *very* well placed."[21]

Trusting that the text we have today is essentially what was written then is not a blind leap of faith. It is an entirely reasonable thing to do.

Three Big Ideas

1. None of the original manuscripts of either the Old or New Testaments is still in existence—all that remains are imperfect copies. But this is exactly the same situation for every other ancient work of literature. In addition, the telephone game is not a helpful analogy when explaining how the New Testament text has been passed down to us—not least of which because multiple lines of written evidence exist and the questions are of eternal significance.

2. When it comes to recovering the text of the New Testament, we need to ask the right questions: *How many manuscripts do we have to work with? How early are the manuscripts we have to work with? How important are the textual variants between these manuscripts?* When we examine these questions, the New Testament is by far the best-attested work of Greek or Latin literature in the ancient world—it's not even close! The gap between the composition of the NT and our first manuscript is only thirty-five years—a blink of an eye in the ancient world. And 99 percent of the "variants" have no bearing on our ability to reconstruct the original New Testament text; the remaining 4,000 occurrences do not affect any central Christian doctrine or practice.

3. The Dead Sea Scrolls discovered in 1947—especially the Isaiah scroll dating to 75 BC—give strong evidence that the OT manuscripts have been accurately preserved for us. Textual critics can confidently reconstruct 99 percent of the original NT and 95 percent of the OT. Given all of the things that could have happened to these texts throughout history, preservation at this level is extraordinary!

Conversation Tips

- Be sure to familiarize yourself with the "telephone game" discussion and the reasons that is not a helpful analogy. Bring up the fact that we (rightly) don't doubt what Livy, Herodotus, or Tacitus wrote. Given that the NT documents are so much better established by the manuscript evidence, why should we not trust them (wait for a response here)?

- Next, emphasize that any classical scholar would love to have the problem that NT scholars have when it comes to number of manuscripts (over 5,700 in Greek alone!).

- Finally, remember that this evidence does not mean that what the apostles said was true. What it does is establish that we are reading and can examine what was originally written. As always, find creative ways to ask questions using your knowledge rather than make statements. Ask people to define their terms and what they mean by them and then also be sure to ask what evidence they have to support their beliefs. (Don't just let them endlessly make unsupported claims about the Bible.)

Digging Deeper

- Paul D. Wegner. *A Student's Guide to Textual Criticism of the Bible: Its History, Methods and Results*. Downers Grove, IL: InterVarsity, 2006.

- Stanley E. Porter. *How We Got the New Testament: Text, Transmission, and Translation*. Grand Rapids: Baker, 2013.

ARE THE GOSPELS FULL OF CONTRADICTIONS?

It is perfectly true that our responsibility is to study the biblical difficulties in order, if possible, to understand and harmonize them. To explain them to everyone's satisfaction however, or to provide a harmony in every instance, is not incumbent upon us.[1]

E. J. Young

hen students are first introduced to the historical, as opposed to a devotional, study of the Bible," writes Bart Ehrman, "one of the first things they are forced to grapple with is that the biblical text, whether Old Testament or New Testament, is chock-full of discrepancies, many of them irreconcilable."[2] Later he writes, "A Christianity dependent on the inerrancy of the Bible probably cannot survive the reality of the discrepancies."[3]

There's a lot wrapped up in these statements—not the least of which is how Ehrman assumes that a devotional or "faith-based" approach is at odds with an historical approach. We will revisit that below. For now, what kind of discrepancies is Ehrman referring to? Here is a typical example. When Jesus asked Peter who people say that he is, what did Peter actually say?

You are the Christ, the Son of the living God. (Matthew 16:16)

You are the Christ. (Mark 8:29)

The Christ of God. (Luke 9:20)

When Peter's confession is presented like this, you can see the issue. This is not the only place in the Gospels where something like this occurs. What are we to make of these kinds of passages? Did God make a mistake while writing His book?

ASKING THE RIGHT QUESTIONS

By now you will have noticed a theme emerging in this book: When you encounter difficult objections to the Bible, you need to make sure that you are asking the right questions. This chapter will be no different. To gain the needed clarity to proceed, we shall ask some important questions of the Gospels, ancient historiography, and the nature of contradictions. The answers that we find will help us engage specific problem texts like Peter's confession mentioned above.

What Is an Actual Contradiction?

If the claim is being made that God has erred and that this is shown because discrepancies in the Bible are irreconcilable, then it would be very helpful to clearly understand the nature of a real contradiction. After all, appearances can be deceiving. One of the foundational laws of logic is called the Law of Noncontradiction: It says that "A" cannot equal "A" and equal "non-A." It is most clearly seen to be true once you try to argue against it.

Also, it is quite difficult to generate a true contradiction. When this law is applied to literature, it means a statement cannot be both true and false at the same time and in the same respect. For example, someone who says both that "the Declaration of Independence was adopted on July 4, 1776" and "the Declaration of Independence was not adopted on July 4, 1776" contradicts himself. It's logically impossible for the Declaration of Independence to have both been adopted on July 4, 1776, and not have been adopted on July 4, 1776. Or take this religious example: "Jesus Christ is God incarnate" (historic Christianity) or "Jesus Christ is not God Incarnate" (Judaism, Islam). Both cannot be true. To sum up, two or more statements are *consistent* when it is possible for them all to be true at the same time. Two or more statements are *inconsistent* when it is not possible for them all to be true at the same time. It is this standard that we need to apply to the Gospels in order to see if statements are truly irreconcilable.

How Does History Work?

Now that we have clarity concerning contradictions, our next important question is the nature of history. At first glance, it seems like an easy question to answer. History is simply what has already happened. But when it comes to writing from a certain perspective about something that has happened and that is also interrelated with other events, things can get a bit more complicated. Our investigating will require more sophistication and nuance. We need a scalpel and not a sledgehammer. New Testament scholar Darrell Bock offers this helpful reminder of what we already know about the past:

> History is not a static entity. Neither are the sayings that belong to it and describe its events. Historical events and sayings do not just happen and then sit fossilized with a static meaning. As events in history proceed, they develop their meaning through interconnected events that give history its sense of flow. Later events impact how previous events and sayings are understood, seen, and appreciated....Sometimes events and sayings are understood better after reflection than when they first took place. The wording of a saying may not change, but what is perceived about it may change.[4]

This is very important to understand as we approach the Bible in general and the Gospels in particular. Some examples will make these observations more vivid. First consider Gandalf talking to Frodo concerning Gollum in J. R. R. Tolkein's *The Fellowship of the Ring.* "My heart tells me that Gollum has some part to play yet, for good or ill . . ." However, if you know the whole story, then this conversation takes on a whole new layer of significance in light of later events (not known at the time of the conversation). Ultimately Gollum himself will destroy the ring. There is a flow of fictional time that informs our later understanding of Gandalf's words. The point to highlight is that history is not a flat, static, and one-dimensional sort of thing. It is multilayered and multidimensional.

Next, imagine the year is 1999 and you were having a conversation with a friend about when his birthday is. He answers, "September 11." Now imagine the year is 2002 and you ask the same question. The cultural context in America following the terrorist attacks on 9/11/2001 will add a layer of significance to that conversation that was not there before. We will develop this idea more below, but this understanding helps us see how an eyewitness writing one of the Gospels after these events have taken place can add or embed layers of significance into the story he is writing.

What Was History Writing Like in the Ancient World?

Our next critical question is to explore the differences in the way that history writing is approached in the modern world versus how it was approached in the ancient world. It will be important to make sure we are not holding ancient historiographers to standards and conventions they did not intend to follow.

Both Greek historians (Thucydides and Polybius) and Roman historians (Livy and Tacitus) are informative. Thucydides writing around the fifth century BC is instructive, "It was difficult for me to remember the exact substance of the speeches I myself heard and for others to remember those they heard elsewhere and told me of . . . I have given the speeches in the manner in which it seemed to me that each of the speakers would best express what needed to be said about the ever-prevailing situation, but I have kept as close as possible to the total opinion expressed by the actual words" (*History of the Peloponnesian War* 1.22). His intention was not to give the words "verbatim" but rather report an accurate summary or gist of what occurred.

This sounds strange to us in our "gotcha" culture of sound bites, because we are used to being bombarded with direct quotations (usually ripped out of context!). It may surprise you to learn that the original languages of the Bible—Greek and Hebrew—do not have punctuation marks. As Craig Blomberg notes, people during that time did not feel "that a verbatim account of someone's speech was any more valuable or accurate than a reliable summary, paraphrase, or interpretation."[5] They were concerned with accurately reporting what occurred. As New Testament historian Ben Witherington notes, "The modern desire for precision must not be imposed on the ancient authors, who often, though not always, preferred to write in a generalizing fashion."[6]

Therefore, if we are to be intellectually responsible when approaching the earliest biographies of Jesus of Nazareth, we need to recognize that it is illegitimate for someone in the twenty-first century to impose modern standards of precision on first-century writers and then dismiss them as inaccurate. There are simply different conventions at play here.

What Are the Key Differences between a Predominantly Oral Culture and a Print Culture?

People in the ancient world were used to remembering things for themselves. We, on the other hand, are used to having things remembered for us. I bring this up because as moderns we tend to project our inability to remember details back on the first-century writers. This is both illegitimate and anachronistic. A strong oral society would have been well positioned—especially the Jewish culture of remembering—to maintain the teaching tradition of Jesus (e.g., received/delivered formula commonly used by rabbis to their disciples we discussed in chapter 3). It seems amazing to us, but "rabbis were encouraged to memorize the entire Hebrew Scriptures (what we call the Old Testament), plus a sizable body of oral laws that grew up around them. Elementary education, mandatory for many Jewish boys from age five to twelve or thirteen, was entirely by rote memory; and only one topic was studied, the Bible."[7]

Another worry that concerns moderns is that if writers were relying predominantly on oral testimony, then there would be nothing controlling the accuracy of the accounts. Indeed, this is one of the central presuppositions of the more skeptical form critics of the early twentieth century. (Form criticism studies the spoken tradition before it became written down.) However this presupposition has been forcefully challenged by the groundbreaking work of Richard Bauckham in his book *Jesus and the Eyewitness*. He is worth quoting here:

> In the period up to the writing of the Gospels, gospel traditions were connected with named and known eyewitnesses, people who had heard the teaching of Jesus from his lips and committed it to memory, people who had witnessed the events of his ministry, death, and resurrection and themselves had formulated stories about these events that they told. These eyewitnesses did not merely set going a process of oral transmission that soon went its own way without

reference to them. They remained throughout their lifetimes the sources and . . . the authoritative guarantors of the stories they continued to tell.[8]

The historical truth was guarded and guaranteed by the community of eye-witnesses. If errors and inaccuracies crept in, they would have been able to set the record straight.

What Kind of Literature Are the Gospels?

While there has been much debate and discussion over the past one hundred years, there is a growing consensus that the Gospels are best understood as ancient biography or *bios*.[9] Here are several important features of this genre, which will help us when we get to the stage of interpretation.

First, the Gospels are the right length. Mark has 11,242 words, which is similar to the average length of *Plutarch's Lives* (Plutarch was a Greek historian and biographer living ca. AD 46–120). Luke weighs in at 19,428 words, which is at the upper limit of what a single scroll could contain.

Second, notice how rarely Jesus is not the center of attention of any given Gospel narrative. The goal was not to give an exhaustive life account—a representative sampling of a person's life activities that revealed character would be more than sufficient.

Third, the Gospels follow the convention of ancient biographies by letting Jesus' words and deeds speak for themselves. As Bock notes, in "ancient biography actions and sayings are the focus of the portrayal. . . . Who the person was emerges from the portrait."[10]

Fourth, the usual subjects of ancient biographies were public figures (e.g., emperors, generals, poet, sages, or philosophers) **and these were written for everyday people** with the goal of creating a lasting impression.

Finally, crucifixion was an ignoble way to die, so the Gospel writers have some explaining to do if their hero figure (Jesus) was to be viewed sympathetically by a first-century audience. "If the person's death took place in some glorious or inglorious fashion, ample space had to explain the significance of the event," New Testament historian Witherington writes, "because it was widely believed in antiquity that how one died revealed one's true character . . . and what God (or the gods) . . . thought about that person."[11] The crucifixion events need the context of the claims and mission of Jesus of Nazareth regarding his atonement and the significance of resurrection.

This discussion is important because we need to establish what kind of literature the Gospels are and how they should be interpreted. This spadework helps us avoid the charge of special pleading when we deal with various alleged discrepancies in the Gospels.

Did the Gospel Writers Intend to Write Accurate History?

Witherington observes, "The most the historian can establish about events in the past is a good probability one way or another that this or that event did or did not happen. There is no such thing as absolute certainty on such matters."[12] Again, this doesn't mean that we should become historical skeptics, only that we should have realistic expectations.

Thucydides, writing in the fifth century BC, stated his approach to history and the importance of eyewitness testimony:

And with regard to my factual reporting of the events of the war I have made it a principle not to write down the first story that came my way, and not even to be guided by my own general impressions; either I was present myself at the events which I have described or else I heard of them from eye-witnesses whose reports I have checked with as much thoroughness as possible. (*History of the Peloponnesian War* 1.22)

Now compare Luke's introduction to his Gospel:

Inasmuch as many have undertaken to compile an account of the things accomplished among us, just as they were handed down to us by those who from the beginning were eyewitnesses and servants of the word, it seemed fitting for me as well, having investigated everything carefully from the beginning, to write it out for you in consecutive order, most excellent Theophilus; so that you may know the exact truth about the things you have been taught. (Luke 1:1–4 NASB)

Luke is an ideal case study, because his approach is very similar to that of Thucydides. Yes, they intended to write accurate history.

Were the Gospel Writers Incapable of Writing Accurate History because They Were Biased?

Another common objection is that the Gospel writers were biased. Wouldn't Jesus' followers have had a theological axe to grind? If by this someone means that the disciples had convictions about the identity and teachings of Jesus, then yes, they were biased. But so is every other writer of history, because everyone has a worldview. The important question is whether being an advocate for a certain point of view necessarily renders that person incapable of recording reliable and accurate history.

Gospels scholar Mark Strauss is helpful on this point: "If an American wrote a history of the United States, would that history necessarily be unreliable or distorted? Or more pointedly, some of the most important accounts of the Nazi Holocaust have been composed by Jews. Does this fact render them inaccurate? On the contrary, those passionately interested in the events are often the most meticulous in recording them. To claim that the Gospels cannot be historical because they were written by believers is fallacious."[13]

DEALING WITH APPARENT CONTRADICTIONS: TWO PRINCIPLES TO REMEMBER

As we begin to turn our attention from more general and foundational questions to more specific challenging texts, the following two principles will serve as reliable guides.

First, differences don't necessarily equal errors. We can easily imagine different perspectives of the same event. For example, let's say you and your friend go and see *The Hobbit* movie and then both of you explain to your friends at different times later that week what happened. Odds are there will be differences in what you chose to share, but that doesn't mean that one of you is mistaken.

This second principle was a game changer for me: *An account can be accurate—a broader category—without being as precise as it could be.* Take the everyday example of a wife asking her husband, "How was your day?" The reply? "Good." Now, this is accurate perhaps, but not precise. There are a lot of details that have been left out, but it is still accurate nonetheless. As an aside, the doctrine of inerrancy requires accuracy but not always precision.[14]

ARE THE RED LETTERS IN MY BIBLE THE EXACT WORDS OF JESUS?

If you have been tracking my discussion so far, then you probably know where I am going with this one. The answer to this question is *maybe*. Jesus probably gave most of his teaching in Aramaic, which was the dominant public language of first-century Palestine. The New Testament is written in Greek, which was the dominant language of the larger first-century Greco-Roman World to which the Gospels were addressed. Therefore, most of Jesus' teaching in the Gospels is already a translation.

When scholars discuss this question, what they are asking is, Do the Gospels record the "words of Jesus" or "the voice of Jesus" (*ipsissima verba* vs. *ipsissima vox*)? Actually we have both (though we are not always sure which is which). As already noted above, the Gospel writers intended in most cases to give us the gist of Jesus' teaching, not a verbatim audio recording. Bock writes:

> Each Evangelist retells the living and powerful words of Jesus in a fresh way for his readers, while faithfully and accurately presenting the gist of what Jesus said. . . . We clearly hear Jesus, but we must be aware that there is summary and emphasis in the complementary portraits that each Evangelist gives to the founder of the faith. Jesus' teaching is both present in the Gospels and reflected on in light of the significance his teaching came to possess.[15]

From a Christian point of view, we have the words/voice of Jesus that God wanted us to have and that we would need for living, spiritual formation, and accomplishing our mission (2 Timothy 3:16–17).

116 QUESTIONING THE BIBLE

A TEST CASE FOR AN APPARENT CONTRADICTION: MATTHEW 8:5–13 VS. LUKE 7:1–10

The time has now come to examine a particular text. Read these two passages, Matthew 8:5–13 and Luke 7:1–10 (NIV) and see if you can find the alleged contradiction.

Chart 8

A TEST CASE FOR AN APPARENT CONTRADICTION

Matthew 8:5–13	Luke 7:1–10
[5]When Jesus had entered Capernaum, a centurion came to him, asking for help. [6]"Lord," he said, "my servant lies at home paralyzed, suffering terribly." [7]Jesus said to him, "Shall I come and heal him?" [8]The centurion replied, "Lord, I do not deserve to have you come under my roof. But just say the word, and my servant will be healed. [9]For I myself am a man under authority, with soldiers under me. I tell this one, 'Go,' and he goes; and that one, 'Come,' and he comes. I say to my servant, 'Do this,' and he does it." [10]When Jesus heard this, he was amazed and said to those following him, "Truly I tell you, I have not found anyone in Israel with such great faith. [11]I say to you that many will come from the east and the west, and will take their places at the feast with Abraham, Isaac and Jacob in the kingdom of heaven. [12]But the subjects of the kingdom will be thrown outside, into the darkness, where there will be weeping and gnashing of teeth." [13]Then Jesus said to the centurion, "Go! Let it be done just as you believed it would." And his servant was healed at that moment.	[7:1] When Jesus had finished saying all this in the hearing of the people, he entered Capernaum. [2]There a centurion's servant, whom his master valued highly, was sick and about to die. [3]The centurion heard of Jesus and sent some elders of the Jews to him, asking him to come and heal his servant. [4]When they came to Jesus, they pleaded earnestly with him, "This man deserves to have you do this, [5]because he loves our nation and has built our synagogue." [6]So Jesus went with them. He was not far from the house when the centurion sent friends to say to him: "Lord, don't trouble yourself, for I do not deserve to have you come under my roof. [7]That is why I did not even consider myself worthy to come to you. But say the word, and my servant will be healed. [8]For I myself am a man under authority, with soldiers under me. I tell this one, 'Go,' and he goes; and that one, 'Come,' and he comes. I say to my servant, 'Do this,' and he does it." [9]When Jesus heard this, he was amazed at him, and turning to the crowd following him, he said, "I tell you, I have not found such great faith even in Israel." [10]Then the men who had been sent returned to the house and found the servant well.

You will have noticed that Matthew says that the centurion came to Jesus himself (8:5), whereas Luke says that he sent some Jewish elders as emissaries to Jesus (7:3). This is a contradiction, right? Actually, no. In this passage,

Matthew, for literary reasons, collapses Jesus' full saying and captures the "gist." Moreover, this is a culturally acceptable move because the Jewish emissaries represented the centurion. Reporters do something similar today when we read, "The president said today." Now this could have been the president himself, but often the president speaks through a press secretary or a press release. And these are all legitimate ways to capture what happened.[16]

MAJOR CATEGORIES OF
APPARENT CONTRADICTIONS[17]

Paraphrasing, Summarizing, and Interpretation

Returning to Peter's confession of Jesus (Matthew 16:16; Mark 8:29; Luke 9:20), we see that all three affirm the historical core that Jesus is the Messiah. Matthew then adds the theological significance as Peter grows in his understanding of Jesus' identity. Matthew's words are pregnant with meaning and are purposely ambiguous—they could refer to the OT conception of a regal son (cf. David in 2 Samuel 7) or the more fully developed idea later made in his Gospel and postresurrection.[18] As Craig Blomberg reminds us, "Many of the seeming discrepancies vanish once we understand the literary conventions for writing history or biography in the ancient world."[19]

Abbreviations and Omissions

How did James and John request the chief seats in the kingdom of God (Matthew 20:20–21 vs. Mark 10:35–37)? In Matthew, the mother asks on behalf of the sons. In Mark, the sons ask. Jesus responds to the sons in both accounts. A reasonable solution is that Mark simplifies/abbreviates the account to suit his purposes and because the context seems to indicate that it was the brothers who put their mother up to asking Jesus.[20]

Reordering of Events/Sayings

The temptations of Jesus are in a different order (Matthew 4:1–11 vs. Luke 4:1–13). This is not unusual as the narrative purpose of each writer is different. In Matthew 4, the temptations proceed with making stones into bread (vv. 3–4), jumping from the temple (vv. 5–7), and receiving the kingdoms of the world (vv. 8–9). In Luke 4, it's stones to bread (vv. 3–4), kingdoms of the world (vv. 5–8), and jumping from the temple (vv. 9–12). Luke probably wanted to emphasize the temple (thematically) and so listed that temptation last.[21]

Reporting of Similar Events/Sayings

Matthew's parable of the talents (Matthew 25:14–30) vs. Luke's parable of the minas (Luke 19:11–27). Jesus was an itinerant preacher and doubtless covered similar material in various towns with different illustrations that would not have been verbatim or that he would have used to emphasize a different point.[22]

Variation in Numbers

A classic objection concerns how many angels the women encountered at the empty tomb (Mark 16:5, Matthew 28:2–3, Luke 24:4). Craig Blomberg offers a possible reading of this text. "Mark 16:5 has them seeing a young man dressed in a white robe, Matthew 28:2–3 refers to an angel with clothing white as snow, while Luke 24:4 speaks of two men in dazzling apparel. Since angels are regularly depicted in the Bible as men, often in white or shining clothing, there is no reason that Mark or Luke needed to mention explicitly that angels were present. As for the number of them, if there were two it is hardly inaccurate to say that the women saw a young man who spoke to them, especially if one was the consistent spokesperson for the two. Only if Mark or Matthew had said that the women saw one person all by himself would there be an actual contradiction."[23] Remember, differences do not necessarily indicate contradictions; this is an example of difference in reporting.

DO WE HAVE TO RESOLVE ALL THE QUESTIONS BEFORE WE CAN TRUST THE BIBLE?

How much is enough? Cold-case detective Jim Wallace helps us here. "It's important to remember that truth can be known even when some of the facts are missing. None of us [has] ever made a decision with complete knowledge of all the possible facts. There are always unanswered questions."[24] Well said. There comes a time when juries have to make up their minds and offer a decision regarding the evidence. This is true for all of us. And as Wallace accurately points out, there will always be some unanswered questions. But have enough pieces of the puzzle been put together for us to reasonably trust the available evidence? I think in the case where the Gospels are concerned, the answer is yes.

The Bible has proven remarkably reliable. So in the very small number of places where we await further light, evidence, or insight, it is reasonable for us to expect that we don't have enough information yet. "Not every proposed harmonization is as credible as every other, but enough are sufficiently credible that it is best to give the text the benefit of the doubt where we are less sure rather than immediately speaking of proven contradictions."[25]

Three Big Ideas

1. A contradiction is a very specific thing: Two or more statements are *consistent* when it is possible for them all to be true at the same time. Two or more statements are *inconsistent* when it is not possible for them all to be true at the same time. (For this reason, it's very difficult to generate an actual contradiction in the Bible.)

2. History is dynamic and three-dimensional, not static and one-dimensional. Also we must make sure we are not imposing twenty-first-century historical standards on a first-century text. We need to pay attention to the differences between an oral and print culture and recognize that the Gospels (based on eyewitnesses cf. Luke 1:1–4) were "ancient biographies" that need to be interpreted as such.

3. More often we probably have the voice of Jesus rather than the precise words of Jesus in the Gospels. The Gospel writers had unique purposes in their writing and therefore were selective by omitting certain details and including features that served their narrative purposes. Remember each author can arrange material topically, chronologically, literarily, or thematically—all are legitimate.

Conversation Tips

How should you respond if you encounter the "But there are so many contradictions in the Bible" claim?

- First, ask them to give you an example. And if they list one, ask them why they think it is a contradiction. (Most people have just heard this slogan and repeat it . . . make them do some work here.)

- Respond to their objection. As you do, use categories about the aims of first-century history writing, define what a real contradiction is, and remind them that differences do not equal errors because of various perspectives at work. Introduce the important distinction between "precision vs. accuracy."

- Then ask them if (1) they have understood your answer and (2) if they are satisfied with your explanation. (Again, wait for a response here.) If so, great. If not, why not?

- It may seem at some point that they are not genuinely interested in an answer—it may be worth asking them what would satisfy them in this case. It may become obvious that they have a very unrealistic (and sometimes naïve) standard they are applying to the historical/biographical writings contained in the Bible. If you have offered a reasonable or plausible solution to the apparent contradiction, then it's up to them at that point. Remember, just because they may not be convinced on the spot, doesn't mean your conclusions are not reasonable.

Digging Deeper

- Jeremy Howard, ed. *The Holman Apologetics Commentary on the Bible: The Gospels and Acts*. Nashville: B & H Publishing, 2013.

- Craig L. Blomberg. *The Historical Reliability of the Gospels*, 2nd ed. Downers Grove, IL: InterVarsity, 2002.

IS THE BIBLE UNSCIENTIFIC?

I am a scientist who believes Scripture to be the Word of God. I am not shy, therefore, of drawing scientific implications from it, where warranted. However, saying Scripture has scientific implications does not mean that the Bible is a scientific treatise from which we can deduce Newton's Laws, Einstein's equations, or the chemical structure of common salt.[1]

John Lennox

We live in the age of science. And to many people, the Bible seems very unscientific. After all, have you ever personally witnessed any of the following?

- A major body of water parts so desert nomads can walk through on dry land while being chased by Pharaoh's army (Exodus 14:21–31).

- A man swallowed by a giant fish stays entombed for three days but lives to preach another day (Jonah 1:17; 2:10–3:15).

- Someone calms a violent storm with just a sentence and later walks on water (Mark 4:35–41; 6:45–50).

- A man who has been dead for a few days is raised from the dead (John 11:38–44).

"The nineteenth century is the last time when it was possible for an educated person to admit to believing in miracles like the virgin birth without embarrassment."[2] Or at least that is what the world's most famous atheist, Richard Dawkins, claims. The Bible is chock-full of miracle claims, and to many scientifically minded people this is a sure sign that the Bible is unreliable. And honestly, sometimes Christians find themselves embarrassed by some of these stories. They find themselves caught flat-footed in a conversation and quickly realize that appealing to blind faith isn't going to cut it. Students who grow up in well-meaning churches that do not train them how to think well about faith and science issues are especially susceptible.

My contention is that Christians shouldn't be embarrassed by the miraculous claims in the Bible. But in the same breath, I also think we can do a much better job when it comes to thinking and talking about science, God's activity in the world, and the Bible.

ARE MIRACLES POSSIBLE?

Christianity is a supernatural religion. As Ronald Nash reminds us, "Miracles are essential to the historic Christian faith. If Jesus Christ was not God incarnate, and if Jesus did not rise bodily from the grave, then the Christian faith as we know it from history and the Scriptures would not—could not—be true. . . . It is, then, easy to see why enemies of the Christian faith direct many of their attacks against these two miracles of Christ's incarnation and resurrection in particular and against the possibility of miracles in general."[3] No miracles, no Christianity.

The reason for Dawkins's confident assertion above is his belief that the writings of the prominent Scottish philosopher David Hume (specifically his essay *Of Miracles*) have forever relegated miracle claims to the irrational dustbin of history. While this is unfortunately a widespread belief today, it also happens to be false.

Hume claimed that belief ought to be justified by probability and that probability is based upon the uniformity or consistency of nature. Nature always behaves in a certain way, Hume said; therefore it is likely that it will always behave that way. Based on this probability, he concluded that exceptions to nature's laws are so infinitely improbable as to be considered impossible. The unchangeable laws of nature outweigh any evidence that could ever be offered for a miracle. Anything that is unique to normal human experience—such as a miracle—should be, according to Hume, eliminated outright. In Hume's own words, "A miracle is a violation of the laws of nature; and as a firm and unalterable experience has established these laws, the proof against a miracle, from the very nature of the fact, is as entire as any argument from experience can possibly be imagined."[4] This is Hume's main objection (his "in principle" objection).

The major (and obvious) problem with this line of reasoning is that it is circular. C. S. Lewis playfully points this out:

> Now of course we must agree with Hume that if there is absolutely "uniform experience" against miracles, if in other words they have never happened, why then they never have. Unfortunately we know the experience against them to be uniform only if we know that all the reports of them are false. And we can know all the reports to be false only if we know already that miracles have never occurred. In fact, we are arguing in a circle.[5]

Hume presented four specific "in fact" arguments against miracles. To each of these arguments we offer a reasoned response.

First, no historical miracle has been sufficiently attested by honest and reliable men who are of such social standing that they would have a great deal to lose by lying. In response to this, we have made the case in this book that the Gospel writers were both interested in and capable of recording accurate history. Further, that Jesus of Nazareth was a miracle worker is well documented both in the literary sources within the Gospel tradition (e.g., number of unique miracles recorded in Mark = 20, John = 7, Q = 1, Matthew = 2, Luke = 3) and in non-Christian sources such as Josephus and the Talmud.[6] Finally, several of the disciples were put to death because of their convictions that Jesus is the risen Lord. While this does not prove the veracity of their beliefs, it does show the depth of their conviction and the level of their sincerity. Liars make poor martyrs.[7]

Second, people crave miraculous stories and will gullibly believe absurd stories, which is evidenced by the sheer number of false tales of miraculous

events. Granted, some people are willing to gullibly follow absurd miracle claims, but are we in a position to say this is true for all people? This certainly doesn't follow logically. Furthermore, perhaps our own personal lack of exposure to stories of and evidence for the miraculous is the limiting factor here? For example, in his two-volume work, *Miracles: The Credibility of the New Testament Accounts*, historian Craig Keener has written almost twelve hundred heavily footnoted and meticulously documented pages exploding the myth that miracles have not occurred in ancient history and are not occurring today. From around the world, he documents numerous kinds of healings, people regaining their eyesight, and even people being raised from the dead (including an account of his own sister-in-law).[8]

Third, miracles only occur among ignorant and uncivilized people. In response, Jesus' miracles did not occur among ignorant and uncivilized people, but among the Jews, who were a highly educated and sophisticated people. Unlike other people groups of the Mediterranean world, the Jews were uniquely committed to studying and following their ancient Scriptures. Again, I would refer you to Keener's book documenting the impressive scope of miracle claims occurring in the world today. I don't think Hume, were he alive today, could make this argument.

Fourth, miracles occur in all religions and thus cancel each other out, since they teach mutually contradictory doctrines. While it is true that other religions have miracle claims, none of the miracles is as powerfully attested as the miracles of Jesus Christ. Moreover, the historical evidence for the resurrection is quite strong.[9] A more rational approach would be to examine the strongest claims and not just dismiss all of them.

For these and other reasons we have not mentioned, Hume's argument against miracles is unsuccessful.[10] Therefore, if it's even possible that God exists, then we can't rule out his intervention in the natural world *before* we consider the evidence. A reasonable approach then is to examine the evidence for miracles on a case-by-case basis (this avoids the charge of gullibility). But we may be getting ahead of ourselves here; after all, hasn't science disproved God? Are there any good reasons to believe in God?

A DIVINE REVOLUTION: RENEWED ARGUMENTS FOR GOD'S EXISTENCE

It may have seemed acceptable in the mid-1960s to argue that religious people were irrational and clinging to blind faith. The now famous *Time* magazine cover of April 1966 with the headline "Is God Dead?" certainly captured the spirit of the age. Philosophers and liberal theologians celebrated the "death of God" movement and believed that Western culture was permanently leaving behind its theistic roots. Yet as philosopher William Lane Craig pointed out in a *Christianity Today* article titled "God Is Not Dead Yet," the news of God's passing was premature.[11] In fact, at the very time theologians were proclaiming the death of God, a new generation of philosophers (like Alvin Plantinga) was launching a quiet revolution in Christian thought. This philosophical revolution over the past few decades has led to the strengthening of the traditional arguments for God's existence with new insights and evidence. Here is a brief summary of just a few of the scientifically oriented arguments that have revitalized Christian theism.[12]

The Cosmological Argument

This argument begins with the observation that the universe had a beginning, which is demonstrable by science and philosophy. Given that something can't begin to exist without a cause, it seems eminently reasonable to believe that a transcendent cause (outside of the universe) is responsible for its existence. Since space, time, matter, and energy simultaneously came into existence at a finite point in the past, the cause is plausibly timeless, immaterial, intelligent, powerful, and personal. Simply put, the beginning of the universe points to a Beginner.

The Design Argument from Physics

Scientists have learned that the laws of physics that govern the universe are exquisitely fine-tuned for the emergence and sustenance of human life. The universe seems to be uniquely crafted with us in mind. If there were the slightest changes in any number of physical constants, our universe would quickly become inhospitable. The most compelling and reliable explanation for why the universe is so precisely fine-tuned is because an Intelligent Mind made it that way. Simply put, the fine-tuning of the universe points to a Fine-Tuner.

The Design Argument from DNA

Since the discovery of the structure of DNA in 1953, scientists have learned that cellular organization and the development of living creatures are orchestrated by genetic information. Human DNA, for example, contains the informational equivalent of roughly eight thousand books. Natural forces such as chance and necessity have overwhelmingly failed to explain the origin of biological information. In our everyday experience, we attribute the origin of information to a mind. Simply put, the vast amount of information contained in living organisms points to an Information Giver.

The Curious Case of Antony Flew

Antony Flew was arguably the most influential atheistic philosopher of the twentieth century. Remarkably, after a lifetime of study, writing, and teaching as an atheist, Flew rejected his atheism and affirmed the existence of God. In his autobiography, *There Is a God*, Flew wrote, "I now believe that the universe was brought into existence by an infinite Intelligence. I believe that this universe's intricate laws manifest what scientists have called the Mind of God. I believe that life and reproduction originate in a divine Source. Why do I believe this, given that I expounded and defended atheism for more than a half century? The short answer is this: this is the world picture, as I see it, that has emerged from modern science."[13] As you can see, the case for God in the age of science is alive and well!

ARE MIRACLES "OFF-LIMITS" TO HISTORIANS?

The conclusion historians are willing to draw concerning the Gospels depends in large part on what presuppositions they bring to their investigation. British New Testament scholar R. T. France captures the situation well:

> At the level of their literary and historical character we have good reasons

to treat the Gospels seriously as a source of information on the life and teaching of Jesus, and thus on the historical origins of Christianity. . . . Beyond that point, the decision as to how far a scholar is willing to accept the record they offer is likely to be influenced more by his openness to a "supernaturalist" world-view than by strictly historical considerations.[14]

In light of Hume's failure and the evidence that God might actually exist after all, the most reasonable approach is not to assume naturalism—the worldview that says physics, chemistry, biology, and genetics explain every aspect of reality—at the outset. In their thoughtful critique of miracles and the critical-historical method, Paul Eddy and Greg Boyd conclude that naturalism "as an unquestioned presupposition . . . is unwarranted and inconsistent with the goal of engaging in a truly critical investigation of history that strives for objectivity." They have "advocated an open historical-critical method that . . . is open to the possibility that evidence from history might require scholars to conclude that an event that defies plausible naturalistic explanation—a *super*natural occurrence—has happened."[15] If the goal really were discovering the truth, then why would the historian intentionally exclude certain explanations from the start—even if they explained the relevant data points the best?

This historical discussion about the biblical material leads us into the larger cultural discussion occurring in science concerning the origin of the universe and humanity. But this is not a science vs. religion issue. It is a worldview issue that needs to be debated, not merely assumed and then used as a club to bludgeon or shame anyone who dissents. Which is the most reasonable philosophical approach to reality? Let the best ideas win!

In his book *Where the Conflict Really Lies: Science, Religion, and Naturalism*, Alvin Plantinga convincingly argues that "there is superficial conflict but deep concord between science and theistic belief, but superficial concord and deep conflict between science and naturalism. Given that naturalism is at least a quasi-religion, there is indeed a science/religion conflict, all right, but it is not between science and theistic religion: it is between science and naturalism. That's where the conflict really lies."[16] What we are seeing play out in the public square today is the clash of worldviews.

Just to make sure I'm not misunderstood, ethically practiced science is a wonderful thing. Christians should study it and go into the field! In fact, the scientific method is part of the heritage of Christianity: "Men became scientific," said C. S. Lewis, "because they expected law in nature and they expected law in nature because they believed in a lawgiver."[17] But there are limits to what science can tell us; it is only one slice of the knowledge pie—other sources include philosophy, history, economics, literature, sociology, and religion. Christians also need to reject one of our culture's most unexamined and influential assumptions—namely that "you can't know something unless you prove it scientifically." Here's the fatal problem for this assumption—*one cannot "scientifically prove" that statement itself*. It fails to fulfill its own standard. This is clearly a self-refuting statement, which means it can't possibly be true. Please spread the word.

CAN GOD'S ACTIONS BE DETECTED SCIENTIFICALLY?

How do we know when God does something or not? Is everything God does a miracle? As Christians we definitely want to avoid falling into the trap of "god of the gaps" reasoning, which says, "We can't understand it; therefore God did it." This is not a helpful approach; nor is it theologically or philosophically accurate. We want to pursue understanding, not champion ignorance. And to so pursue, I want to suggest some helpful categories and make sure we are accurately defining our terms.

According to philosopher Stephen Davis, God relates to the world in four primary ways: "(1) God brings the world into existence; (2) God sustains or upholds the world in existence; (3) God acts through natural causes in the world; and (4) God acts miraculously or outside of natural causes in the world."[18]

Numbers (1) and (2) are foundational truths clearly taught in Scripture: "For by him [Christ] all things were created, in heaven and on earth, visible and invisible, whether thrones or dominions or rulers or authorities—all things were created through him and for him. And he is before all things, and in him all things hold together" (Colossians 1:16-17). Most of the action when it comes to the miracles discussion revolves around (3) and (4).

Old Testament scholar C. John Collins offers the most helpful way I've come across to explain the proper distinctions between God's natural and supernatural actions:

> After the creation, God works in two ways. First, He maintains the things He created, along with their powers to cause things. Apples keep on tasting good and nourishing us because God keeps maintaining their properties. A soccer goalie deflects the ball because God maintains the properties of the ball, the air, and the goalie's body. Second, God is not limited by the powers of created things. Sometimes He goes beyond their powers if it suits His purpose. We can call the first kind of action the *natural* (since it works with created natures) and the second the *supernatural* (since it goes beyond natural powers). Let's be clear about this: *Both* kinds are God's actions and both serve His purpose.[19]

In this explanation, Collins is combining categories (2) and (3) above. To put it simply, God can either work with created natures (natural properties) or go beyond their natural capacities to accomplish his purposes. Collins goes on to clarify:

> Because God made His world "very good" (Genesis 1:31), it needs no tinkering to keep in operation, so we don't expect that the sciences will "detect" God's natural actions. The reason that an atom's electrons don't crash into the nucleus is not that God holds them apart by a miracle but that He made their properties so that they don't crash. On the other hand, the sciences may sometimes help us detect a supernatural event because in knowing the properties of natural things, we can tell when these have been transcended. For example, the more we know about how babies come about, the more clearly supernatural becomes the conception of Jesus: There is no natural explanation for it.[20]

These distinctions are extremely helpful because we may come across situations where a supernatural explanation is necessary precisely because of our knowledge of what natural powers are capable of. This is not a gap of ignorance that we are trying to fill with God's activity; rather it's a gap that has been created through our scientific understanding of the world, our growing understanding of the nature of things. The classic example of this would be the resurrection. We know that dead bodies stay dead "unless someone with extraordinary powers intervenes."[21] We could also apply the same to the prophet Jonah. We are not looking for a natural explanation of how a man can stay alive in the belly of a great fish for three days because we know what our natural capacities are as humans along with very large fish; clearly a supernatural explanation is warranted.

Understood this way, God is not in competition with scientific explanation. For as Oxford professor John Lennox puts it, to understand them to be in competition "is as wrong-headed as thinking that an explanation of a Ford car in terms of Henry Ford as inventor and designer competes with an explanation in terms of mechanism and law. God is not a 'God of the gaps,' he is God of the whole show."[22]

HELPING A NEW GENERATION THINK ABOUT GOD, SCIENCE, AND GENESIS 1–2

Whenever I speak to students on God and science, questions about Genesis and the age of the earth inevitably come up. When I am asked my opinion on what Genesis teaches regarding the age of the earth and if that conflicts with modern science, I don't give them a straight answer. Not because I don't have a view on the matter but because I would rather give them a framework with which to think carefully and biblically about a question like this. That is what I would like to do here.

First, creationism begins not with the observable evidence discovered from creation but with the biblical text of Genesis that affirms, "in the beginning, God created" (Genesis 1:1). Creationism affirms the truthfulness of a literal (that is, historical-grammatical-literary) interpretation of Genesis and the existence of the biblical God. It certainly is consistent with what we discover about the universe, but creationism is, first and foremost, a *theological* doctrine, and it reasons outward from that starting point. (This stands in contrast to intelligent design and Darwinian evolution, which both begin with the available empirical data and then reason backwards to the best explanation.)

The progression goes something like this: A Christian accepts the teachings and worldview of Jesus, who affirmed the doctrine of creation recorded in Genesis. The Christian then compares the biblical text and the physical universe and sees confirmation of this worldview (Psalm 19:1–4; Romans 1:19–20). For this reason, I suggest that it is most prudent for Christians to have the public discussion of origins at the level of naturalism versus theism and not creationism versus evolution, because one's worldview commitments will shape which interpretations of the available evidence will be allowed. Furthermore, I think the debate going on between intelligent design and Darwinian evolution is healthy for science and profitable because it is clarifying the nature and extent of the available evidence and the role that worldview plays in the cultural discussion.

Once Christians recognize that the fundamental battle exists between theism and naturalism (as Plantinga stated above), we can put the current debate about origins into perspective. I have two suggestions that may help us better navigate these issues. First, Christians need to present a united front opposing naturalism in the public square while also standing up for academic freedom so that questions of origins can be rigorously discussed without fear of censorship, denial of tenure, or the loss of research money.

Second, and closely related, Christians must be charitable toward other Christians who disagree about which particular interpretation of Genesis is the most accurate (for example, the young earth, old earth debate). This is especially true when we discuss this topic on the Internet, on TV or radio, or in print. All the watching world sees is angry Christians not loving one another and bickering over which view of the flat-earth theory is correct. But in the same breath, we can and should develop careful exegetical and theological views on creation. All Christians who take the Bible seriously should be able to agree that God purposefully created, even if they disagree concerning the *how* and the *when*.

What are the Options?

Whole books have been written on the various understandings of Genesis 1–2. But I think it is helpful to get a bird's-eye view of the landscape and chart 9 accomplishes that purpose. These are the four major views held to by evangelical scholars today.[23]

Things We Can All Agree On

First, the goal is to understand what the text meant to its original audience before trying to make it fit with the prevailing scientific views of our day. Miller and Soden offer a nice summary of some of the main things an ancient Israelite would have learned from reading the opening chapters of Genesis: (1) God in Genesis exists independently of creation and is not created or self-created; (2) God transcends creation; (3) God is effortlessly sovereign over all creation without struggle; (4) God alone is deity; (5) Israel was to celebrate the rule of God in their lives by imitating their creator in work and rest each week; and (6) man does not provide for God, but God provides for man.[24]

Chart 9

FOUR INTERPRETATIONS OF GENESIS 1–2 THAT TAKE THE BIBLE SERIOUSLY

Interpretations and Major Proponents	Summary of the View	Further Reading
The "Calendar-Day" Interpretation (often called the literal view, the traditional view, or the twenty-four-hour view) Proponent: Todd Beall	The Calendar-Day view accepts the first chapter of Genesis as historical and chronological in character and takes the creation week as consisting of six twenty-four-hour days, followed by a twenty-four-hour Sabbath. Since Adam and Eve were created as mature adults, so the rest of creation came forth from its Maker. The garden of Eden included full-grown trees and animals, which Adam named. Those holding this view believe this is the normal understanding of the creation account and that this has been the most commonly held understanding of this account both in Jewish and Christian history.	"Reading Genesis 1–2: A Literal Approach" in *Reading Genesis 1–2: An Evangelical Conversation,* ed. J. Daryl Charles
The "Day-Age" Interpretation Proponent: Hugh Ross	The six days of the Day-Age view are understood in the same sense as "in that day" of Isaiah 11:10–11—in other words, as periods of indefinite length and not of 24 hours' duration. The six days are taken as sequential but as overlapping and perhaps merging into one another. The Genesis 1 creation week describes events from the point of view of the earth, which is being prepared as the habitation for man. In this context, the explanation of day four is that the sun only became visible on that day, as atmospheric conditions allowed the previous alternation of light and darkness to be perceived as coming from the previously created sun and other heavenly bodies. The Day-Age construct preserves the general sequence of events as portrayed in the text and is not merely a response to Charles Darwin and evolutionary science.	*A Matter of Days: Resolving a Creation Controversy,* by Hugh Ross

FOUR INTERPRETATIONS OF GENESIS 1–2
THAT TAKE THE BIBLE SERIOUSLY   *(continued)*

Interpretations and Major Proponents	Summary of the View	Further Reading
The "Framework" Interpretation Proponent: John Walton	The distinctive feature of the Framework view is its understanding of the week (not the days as such) as a metaphor. According to this interpretation, Moses used the metaphor of the week to narrate God's acts of creation. Thus, God's supernatural creative words or fiats are real and historical but the exact timing is left unspecified. The purpose of the metaphor is to call Adam to imitate God in work, with the promise of entering His Sabbath rest. Creation events are grouped in two triads of days: Days 1–3 (creation's kingdoms) are paralleled by Days 4–6 (creation's kings). Adam is king of the earth; God is the King of Creation.	*The Lost World of Genesis One: Ancient Cosmology and the Origins Debate*, by John H. Walton
The "Analogical Days" Interpretation Proponent: C. John Collins	According to the Analogical view, the "days" of Genesis 1 are God's workdays, analogous (but not necessarily identical) to human workdays. They set a pattern for our rhythm of work and rest. The six days represent periods of God's historical supernatural activity in preparing and populating the earth as a place for humans to live, love, work, and worship. These days are broadly consecutive. That is, they are successive periods of unspecified length. They may overlap in part, or they may reflect logical rather than chronological criteria for grouping certain events on certain days.	*Science and Faith: Friends or Foes*, by C. John Collins and "Reading Genesis 1–2 with the Grain: Analogical Days" in *Reading Genesis 1–2: An Evangelical Conversation*, ed. J. Daryl Charles

Second, and a good qualification of the first point, history reminds us to be humble in our interpretations. We don't want to say anything less than the Bible says, but we don't want to say any more than it says either. While the Bible is infallible, our interpretations of the Bible certainly are not. Humility is important here because the "biblical text just might be more sophisticated than we first imagined, and we might therefore be in danger of using it to support ideas that it never intended to teach."[25] John Lennox, Oxford University professor of mathematics and adjunct lecturer at the Oxford Centre for Christian Apologetics, cites as an example the controversy in the sixteenth century between the "fixed earthers" and the "moving earthers."[26] Certain passages of the Bible (e.g., Psalm 93:1; 104:5; 1 Samuel 2:8, etc.) could be read to mean that the earth was fixed (i.e., it did not move around the sun)—but the verses didn't have to be read that way. Since we believe that God is the author of both the book of nature and the book of Scripture, we believe they will ultimately agree when all the facts are known. But we have incomplete information with which to work. So we do our best and remain humble in the process. We can at least be grateful that after hundreds of years, we can rule out the fixed-earth interpretation!

Next, and a little more controversially, we need to have conversations in the public square and in our churches and youth groups about the significant scientific evidence that undermines the plausibility of Darwinian evolution and points toward Intelligent Design.[27] I find that many are unaware of the academic debate that is occurring today.

Finally, these things matter—but there is a right and wrong way to go about it. David Hagopian helpfully summarizes, "This debate has important ramifications for how we interpret Scripture, proclaim the faith, embrace science, and stand on the shoulders of those who have preceded us in the faith. We all would do well to remember that we agree on far more than we disagree, but we also must remember that we gain nothing by ignoring our differences or sweeping them under the rug. In fact, we stand to gain quite a bit by discussing our differences openly, honestly, and charitably."[28]

Three Big Ideas

1. Hume did not disprove miracles. In fact, in his major argument he begged the question (assumed what he was trying to prove). Moreover, if God exists—and there is good reason to believe that he does—then miracles become possible. At that point we examine events on a case-by-case basis and come to a conclusion based on the evidence.

2. When we talk about miracles, we need to remember that God can either work with created nature or go beyond its natural capacities to accomplish his purposes. It is our knowledge of science that allows us to know what something's natural capacities are and what it would not normally be capable of. Having these distinctions and definitions in mind will help us avoid the "God of the gaps" charge because we will making an argument from evidence, not ignorance.

3. Questions of origins can be very contentious. However as Christians, we are to model thoughtful, loving engagement with those with whom we disagree. We need to remember that the world is watching.

Conversation Tips

- When talking about God and science, be on guard for those trying to smuggle naturalism into the conversation and then trying to equate it with "good science." The major source of conflict is between naturalism and theism—if miracles are possible then the Bible would not be unscientific just because it contains miraculous claims.

- Be sure you are asking a lot of questions to ensure that the terms being thrown around are clearly defined.

- If you are interacting with someone who does not take the Bible seriously, don't get bogged down in the how-God-created discussion. It is much more productive to focus on the powerful evidence that God created.

Digging Deeper

- Douglas Geivett and Gary R. Habermas, eds. *In Defense of Miracles: A Comprehensive Case for God's Action in History.* Downers Grove, IL: InterVarsity, 1997.

- John C. Lennox. *Seven Days That Divide The World: The Beginning According to Genesis and Science.* Grand Rapids: Zondervan, 2011.

IS THE BIBLE SEXIST, RACIST, HOMOPHOBIC, AND GENOCIDAL?

One possibility I urge them to consider is that the passage that bothers them might not teach what it appears to them to be teaching. Many of the texts people find offensive can be cleared up with a decent commentary that puts the issue into historical context.[1]

Tim Keller

The simple fact of the matter is that a lot recorded in the Bible—especially in the Old Testament—is shocking, confusing, and honestly makes the modern reader uncomfortable. Many Christians simply pretend it's not there. However, that tactic will no longer work because the so-called New Atheists, such as Richard Dawkins, are shouting it from the rooftops:

The God of the Old Testament is arguably the most unpleasant character in all fiction: jealous and proud of it; a petty, unjust, unforgiving control-freak; a vindictive, bloodthirsty ethnic cleanser; a misogynistic, homophobic, racist, infanticidal, genocidal, filicidal, pestilential, megalomaniacal, sadomasochistic, capriciously malevolent bully.[2]

Those are some pretty heavy accusations to be making about the Almighty. Scientific objections to the Bible are challenging because Christians don't want to appear ignorant or irrational. But moral challenges to the Bible are often harder to answer because they must be dealt with at both the rational and emotional level. To make matters worse, moral objections like the ones Dawkins mentions can be thrown out quickly in conversation or on Facebook as short sound bites with devastating effect if not responded to. However, to respond to these challenges takes time and usually there are no pithy responses that capture the complexities and nuance necessary to do the biblical accounts justice.

In this chapter, I am going to respond to four of the most visceral and culturally taboo issues of our day—that the Bible is sexist, racist, homophobic, and genocidal. I have written in more detail on these topics elsewhere,[3] so in what follows I want to summarize the key arguments you need to know in order to thoughtfully, lovingly, and biblically respond when you encounter these objections and don't have a whole lot of time. We are now on the clock . . .

DOES THE BIBLE ENDORSE SLAVERY?

Sam Harris is one of the more vocal critics of Christianity and the Bible today. In his *Letter to a Christian Nation* he claims, "Consult the Bible and you will discover that the creator of the universe clearly expects us to keep slaves."[4] Of course you could have never heard of Harris and still encountered this idea in your quiet time: "Slaves, obey your earthly masters in everything; and do it, not only when their eye is on you and to curry their favor, but with sincerity of heart and reverence for the Lord" (Colossians 3:22 NIV).

Who doesn't squirm a little bit reading those words today? After all, I thought the Bible taught kindness and love, but slavery?

Setting the Biblical Record Straight on Slavery

Here are five things you need to know in order to set the record straight on the Bible and slavery.

First, Christianity did not invent slavery. Virtually every society has had slavery; this was a universal problem. It's simply false to imagine that all the other nations were looking to Israel to morally justify slavery. We need to understand Christianity as entering into an existing situation—not creating it. If we do this, then we will see just how revolutionary and countercultural the message of the Bible really was during the time it was composed.

Second, the biblical discussion must appear within its cultural context. The ancient Near Eastern cultural context was very different from the modern postcolonial context. The two biggest causes of slavery in the ancient world were war and poverty, not skin color. Old Testament scholar Christopher J. H. Wright helpfully reminds that the slavery found in ancient Israel was:

> qualitatively vastly different from slavery in the large imperial civiliza-tions—the contemporary ancient Near Eastern empires, and especially the latter empires of the Greeks and Romans. There the slave markets were glutted with captives of war and displaced peoples, and slaves were put to degrading and dehumanizing labour. And, of course, Israelite slavery was even more different from the ghastly commercialized and massive-scale slave trade that Arabs, Europeans, and Americans perpetrated upon Africa.[5]

In drawing attention to this contrast, I am by no means trying to justify slavery, absolve any Christians for their participation in it, or mitigate the dehumanization that occurred in the African slave trade. The main point here is merely that slavery in ancient Israel and the laws pertaining to it recorded in the Old Testament need to be understood within an ancient Near Eastern context because they were very different. The fact that we see laws in Exodus and Deuteronomy regulating slavery at all is striking given the moral poverty of surrounding nations.

We need to remember that Israel was not God's ideal society. Israel was already corrupt and broken like the rest of the peoples of the world when God began his redemptive work in and through them. The people of Israel were called to be progressively different than the surrounding nations. Israel was to begin shining light into a very dark world.

Third, Christianity tolerated slavery until it could be abolished. Since human beings are involved—and free moral agents embedded in cultures are involved—change takes time. The creational norm was that everyone bears the image of God (cf. Genesis 1:26–27). As we just discussed, the laws you find in the Old Testament actually were an improvement compared to the other ancient Near Eastern nations.

There are passages that embody the creational norm in the post-fall world.

For example, Job recognized that his bondservants were created by God just like he was, and therefore he would have to answer to God if he mistreated them (Job 31:13–14). This passage points back to God's original design of humankind in his image before sin's corrupting effects set in. In the New Testament, we see passages like Galatians 3:28: "There is neither Jew nor Greek, there is neither slave nor free, there is no male and female, for you are all one in Christ Jesus." Moreover, we see Paul urging Onesimus that his slave Philemon must be treated as a brother (Philemon 1:16).

In a fallen world where evil has infected people as well as social structures, commentator John Mark Reynolds is right to remind that, "Economic slavery is evil, but immediate abolition could have been a worse evil, possibly leading to violence, starvation, and total societal collapse."[6] The immediate abolition of slavery would have created serious cultural problems. For lasting change to occur and be sustained, a moral tipping point had to be reached over time. One need look no further than how William Wilberforce, as a member of the British parliament, thoughtfully approached the abolition of the slave trade in England. He knew that slave owners would not give up their slaves without compensation, so he incrementally worked over time to address this and other societal conditions that would allow the abolition of slavery to be accomplished and sustainable.[7]

Fourth, Jesus was not silent on slavery; he simply understood what the root issues were—and they all reside in the human heart. Jesus' mission was to set spiritual captives free, and this freedom would come to have real-world effects. When Jesus began his public ministry, he stood in the synagogue to read the following passage: "The Spirit of the Lord is upon me, because he has anointed me to proclaim good news to the poor. He has sent me to proclaim liberty to the captives and recovering of sight to the blind, to set at liberty those who are oppressed" (Luke 4:18, quoting Isaiah 61:1–2).

Jesus came to set captives free, restore, heal, and transform—that is the good news of the kingdom of God. It has already begun and we await its full and final consummation.

Fifth, the Christian worldview best accounts for human rights and dignity. "Human rights" are buzzwords today and rightly so. The Bible unequivocally teaches universal human dignity and equality because all are made in the image of God. Racism is completely at odds with this foundational truth. What is often forgotten is that atheism rose to prominence only after centuries of Judeo-Christian ethic and thought had shaped modern civilization. Atheism did not lay the groundwork for inherent human dignity and equality; it borrows that from a Judeo-Christian worldview. If you remove God from the equation, you also remove inherent human dignity and equality.

DOES THE BIBLE APPROVE OF GENOCIDE?

If you happen to make it to Deuteronomy in your read-through-the-Bible in a year, you will be jolted by this passage:

> But in the cities of these peoples that the Lord your God is giving you for an inheritance, you shall save alive nothing that breathes, but you shall devote them to complete destruction, the Hittites and the Amorites, the Canaanites and the Perizzites, the Hivites and the Jebusites, as the Lord your God has commanded, that they may not teach you to do according to all their abominable practices that they have done for their gods, and so you sin against the Lord your God. (Deuteronomy 20:16–18)

The language of genocide and ethnic cleansing is emotionally charged and employed with rhetorical flourish by the New Atheists. But these words are not accurate descriptions of what really happened in what scholars refer to as the "conquest narratives." While we are not going to try to make these events seem nice or sanitized (there is nothing nice or sanitized about war of any kind—even if justified or necessary[8]), we do want to set the discussion within a biblical framework and the cultural context of the ancient Near East.

Setting the Biblical Record Straight on Genocide

Here are five things you need to know to set the record straight about the Bible and genocide.

First, things are not the way they ought to be. This should go without saying, but war was not God's idea. Rather, God's ideal in creation can best be expressed in the Hebrew word *shalom*. And it carries the idea of universal human flourishing, joy, and delight. In light of that, it is essential that we understand a critical principle of interpretation as we engage all of these strange and violent Old Testament passages: *Israel as described in the Old Testament is not God's ideal society.* To use an analogy from the computer industry, they were God's people version 1.0 because they were a work in progress (just as you and I are). From the Christian perspective, all of humanity is made in God's image—that is God's ideal. When sin entered and perverted the good world God created, that ideal was violated and the ancient world was from then on perpetually plagued by war and poverty. It was within the volatile kill-or-be-killed world of the ancient Near East that God *began* the process of restoration and redemption through the people of Israel (who, by the way, would have been just like everyone else in that culture were it not for God's grace and revelation). Needless to say, there was no United Nations or diplomacy over high tea in this violent culture.

Second, the divinely given command to Israel of *herem* (Yahweh War) concerning the Canaanites was unique, geographically and temporally limited, and not to be repeated. On this point Old Testament scholar Christopher Wright is worth quoting at length because the historical context he develops is imperative to grasp:

> The conquest was a single episode within a single generation out of all the many generations of Old Testament history. Of course it spans a longer period than that if one includes the promise and then completion. The conquest of Canaan was promised to Abraham, anticipated as the purpose of the exodus, delayed by the wilderness rebellion, accomplished under Joshua, and brought to provisional completion under David and Solomon. Even including all this, though, it was limited in the specific duration of the warfare involved. Although the process of settling and claiming the land took several generations, the actual invasion and destruction of key fortified cities took place mostly within a single generation. And it is this event, confined to one generation, which constituted the conquest. . . . Some . . . other wars also

had God's sanction—especially those where Israel was attacked by other nations and fought defensively to survive. *But by no means are all the wars in the Old Testament portrayed in the same way as the conquest of Canaan.* Some were clearly condemned as the actions of proud and greedy kings or military rivals. It is a caricature of the Old Testament to portray God as constantly on the warpath or to portray it as "typical" of the rest of the story. . . . So the conquest of Canaan, as a unique and limited historical event, was never meant to become a model for how all future generations were to behave toward their contemporary enemies. (italics added)[9]

Third, *genocide* and *ethnic cleansing* are inaccurate terms for the conquest of Canaan. The long list of Canaanite depravity—idolatry, incest, temple prostitution, adultery, child sacrifice, homosexuality, and bestiality (Leviticus 18:24–25; 20:22–24; Deuteronomy 9:5; 12:29–31) have been well documented, but let's limit our discussion to their despicable practice of child sacrifice: "Molech was a Canaanite underworld deity represented as an upright, bull-headed idol with human body in whose belly a fire was stoked and in whose arms a child was placed that would be burnt to death. It was not just unwanted children who were sacrificed. Plutarch reports that during the Phoenician (Canaanite) sacrifices, 'the whole area before the statue was filled with a loud noise of flutes and drums so that the cries and wailing should not reach the ears of the people.'"[10]

The conquest of the land of Canaan "is repeatedly portrayed as God acting in judgment on a wicked and degraded society and culture—as God would do again and again in Old Testament history, *including against Israel itself.*"[11] God had given them 430 years to change their ways, but their wickedness finally reached the tipping point for God to judge (cf. Exodus 15:6). In the biblical narrative, the actions of the Israelites are "never placed in the category of oppression but of divine punishment operating through human agency,"[12] Wright notes. God as the creator of life has the right to take life and during this unique occasion of judgment, that prerogative was temporarily extended to the people of Israel since Yahweh was their king (e.g., a theocracy). While Israel carried out this judgment against a specific people—the Canaanites—

their actions were *not* motivated by racial superiority or hatred. Therefore the language of ethnic cleansing and genocide is inaccurate. Idolatry, not ethnicity, is the issue here.

Fourth, we must allow for the possibility of rhetorical generalization in ancient Near Eastern "war language." When it comes to the destruction of Canaanites, there are two main interpretive options. First, as we have seen, Canaan was a wicked nation that God had graciously given over four hundred years to repent. They did not repent and clearly deserved God's judgment. The second option is very similar, but rather than the total destruction of everything that breathes, the main targets were the key military centers. They were to be destroyed in the region with the goal of eradicating the Canaanite religion. On this view, it is very likely that many if not most of the women and children would have fled these cities as the warriors fought. Judgment was still occurring but exaggerated language was used in the biblical text as a common literary convention of the day: "Texts from other nations at the time show that such total destruction in war was practiced, or at any rate proudly claimed, elsewhere." "But we must also recognize that the language of warfare had a conventional rhetoric that liked to make absolute and universal claims about total victory and completely wiping out the enemy . . . which often exceeded reality on the ground."[13] Accordingly this ancient Near East rhetorical generalization allows for exaggerated language and "enables us to allow for the fact that descriptions of destruction of 'everything that lives and breathes' were not intended literally."[14] This is certainly a legitimate possibility. Again, the goal here is not to make it more palatable. The goal is an accurate understanding of what the biblical text teaches.

Fifth, the Canaanite incident should be read against the backdrop of God's promise of blessing for all the nations. Rebellion, depravity, and the violation of shalom had become so rampant among all the nations of the earth that God decided to work his plan of redemption through one nation. Paul Copan notes, "National Israel was established by God to help set the religious, cultural, and historical context for the saving work of Jesus the Messiah later in history. The ultimate goal is nothing less than God's salvation being brought to all the nations and seeing his righteous rule finally established."[15] Because of this role, God providentially protected the nation of Israel, from whom the Messiah would eventually come.

IS THE BIBLE HOMOPHOBIC?

In a *Newsweek* cover story in December 2008, Lisa Miller wrote the following:

> Most of us no longer heed Leviticus on haircuts or blood sacrifices; our modern understanding of the world has surpassed its prescriptions. Why would we regard its condemnation of homosexuality with more seriousness than we regard its advice, which is far lengthier, on the best price to pay for a slave? . . . A mature view of scriptural authority requires us, as we have in the past, to move beyond literalism. The Bible was written for a world so unlike our own, it's impossible to apply its rules, at face value, to ours.[16]

This quote by Miller is rhetorically effective but factually incorrect. (Hopefully you noticed how she inaccurately portrays the issue of slavery in the Bible.) That being said, it makes one point loud and clear: When it comes to the issue of homosexuality, the Bible is clearly out of step with today's culture.

Setting the Biblical Record Straight on Homosexual Behavior

While ultimately the Bible does teach that homosexual behavior is sinful, there are some very significant misunderstandings both inside and outside the church when it comes to this issue that we need to do our best to correct. Here are five things that you need to know in order to set the record straight concerning the Bible and homosexual behavior.

First, the Bible includes homosexual behavior among a long list of sinful behaviors outside of God's design for human sexuality. God designed sex to be between one man and one woman for a lifetime so that they can experience love, intimacy, oneness, safety, trust, pleasure, and delight, and for this to serve as the context in which children can grow up in a safe, loving environment where they will have the best opportunity to flourish as humans. This is the compelling vision we get to say yes to and that makes sense of all the no's in the Bible. Therefore any behavior contrary to this vision is sinful and ultimately harmful. That is why we are commanded to "flee from sexual immorality. Every other sin a person commits is outside the body, but the sexually immoral person sins against his own body" (1 Corinthians 6:18). The Scripture also declares, "For this is the will of God, your sanctification: that you abstain from sexual immorality" (1 Thessalonians 4:3). And finally, "Let marriage be held in honor among all, and let the marriage bed be undefiled, for God will judge the sexually immoral and adulterous" (Hebrews 13:4). We could cite many more passages, but this point is well established.

The disputed point is whether homosexual behavior falls into the category of sexual immorality. Homosexual behavior is specifically addressed as sinful in Genesis 19:4–9; Leviticus 18:22; 20:13; Romans 1:26–27; 1 Corinthians 6:9–10, and 1 Timothy 1:9–10). The clearest declaration is in Romans 1:26–27; however, the traditional understanding of this passage has been challenged recently. The revisionist interpretation is summarized as follows: Paul was not talking about homosexuals here, but (1) heterosexuals who abandon their "nature" (that is, sexual orientation) by practicing homosexuality; (2) homosexuality within the context of idolatrous worship; or (3) sex with boys (pederasty) or multiple-partner, risky sexual relationships (that is, noncommitted homosexual relationships).

Here is why these interpretations fail. As we mentioned, Romans 1:26–27 is the clearest and most comprehensive treatment of homosexual behavior in the Bible. It's also the only passage that specifically addresses female homosexuality. The biblical context is important when addressing various revisionist interpretations. In Romans 1–3, Paul demonstrates the *universality* of human sinfulness and that *every person* is under God's righteous judgment. This is the main point—homosexual behavior is just one of many illustrations:

1. This argument, if it invokes sexual orientation, is highly anachronistic. Scientific discussions about being "born gay" began only in the late twentieth century, and the available data is highly inconclusive. Furthermore, "natural desires" are not what Paul is discussing here. "Against nature" (*para physis*) in this context refers to the created order. Furthermore, Paul appeals to the natural "function" (*chresis*) of males and females. The vocabulary he uses for male (*arsen*) and female (*thelys*) highlights their specific genders. Paul is arguing on the basis of how males and females are biologically and anatomically designed to operate sexually. Men were designed to function sexually not with men but with women. Males and females were designed by God to "function" together in a sexually complementary way. Paul's word choice could not have been clearer. Homosexual behavior is a clear violation of God's creational order and complementary design of male and female, along with the command to be fruitful and multiply (Genesis 1:26–27; 2:18–24).

2. If idolatry was the only moral limitation of homosexual behavior, then what of the other twenty-three sins addressed between verses 20 and 31? The logic would seem to require them being morally acceptable as long as they're not practiced in an idolatrous manner—which is absurd. Regarding the "doing what comes naturally" argument, these other sins come naturally to us as well; we're all inclined toward pride, lying, envy, greed, etc. An inclination or even strong desire does not make a behavior morally right or authorize us to act on it.

3. If Paul was concerned only with condemning adult male sex with young boys (pederasty), then he would have chosen the Greek word commonly used for this practice. Finally, Paul's argument leaves no room for "loving, committed, and responsible homosexual relationships" because he uniformly condemns the *behavior itself*, not merely what are described as risky or irresponsible expressions of certain homosexual behaviors.[17]

Mark Mittelberg rightly reminds us, "We should . . . be honest about God's clear prohibition against homosexual behavior expressed in both the Old and New Testaments of the Bible. It isn't listed as being worse than other sins, but it's clearly on the list. As followers of Christ we need to tell people what God says about it."[18]

Second, the Bible does not teach that God created people to be gay. It is sometimes claimed that Jesus never addressed the topic of homosexuality. Actually that is not technically true. On this occasion Jesus reaffirms God's original design for sexuality grounded in creation:

Some Pharisees came to Jesus, testing Him and asking, "Is it lawful for a man to divorce his wife for any reason at all?" And He answered and said, "Have you not read that He who created them from the beginning made them male and female, and said, 'For this reason a man shall leave his father and mother and be joined to his wife, and the two shall become one flesh'? So they are no longer two, but one flesh. What therefore God has joined together, let no man separate." (Matthew 19:3–6 NASB; cf. Genesis 1:27; 2:24)

Jesus affirmed that God's intention was the complementary sexes of male and female committing to a permanent one-flesh union. This was the pre-fall standard that Jesus, the most loving man who ever lived, appealed to.

Third, while the Bible does not teach that people are born gay, it does teach that all people are born sinful. As we just mentioned, we no longer inhabit a sin-free garden. The reality is that we live in a fallen world in which sin affects all of us at physical, genetic, psychological, relational, and emotional levels (cf. Romans 3:23; 5:12–21). There are plenty of sinful desires we should not act on or consider "natural" that can be overcome as we grow more like Christ. This is the hope and power of the gospel—we can struggle well. As Mittelberg states, "We must correct the idea that because a desire seems natural it must be from God and is therefore okay. As fallen humans we all have many desires that seem natural to us but that are not from God."[19]

But hasn't science shown that people are born gay? Actually, no. Alan Shlemon summarizes the state of the scientific evidence:

The American Psychological Association (APA), for example, once held the position in 1998 that, there is "evidence to suggest that biology, including genetic or inborn hormonal factors, play a significant role in a person's sexuality." However, a decade of scientific research debunked this idea and caused the APA to revise their view in 2009. Their new position reads: "Although much research has examined the possible genetic, hormonal, developmental, social, and cultural influences on sexual orientation, no findings have emerged that permit scientists to conclude that sexual orientation is determined by any particular factor or factors."[20]

You can be sure that if the evidence did exist, the APA would have cited it. The point to be made here is that even if someone was more genetically predisposed toward certain desires/behaviors, that does nothing to alter what God has already revealed about his design for sexuality. Because of the fall, it is entirely possible that we may discover the effects of sin to be deeply bound up in our genetic information. To recognize this fact does not legitimatize the behavior.

Fourth, the Bible teaches that change is possible for all those who struggle with sin. One of the most hope-filled passages in the entire Bible is 1 Corinthians 6:9–11:

> Or do you not know that the unrighteous will not inherit the kingdom of God? Do not be deceived: neither the sexually immoral, nor idolaters, nor adulterers, nor men who practice homosexuality, nor thieves, nor the greedy, nor drunkards, nor revilers, nor swindlers will inherit the kingdom of God. *And such were some of you. But you were washed, you were sanctified, you were justified in the name of the Lord Jesus Christ and by the Spirit of our God.* (emphasis mine)

When it comes to the biblical message on sin and the Christian life, it's pretty simple—all are broken, all are welcome, and all are called to repentance. First, we are all sinful and no one is exempt from this. But second, the Gospel is good news for everyone! Grace is available to all. And finally, all of us as Christ-followers are called to conform our way of life to God's design for human flourishing. No one is excluded from this either.

With this in mind, we are better positioned to engage the claim that "gay people can't change." The first thing to point out is that Paul and the Bible teach that change had happened in Corinth. Moreover there are plenty of people who have struggled with and overcome same-sex attraction.[21] And as long as at least one has "changed" then change is at least possible for those who struggle with same-sex attraction. Shlemon's comments are helpful here:

> Does everyone who tries to change succeed? No. In fact, most people fail. Is it an easy process for those who achieve a measure of change? Absolutely not.

Does change always entail complete transformation? Rarely. Do some people return to homosexuality? Of course. But is it possible for some to experience substantial and enduring change? Yes. That's good news, given that there are many people with unwanted SSA [same sex attraction]. They have hope.[22]

Fifth, the Bible teaches that holiness, not heterosexuality, is the goal of the spiritual life. All of us are broken; we just express our brokenness in different ways. As we repent and are empowered by the Holy Spirit, we pursue holiness. The goal is being conformed to the image of Jesus Christ (cf. Romans 8:29). Unfortunately, when these goals get talked about in the context of homosexual sin, some well-meaning Christians have indicated that the goal is for this person to live a heterosexual lifestyle. This may or may not happen. But we need to be clear that whatever our struggle, holiness is the goal.

Moreover, "We need to explain that someone's orientation toward or temptation by same-sex attractions is not in and of itself sin. The problem, biblically defined, is not with homosexual inclinations, but with actual homosexual behaviors. However, many people with these inclinations do, with God's help, find ways to honor God either through celibacy or eventual heterosexual marriage."[23] A Christian may find that he still struggles with same-sex attraction but is convinced that this is contrary to God's design and will.[24] Therefore, under the lordship of Jesus, he says no to his desires. But saying no to sinful desires is not a specifically homosexual issue; it is a fallen human issue. Recognizing this dynamic will help us have appropriate compassion with each other as we struggle toward holiness and Christlikeness together.

IS THE BIBLE SEXIST?

If you look up *sexism* in the dictionary, you will find words like *discriminate*, *demean*, and *devalue*. Does the Bible really demean women? It won't surprise you that my answer is no, but it's really important how we arrive at this conclusion, because you will encounter some Bible passages that seem to teach just the opposite. For example, did you know that there are over thirty references to polygamy in the Old Testament?[25]

Setting the Biblical Record Straight on Sexism

Here are five things you need to know in order to set the record straight about the Bible and the charge of sexism.

First, God's creational ideal is that women are made in the image of God and therefore possess the same dignity, honor, and value as men. God created humanity as male and female in his own image (Genesis 1:27; 2:24). Theologian Bruce Ware summarizes this exalted position: "The image of God in man as functional holism means that God made human beings, both male and female, to be created and finite representations (images of God) of God's own nature, that in relationship with Him and each other they might be His representatives (imaging God) in carrying out the responsibilities He has given to them. In this sense, we are images of God in order to image God and His purposes in the ordering of our lives and the carrying out of our God-given responsibilities."[26] The book of Exodus recalls this idea as it commands honor be given to both mother and father (Exodus 20:12).

Second, polygamy was tolerated and regulated in order to offer some measure of protection for women in an ancient Near Eastern context. By now you should be seeing a pattern develop as we approach texts that seem to be at odds with God's ideal (e.g., slavery). Copan helpfully summarizes: "Although Genesis 1–2 spells out the ideal of male-female equality, laws regarding women in ancient Israel take a realistic approach to the fallen human structures in the ancient Near East. In Israel's legislation, God does two things: (1) he works within a patriarchal society to point Israel to a better path; and (2) he provides many protections and controls against abuses directed at females in admittedly substandard conditions."[27] Regarding the sometimes disturbing nature of reading the Old Testament, Tim Keller shares how knowing the context and background really changes everything:

> Many years ago, when I first started reading the Book of Genesis, it was very upsetting to me. Here are all these spiritual heroes—Abraham, Isaac, Jacob, and Joseph—and look at how they treat women. They engage in polygamy, and they buy and sell their wives. It was awful to read their stories at times.

But then I read Robert Alter's *The Art of Biblical Narrative*. Alter is a Jewish scholar at Berkeley whose expertise is ancient Jewish literature. In his book he says there are two institutions present in the Book of Genesis that were universal in ancient cultures: polygamy and primogeniture. Polygamy said a husband could have multiple wives, and primogeniture said the oldest son got everything—all the power, all the money. In other words, the oldest son basically ruled over everyone else in the family. Alter points out that when you read the Book of Genesis, you'll see two things. First of all, in every generation polygamy wreaks havoc. Having multiple wives is an absolute disaster—socially, culturally, spiritually, emotionally, psychologically, and relationally. Second, when it comes to primogeniture, in every generation God favors the younger son over the older. He favors Abel, not Cain; Isaac, not Ishmael; Jacob, not Esau. Alter says that you begin to realize what the Book of Genesis is doing—it is subverting, not supporting, those ancient institutions at every turn.[28]

Finally, we hear echoes of God's ideal when he warns that Israel's king should not "acquire many wives for himself, lest his heart turn away" (Deuteronomy 17:17).

Third, the realities of women in the Greco-Roman world were harsh. To say that being a woman was extremely challenging would be an understatement. In Athens, "women were in relative short supply owing to female infanticide, practiced by all classes, and to the additional deaths caused by abortion. The status of women was very low. Girls received little or no education [and] were married at puberty and often before. Under Athenian law a woman was classified as a child, regardless of age, and therefore was the legal property of some man at all stages of her life. Males could divorce by simply ordering a wife out of the household."[29]

Women did not fare much better in Rome as indicated by two laws. *Manus* "placed her under the absolute control of her husband, who had ownership of her and all her possessions."[30] In addition, *patria potestas* and *paterfamilias*, which were spelled out in Table 4 of the Twelve Tables of Roman Law, the husband and father "had supreme, absolute power over his children, even grown, including grandchildren. He alone had the power to divorce his wife, and he also possessed the power to execute his children. He could even execute his married daughter if she committed adultery in his or her husband's house."[31] Incidentally, you can see how radical the apostle Paul's teaching to fathers would be: "Fathers, do not exasperate your children; instead, bring them up in the training and instruction of the Lord" (Ephesians 6:4 NIV). And Jewish rabbinical tradition (i.e., not the Bible) taught, "Let the words of law [Torah] be burned rather than committed to a woman" (*Sotah* 3.4).[32]

Fourth, the apostle Paul had a high view of women, and the teachings of Christianity began to elevate their status.[33] Sociologist Rodney Stark summarizes the views of the apostle Paul and the early church toward women:

> Paul, who often gets a bad rap for his *perceived* low view of women, considered at least twelve women coworkers in his ministry (cf. see Rom. 16:1–16; Phil. 4:2–3; 1 Cor. 1:11; Col 4:15; Acts 16:14–15, 40). Paul clearly had a high view of women, "There is neither Jew nor Greek, slave nor free, male nor female, for you are all one in Christ Jesus" (Gal. 3:28). The earliest Christians frequently recited these remarkable, counter-cultural words as a baptismal confession. Widows, far from being abandoned were cared for and older women were given a place of honor (cf. 1 Tim:6). In light of all of this, is it any wonder "the ancient sources and modern historians agree that primary conversion to Christianity was far more prevalent among females than males"?[34]

Fifth, Jesus is good news for women. With the harsh Greco-Roman backdrop in mind, we can see how radical Jesus' view of women really was. First, he healed several women of diseases (Matthew 9:18–26), interacted with women of different races (John 4:9), and extended forgiveness to women who had committed sexual sin (Luke 7:36–50). Jewish rabbis of the day would not teach women, but Jesus had many women followers and disciples (cf. Mark 15:41) and he taught them (Luke 10:39). Women supported his ministry financially (Luke 8:1–3), and he used women as positive examples in his teaching (Luke 18:1–8). Jesus' women followers were the last to leave at his crucifixion and the first at his empty tomb.

New Testament scholar D. M. Scholer concludes, "Jesus' respect for and inclusion of women as disciples and proclaimers provided the foundation for the positive place of women in the earliest churches and their ministry."[35]

LIFE IN A FALLEN WORLD IS MESSY

In this chapter we have seen that appearances can sometimes be deceiving and that sound bites don't do justice to how messy life can be in a fallen world. We have also seen that God has given humanity significant freedom and because of this, moral change is often painfully slow. Thankfully God has not left us to die in our brokenness and rebellion; he has redemptively pursued us with the everlasting love of a heavenly father (Jeremiah 31:3).

Three Big Ideas

1. When engaging emotional topics like these, we must locate the discussion within its cultural and theological context. When sin entered and perverted the good world God created, that ideal was violated; from then on war and poverty would perpetually plague the ancient world. Within the volatile kill-or-be-killed world of the ancient Near East, God *began* the process of restoration and redemption through the people of Israel (who, by the way, would have been just like everyone else in that culture were it not for God's grace and revelation). Israel was a work in progress and so are we.

2. Since human beings are involved, moral change takes time and the process is always messy. There are very real historical factors at work that must be accounted for.

3. Sin is very real and a just God must judge. But a gracious and loving God offers forgiveness and redemption to anyone who would accept it on the basis of Christ's work. All of us are broken, all of us are welcome through the Gospel, and all of us are called to repentance.

Conversation Tips

When it comes to discussing these emotionally charged issues you need to do your homework. This means:

• Context will be your greatest ally. Many times the person you are talking with will not know the context of life in the war-torn world of the ancient Near East. Let's take the slavery issues as an example. In the ancient Near East, slavery was most often the result of war and poverty. In other words, those conquered often became enslaved, and in free areas those who could not find work to feed their family typically became slaves to provide sustenance. Ask the person you are talking with if there are still poor people in America, the wealthiest country on earth? (The answer is yes.) If we haven't solved poverty in the most prosperous country the world has ever seen, then how much more challenging would war and poverty be in a severely under-resourced community.

- Know that your responses may not convince everyone. Still, if they are reasonable and coherent with the rest of the teachings of the Bible, many will consider them.

Digging Deeper

- Paul Copan. *Is God a Moral Monster?: Making Sense of the Old Testament God*. Grand Rapids: Baker, 2010.

- Alvin J. Schmidt. *How Christianity Changed the World*. Grand Rapids: Zondervan, 2004.

WHAT DO CHRISTIANS BELIEVE ABOUT THE BIBLE?

Knowing God is the most important thing in life. God created people fundamentally for relationship with himself. This relationship depends on knowing who he is as he has revealed himself. God is personal, which means he has a mind, will, emotions, relational ability, and self-consciousness. Because he is personal, and not merely an impersonal object, God must personally reveal himself to us.[1]

Erik Thoennes

In many cases, people who reject the Bible aren't sure what they are rejecting. Whether you are a skeptic who is looking for reasons to dismiss the Bible or a seeker looking for reasons to accept the Bible, intellectual honesty requires that we seek to understand what the Bible actually claims of itself. Historians and theologians use the word *doctrine* to capture what the Bible teaches on various subjects. In what follows, I want to introduce you to the doctrine of the Bible.

WHY STUDY THEOLOGY?

Theology has a public relations problem. Many view theology as a discipline that academics think about locked up in a dusty library cubicle somewhere.

The rest of us need to just love Jesus and live life. This is mistaken because theology is about the knowledge of God. We need both. As Thoennes reminds us, "Knowledge without devotion is cold, dead orthodoxy. Devotion without knowledge is irrational instability."[2]

The words of the prophet Jeremiah come to mind when we think of the importance of theology: "Thus says the Lord: 'Let not the wise man boast in his wisdom, let not the mighty man boast in his might, let not the rich man boast in his riches, but let him who boasts boast in this, that he understands and knows me, that I am the Lord who practices steadfast love, justice, and righteousness in the earth. For in these things I delight, declares the Lord'" (9:23–24).

Here are five reasons Christians should study theology:

1. To obey the Greatest Commandment. "And you shall love the Lord your God with all your heart and with all your soul and with all your mind and with all your strength" (Mark 12:30). God wants all of us. Part of loving God means loving the truth. We are called to an integrated devotion to the Lord Jesus Christ.

2. To obey the Great Commission. "Go therefore and make disciples of all nations, baptizing them in the name of the Father and of the Son and of the Holy Spirit, teaching them to observe all that I have commanded you" (Matthew 28:19–20). It's that last part that is so often neglected today. For how can we teach people to obey all that God has commanded unless we know what he has commanded ourselves? Theology is essential for this task.

3. To help us grow in our personal relationship with God. "Therefore, as you received Christ Jesus the Lord, so walk in him, rooted and built up in him and established in the faith, just as you were taught, abounding in thanksgiving" (Colossians 2:6–7). God is personal and we cannot grow in our faith apart from his special communication to us through the Bible.

4. To guard, defend, and impart "the faith." "Beloved, although I was very eager to write to you about our common salvation, I found it necessary to write appealing to you to contend for the faith that was once for all delivered to the saints" (Jude 3). As we have already seen, there is an apostolic deposit of truth that has already been delivered to us. We are responsible to safeguard the integrity of this New Covenant message. In addition, we can't guard or defend something we don't understand. Confidence flows from understanding.

5. To not be deceived by false ideas. "Until we all attain to the unity of the faith and of the knowledge of the Son of God, to mature manhood, to the measure of the stature of the fullness of Christ, so that we may no longer be children, tossed to and fro by the waves and carried about by every wind of doctrine, by human cunning, by craftiness in deceitful schemes" (Ephesians 4:13–14).

Everyone is a theologian because everyone has thoughts about God and "what comes into our minds when we think about God," reminds A. W. Tozer, "is the most important thing about us." The only question that remains then is what kind of theologian we will become. Now that we have set the table, let's dig in.

GOD'S TWO BOOKS: NATURE AND SCRIPTURE

God's first book revealing himself is nature. This is often referred to as God's *general revelation* because it is available to all people, at all times, and in all places. To "reveal" simply means to unveil or disclose something not already known. This revelation is general in that everyone has access to it. From several New Testament passages we learn that God has revealed himself through what has been made in creation and placed on the human heart:

> For what can be known about God is plain to them, because God has shown it to them. For his invisible attributes, namely, his eternal power and divine nature, have been clearly perceived, ever since the creation of the world, in the things that have been made. So they are without excuse. (Romans 1:19–20)

> The heavens declare the glory of God, and the sky above proclaims his handiwork. Day to day pours out speech, and night to night reveals knowledge. There is no speech, nor are there words, whose voice is not heard. Their voice goes out through all the earth, and their words to the end of the world. (Psalm 19:1–4)

Indeed, when Gentiles, who do not have the law, do by nature things required by the law, they are a law for themselves, even though they do not have the law. They show that the requirements of the law are written on their hearts, their consciences also bearing witness, and their thoughts sometimes accusing them and at other times even defending them. (Romans 2:14–15 NIV)

Theologian Bruce Demarest describes the content of what can be known through God's general revelation. "While not imparting truths necessary for salvation—such as the Trinity, the incarnation, or the atonement—general revelation conveys the conviction that God exists and that he is transcendent, immanent, self-sufficient, eternal, powerful, good and a hater of evil."[3]

We now turn our attention to God's second book that reveals much more about himself, Scripture. While general revelation is wonderful, it is not enough to allow us to have a personal relationship with God. Think of looking at a magnificent painting in a museum. You can appreciate the skill of the artist and the beauty of the painting, but you could never know the artist unless he spoke to you. And that's how God's *special revelation*—the Bible—is to us. God has graciously taken the initiative to make himself known to us. To better understand all that this entails, we will explore six essential aspects of the Bible: Inspiration, Authority, Inerrancy, Infallibility, Clarity, and Sufficiency (shown in chart 10).

Chart 10

THE BIBLE: GOD'S SPECIAL REVELATION
Key Passage: Hebrews 1:1–2

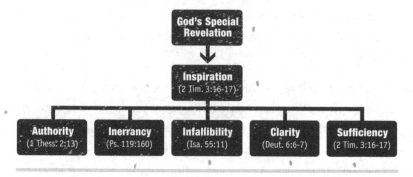

THE INSPIRATION OF THE BIBLE

The classic passage on the doctrine of inspiration of the Bible is 2 Timothy 3:16–17. This passage holds a special place for me because it is the first verse that I memorized as a Christian. Within a month or two of becoming a Christ-follower in high school, my mentor Neal and I memorized this together and it has been foundational in my life ever since: "All Scripture is breathed out by God and profitable for teaching, for reproof, for correction, and for training in righteousness, that the man of God may be complete, equipped for every good work."

The key to understanding inspiration is that the source of the Bible is God's Spirit. Scripture originates with God, not men. The apostle Peter added a layer of clarity here: "Knowing this first of all, that no prophecy of Scripture comes from someone's own interpretation. For no prophecy was ever produced by the will of man, but men spoke from God as they were carried along by the Holy Spirit" (2 Peter 1:20–21).

This passage reveals a concept called dual authorship. "On the one hand, God spoke, revealing the truth and preserving the human authors from error, yet without violating their personality. On the other hand, men spoke, using their own faculties freely, yet without distorting the divine message. Their words were truly their own words. But they were (and still are) also God's words, so that what Scripture says, God says."[4] An analogy might help here. Think of a cruise ship that departs from a port in Miami and arrives in the Bahamas. While the passengers have freedom to walk around the ship, the ultimate destination is set by the captain.

The Authority of the Bible

When we talk about authority we are raising the "who says so" question. Frankly, we all have a cosmic authority problem; we want to do things the way we want, when we want, and how we want. But if God exists and has spoken, then he wins the "who says so" argument hands down: "The Lord has established his throne in the heavens, and his kingdom rules over all" (Psalm 103:19). When Scripture speaks, God speaks. Because the source of Scripture is God, it bears his authority. John Stott captures this sentiment well: "If it is a word from God, it has authority over men. For behind every word that anybody utters stands the person who speaks it. It is the speaker himself (his character, knowledge and position) who determines how people regard his words. So God's Word carries God's authority. It is because of who he is that we should believe what he has said."[5] Paul celebrated when the Thessalonians came to understand this great truth. "And we also thank God constantly for this, that when you received the word of God, which you heard from us, you accepted it not as the word of men but as what it really is, the word of God, which is at work in you believers" (1 Thessalonians 2:13).

As we conclude this brief discussion of the authority of Scripture, it is also critical to note that Jesus of Nazareth submitted to the authority of God's Word (see appendix 1 for more on this). And if he did, how much more so should we?

The Inerrancy of the Bible

If the Bible originated from the Spirit of God (i.e., is "God-breathed") then it flows from this fact that it is also inerrant. Or to put it differently, inerrancy refers to the end result or product of the Spirit's inspiration. But what does it mean to say the Bible is inerrant? Given that this term is so often misunderstood, we will want to be careful in how we define and explain it. A standard way to understand inerrancy is that the Bible is fully truthful in all that it affirms.[6] Christian philosopher and theologian Doug Blount translates this into a philosophically precise definition[7] [where df. means "by definition"]:

"Scripture is inerrant" =df. "for any proposition p [e.g., Jesus walked on water], if the Bible asserts that p, then p."

Three points of clarification are necessary, and then we will more fully explain this doctrine. First, by "fully truthful" inerrantists limit this claim to the original manuscripts (i.e., autographs) themselves and not the copies of original manuscripts. From our earlier discussion, you will recall that truth is what corresponds to reality or rather "telling it like it is."

David Dockery gives this complete definition of biblical inerrancy: "When all the facts are known, the Bible (in its original writings) properly interpreted in light of which culture and communication means had developed by the time of its composition will be shown to be completely true (and therefore not false) in all that it affirms, to the degree of precision intended by the author, in all matters relating to God and his creation."[8]

Next, the Bible makes no false assertions or factual errors in what it claims—though it may accurately record false statements made (e.g., when Satan deceives Adam and Eve). In short, the Bible does not necessarily endorse everything it faithfully records.

Finally, a distinction needs to be made between inerrancy and interpretation. Interpretation seeks to ensure we understand what the Bible is actually asserting in a given passage and what level of precision is intended by the author of that passage. (We will discuss this in more detail in the next chapter.) For example, as we saw earlier in our chapter on science, evangelical scholars who hold to inerrancy can arrive at different interpretations of Genesis 1 (i.e., they differ over what they think the text is actually asserting) and still call themselves inerrantists.

Here then is the logic of the inerrantist's position.[9]

1. The Bible as it was originally written is God's Word.

2. God's Word is wholly truthful.

3. Therefore, the Bible as it was originally written is wholly truthful.

Regarding the first premise (1), that is just a summary statement of what we discussed about inspiration. The second premise (2) has to do with the perfections of God's own nature. We will just highlight a few of the many passages addressing this:

The sum of your word is truth, and every one of your righteous rules endures forever. (Psalm 119:160)

And now, O Lord God, you are God, and your words are true, and you have promised this good thing to your servant. (2 Samuel 7:28)

Paul, a servant of God and an apostle of Jesus Christ . . . in hope of eternal life, which God, who never lies, promised before the ages began and at the proper time manifested in his word through the preaching with which I have been entrusted by the command of God our Savior. (Titus 1:1–3)

The Bible clearly teaches that God is wholly truthful. Which means that the conclusion (3) follows necessarily from the premises (1) and (2)—like intellectual gravity. (This is a logically valid and, I think, successful argument.)

Blount then states, "As long as we have good reason to believe the biblical text as we know it accurately reflects the *autographa* [original manuscripts], we have good reason to believe the Bible is inerrant" (which is what we demonstrated in chapter 6).

But a common objection is often raised against the Bible at this point: Wouldn't the Bible be full of errors because human beings wrote the Bible? The key to responding to this objection is exposing the (incorrect) assumptions behind this question. That men *necessarily* make mistakes is in the end self-defeating. Are men capable of saying or writing anything that is true? (Insert "yes" here unless you think you are never capable of saying or writing anything that is true!)

Greg Koukl exposes the flaw in this way of thinking by asking a series of questions: "Do you have any books in your library? Were those books written by humans? Do you find any truth in them? Is there a reason you think the Bible is less truthful or reliable than other books you own? Do people always make mistakes in what they write? Do you think that if God did exist, he would be capable of using humans to write down exactly what he wants? If not, why not?"[10] Upon further review, this oft-repeated litany should not slow us down.

John Stott offers a concise summary of the doctrines we have covered so far: "Our claim, then, is that God has revealed himself by speaking; that this divine ("God-breathed") speech has been written down and preserved in Scripture; and that Scripture is, in fact, God's Word written down, which therefore is true and reliable and has divine authority over us."[11]

The Infallibility of the Bible

Given God's special revelation and our understanding of what the Bible teaches concerning inspiration and inerrancy, the doctrine of infallibility is entailed as well. There are two senses of infallibility: one from a human perspective and one from a divine perspective. From the human perspective, infallibility refers to "the quality of neither misleading nor being misled and so safeguards in categorical terms the truth that Holy Scripture is a sure, safe, and reliable rule and guide in all matters."[12] Regarding the divine perspective, the prophet Isaiah records:

> For my thoughts are not your thoughts, neither are your ways my ways,
> declares the Lord. For as the heavens are higher than the earth, so are my
> ways higher than your ways and my thoughts than your thoughts. For as
> the rain and the snow come down from heaven and do not return there but
> water the earth, making it bring forth and sprout, giving seed to the sower
> and bread to the eater, so shall my word be that goes out from my mouth;
> it shall not return to me empty, but it shall accomplish that which I pur-
> pose, and shall succeed in the thing for which I sent it. (Isaiah 55:8–11)

Infallibility in this sense describes the result of what God intends to accomplish with his Word.[13] But a question arises: aren't God's revealed intentions (in
at least some sense) blocked by stubborn sinful people? Has God failed? I don't
think it means that God has failed in his intention any more than when God
says that he desires all to be saved and all aren't saved that he has failed. He has
simply built creaturely freedom into his design of the world and has chosen to
providentially operate within realities he intended according to his good pleasure
and for his glory from the beginning. The bottom line here is that obeying God's
(properly understood) Word will always and reliably lead to human flourishing
according to God's design and that God will accomplish—either actively or pas-
sively—all that he has intended with, in, and through his Word. Paul's words to
Timothy help make this point: "But as for you, continue in what you have learned
and have firmly believed, knowing from whom you learned it and how from
childhood you have been acquainted with the sacred writings, which are able to
make you wise for salvation through faith in Christ Jesus" (2 Timothy 3:14–15).

THE CLARITY OF THE BIBLE

I find it comforting that the apostle Peter found Paul difficult to understand
at times:

> And count the patience of our Lord as salvation, just as our beloved brother
> Paul also wrote to you according to the wisdom given him, as he does in all
> his letters when he speaks in them of these matters. There are some things

in them that are hard to understand, which the ignorant and unstable twist
to their own destruction, as they do the other Scriptures. (2 Peter 3:15–16)

The doctrine of the clarity[14] of the Bible does not mean that everything will
be equally easy to understand. We will have to work hard at understanding.
That is why we are commanded to "be diligent to present yourself approved to
God as a workman who does not need to be ashamed, accurately handling the
word of truth" (2 Timothy 2:15 NASB). Moreover, we must rely on God to give
us understanding (cf. 2 Timothy 2:7).

With that said, however, the main themes and teachings of the Bible are clear.
One of the reasons we know this is that children are capable of grasping them:

And these words that I command you today shall be on your heart. You shall
teach them diligently to your children, and shall talk of them when you sit
in your house, and when you walk by the way, and when you lie down, and
when you rise. (Deuteronomy 6:6–7)

At least a basic comprehension must be possible; otherwise this command
would not make any sense and it would also be illegitimate as well.

Finally, we should note that Jesus assumed that people should be able to
understand what was being said in the Hebrew Scriptures. On one occasion
when asked about marriage and divorce, he said, "Have you not read that
he who created them from the beginning made them male and female . . . ?"
(Matthew 19:4). The clear implication is that you should have understood this
one. In summary then, this doctrine is foundational for questions of interpretation
(i.e., hermeneutics) in the next chapter.

THE SUFFICIENCY OF THE BIBLE

Enough is a great word; we just don't like it very much. We prefer the word
more. When it comes to God's special revelation, he has given us enough.
But we still want more information. We don't know everything we would
like to know about the world or our lives. And we certainly don't know God
exhaustively (though we know him truly through his Word). Returning to
our familiar touchstone, we see that "all Scripture is breathed out by God and

profitable for teaching, for reproof, for correction, and for training in righteous-ness, *that the man of God may be complete, equipped for every good work"* (2 Timothy 3:16–17, emphasis mine). Moreover, when God gives revelation, it does not need to be supplemented: "You shall not add to the word that I command you, nor take from it, that you may keep the commandments of the Lord your God that I command you" (Deuteronomy 4:2). Affirming this is not to say that we don't need community or the Spirit's enablement. On the contrary these are essential resources that God has revealed that we need.

As we conclude this discussion of what Christians believe about the Bible, Thoennes explains the benefits of the sufficiency of Scripture for us:

> We should find freedom and encouragement in the knowledge that God has provided all of the absolutely authoritative instruction that we need in order to know him and live as he intends. God's people should never fear that he has withheld something they might need him to say in order for them to know how to please him, or that he will have to somehow supple-ment his Word with new instructions for some new situation that arises in the modern age.[15]

Three Big Ideas

1. We listed five reasons to study theology:

   1- to obey the Greatest Commandment,

   2- to obey the Great Commission,

   3- to help us grow in our personal relationship with God,

   4- to guard, defend, and impart "the faith," and

   5- to not be deceived by false ideas.

2. There are six doctrines Christians need to know when it comes to thinking about the Bible as God's special revelation:

   1- inspiration—the Bible is from God;

   2- authority—the Bible is God's Word;

   3- inerrancy—the Bible is wholly truthful;

   4- infallibility—the Bible is reliable and accomplishes all that God intends;

   5- clarity—the Bible can be understood; and

   6- sufficiency—the Bible is enough.

3. The logic of inerrancy is as follows:

   1- The Bible as it was originally written is God's Word.

   2- God's Word is wholly truthful.

   3- Therefore, the Bible as it was originally written is wholly truthful. Inerrancy only applies to the original autographs; it does not extend to manuscript copies (as reliable as those have proven to be).

Conversation Tips

- When having a conversation about what Christians believe about the Bible, the first thing you need to do is clarify who your audience is. If you are talking with someone more skeptical about the Bible, then inerrancy is not where you want to start. The reason for this is that you will get bogged down in a lot of details and probably never get to Jesus and the Gospel.

- Begin with the (general) historical reliability of the New Testament and the resurrection timeline to get the core teachings and claims of Jesus front and center. The only exception to this would be if the skeptic is sincerely asking for information. They want to know what the Bible teaches concerning itself. If this is the case, by all means engage them and clarify any misconceptions they may have.

Digging Deeper

- Millard J. Erickson. *Introducing Christian Doctrine*, 2nd ed. Grand Rapids: Baker, 2001.

- Stephen J. Nichols and Eric T. Brandt. *Ancient Word, Changing Worlds: The Doctrine of Scripture in a Modern Age.* Wheaton, IL: Crossway Books, 2009.

WHICH INTERPRETATION OF THE BIBLE IS CORRECT?

Biblical authority is an empty notion unless we know how to determine what the Bible means.[1]
James Packer

I have the privilege of working with students.[2] And students usually ask the best questions. I recall spending one afternoon with a recent high-school graduate we'll call Jim, talking about his faith. Jim grew up in a Christian home, attended church, and attended the youth group. He now attended a liberal arts college and was exposed to a lot of new ideas. He also made a lot of friends who were funny, well-educated, and believed very differently than he did. That's when the doubts began. How could so many sincere and intelligent people be wrong? He began asking himself hard questions like "Who am I to judge them?" and "Am I wrong about what I believe?"

As we've said before, Christianity welcomes tough questions. And all of these are fair questions to ask—and I think there are reasonable responses to them from a Christian perspective.[3] But the question that he was really struggling with and that we spent the next few hours discussing was how do we know what the Bible really says? Throughout church history and even today, Christians disagree; how do we know which interpretation is correct? For that matter, how do we know *any* interpretation is correct?

THREE OBJECTIONS THAT NEED TO BE DEALT WITH

Our family likes to go on hikes and discover new trails at the various state parks in the area. From time to time we come upon a trail that doesn't look like it has been walked on in a while. The reason becomes obvious—some debris has fallen across the path or some of the weeds and briars have grown up. But it looks like an interesting path with things we would like to see, so I clear the path. This takes a little time and you have to be careful with the thorns, but it's worth it. When it comes to the problem of interpretation, we need to clear the path of three objections before we can discover a way out of this maze. The time invested here will be worth it as well.

1. The "That's Just Your Interpretation" Objection

Religious topics are in the headlines these days and so the different TV news networks have various experts on to discuss what they believe. The guests may change, but one thing stays the same; inevitably someone throws out the "but that's just your interpretation" line and the conversation comes to a screeching halt. (This usually happens when a moral or religious topic is brought up like "abortion is wrong" or "Jesus is the only way of salvation.") Perhaps you have found yourself in a conversation like that and thought you were making progress only to be dismissed with a slogan. What do you do?

First of all, don't allow yourself to be dismissed so easily. Very politely ask a question. "Do you mean that your interpretation should be preferred over mine? If so, I'd like to know why you have chosen your interpretation over mine. You must have a good reason."[4] And then wait for a response. There are two ways this can go. First, it becomes clear that this person really hasn't thought through their position that much and is unable to provide reasons for their interpretation. They were simply using the "that's just your interpretation" slogan to dismiss you without argument. At this point, you can clarify what they mean by asking, "Are you saying you don't like my interpretation or that you think it's false?" If they think it's false, great. You can then ask them the reasons they have for thinking that it's false and have a productive spiritual conversation.

However, more often than not it will become obvious that this person simply doesn't like the implications of your view. Maybe if your view is correct, they might have to alter a behavior they enjoy or change their mind about a controversial social issue.

Philosopher Paul Copan suggests a reasonable response in situations like these: "There are many truths that I myself don't like or find difficult to accept, but not liking them doesn't give me the freedom to reject them. I have to accept that they are true."[5] Reality is indifferent to our preferences.

If you are a Christian, then the Bible explains why we all do this at some level: "For the wrath of God is revealed from heaven against all ungodliness and unrighteousness of men, who by their unrighteousness suppress the truth" (Romans 1:18). When an uncomfortable or inconvenient truth begins to bubble up to the surface, we squash it back down to avoid having to fall under its authority. While this theological principle is true, in most conversations you won't want to lead with this one and tell them, "You know what your problem is . . . you are suppressing the truth in unrighteousness." It's more effective (with the aid of the Holy Spirit) to help someone become aware of what they are doing by asking them questions they must process and respond to.

A final version of this objection can be seen when the famous atheist philosopher Friedrich Nietzsche stated, "There are no facts—only interpretations." Is this itself a fact or merely an interpretation? It sounds clever, but it's actually self-defeating. In the end, while everyone has a point of view, reason and experience repeatedly show that every point of view is not equal.

2. The "Biased Interpreter" Objection

The objection here is that no one is neutral and therefore no person can arrive at an objective interpretation of the text. This is one of the hallmarks of the postmodern perspective in philosophy and is very common on college campuses. We will want to distinguish between *psychological* and *rational* objectivity because many postmoderns have conflated the two. Psychological objectivity concerns an issue a person may or may not care about and this isn't necessarily a virtue. It is simply achieved when someone doesn't know much about an issue or simply doesn't care. Rational objectivity on the other hand concerns having "accurate epistemic access to the object itself" with the ability (not with infallibility, not standing outside the flux of history, and not with 100 percent certainty) to weigh the evidence or reasons concerning a particular issue.[6] William Dembski brings clarity by suggesting a more modest approach:

> Moderate contextualism, as we may call it, uncovers the pretensions of positivism, which in line with the Enlightenment vision of reason, claims the ability to settle all our questions at the bar of disembodied reason writ large. Against this inflated view of reason, moderate contextualism, affirms that all human inquiry occurs within contexts and must therefore acknowledge the role of contexts in shaping how we view the world. Reason functions in contexts and cannot be divorced from contexts. According to moderate contextualism, reason is to context as soul is to body. *Objectivity is not lost by acknowledging the role that contexts play in shaping how we learn about the world.* Moderate contextualism, while acknowledging the obvious, does not open the door to unbridled skepticism or relativism.[7] (emphasis mine)

I know there is a lot packed into that quote, but it is a very important point to make in today's culture. Insofar as Christians have bought into enlightenment rationalism where they understand themselves to be purely disinterested readers of the text, they should reject it. But simply recognizing that we are limited, have biases and preunderstandings (some good, some bad), and are historically situated does not entail that we are unable to be objective. This is also another reason we need to be careful to read the Bible in community, listen to the voices of the past throughout church history as they have wrestled with texts, and sit under Spirit-empowered teachers (cf. 1 Corinthians 12:27–28; Romans 12:7; Ephesians 4:12–16).

3. The "Pervasive Interpretive Pluralism" Problem

Another objection has recently emerged from some Christian circles of thought that are challenging the authority of Scripture. In his book *The Bible Made Impossible: Why Biblicism is Not a Truly Evangelical Reading of Scripture*, sociologist Christian Smith puts the question this way: "If the Bible is given by a truthful and omnipotent God as an internally consistent and perspicuous text precisely for the purpose of revealing to humans correct beliefs, practices, and morals, then *why is it that the presumably sincere Christians to whom it has been given cannot read it and come to common agreement about what it teaches?*[8] The most serious implication of this view—if true—is that it undermines the authority of the biblical text. However, all I think that Smith has effectively shown in his book is that people can and do disagree. Curiously, he assumes he can come to correct interpretations about the biblical text, suggests what we should really focus on, and even suggests some ways forward in his book. But many other Christian scholars disagree with him and have argued against his interpretation, so where does that leave us?[9] Despair?

This mindset is not unlike the situation we encounter in religious pluralism. If Christianity really is true and if Jesus really is the Son of God, wouldn't everyone presented with this claim accept it? Moreover, disagreement by itself proves nothing. How does it follow from the fact that there are *many* answers to a question, that there is *no* answer to a question? This is just basic logic. In this case I also think that Smith's standard is an unreasonable one. I think it's René Descartes' quest for absolute certainty in knowledge applied to textual (in this case biblical) interpretation. Since we can obviously know things we are not 100 percent certain of, shouldn't our interpretive goal be something less than absolute 100 percent agreement? And then there is the reality that you can have the right interpretation of a text, do your best to explain it to someone, and they still remain unconvinced.

In addition, I think Smith makes the kind of faulty assumption that Ehrman makes in his writings. One of the undercurrents in Ehrman's writings is that he seems to assume that if God really had spoken in the Bible, then it would have been preserved for us without error (even in the copied manuscripts). Since he didn't preserve the text with 100 percent certainty, God must not have spoken. Similarly, Smith seems to think that if we are to understand the Bible in traditional categories (e.g., the ones we explained in the previous chapter like inspiration, inerrancy, clarity, and sufficiency), then all Christians everywhere would agree. Since they don't—and we can empirically verify this—then we need to start with different assumptions and reject these traditional biblical categories (which Smith calls "Biblicism"). The logic is parallel in each case.

But universal agreement certainly isn't the biblical expectation. Note these two examples. First, when Paul and Silas came to town, the Jews of Berea "received the word with all eagerness, examining the Scriptures daily to see if these things were so" (Acts 17:11). In other words they were searching and studying the text to see if Jesus really was the Messiah. A correct interpretation is understood to be possible here. But lots of other people didn't come to this conclusion in the book of Acts. Does that mean that because universal agreement was not reached that either God had not spoken or that this interpretation was not true? Certainly not! Or take Paul's reminder concerning the day of the Lord. He urges the Thessalonians not to be taken in by differing interpretations of what is to come:

> Now concerning the coming of our Lord Jesus Christ and our being gathered
> together to him, we ask you, brothers, not to be quickly shaken in mind or
> alarmed, either by a spirit or a spoken word, or a letter seeming to be from us,
> to the effect that the day of the Lord has come. Let no one deceive you in any
> way. For that day will not come, unless the rebellion comes first, and the man
> of lawlessness is revealed, the son of destruction, who opposes and exalts him-
> self against every so-called god or object of worship, so that he takes his seat
> in the temple of God, proclaiming himself to be God. (2 Thessalonians 2:1–4)

In communities that still had an apostolic witness around to ask, they still had interpretive disagreement. I don't think Paul would have expected any different were he alive today.

Why don't Christians all agree? Erik Thoennes suggests some possible reasons. Primarily we "can assume that the problem is not with the Bible but rather with us as interpreters. Misunderstandings may be due to various factors such as human sin, ignorance of enough of the relevant data, faulty assumptions, or trying to reach a definite conclusion about a topic for which the Bible has not given enough information to decide the question."[10] In the end, I think the way forward is to accept the inherent messiness that comes with human interpretation in a fallen world and then humbly and diligently seek to discover the best interpretation. But how do we do that in any reliable way?

MIND THE GAP

In the London underground you will find an unusual sign—*Mind the Gap*. There is a unique danger that passengers need to be aware of; if the train stops on a curve, then there will be a gap between the platform and the train and this could be harmful for the passenger if he or she would accidentally fall into it. It was impractical for attendants to warn the passengers each time they boarded the train, so they developed the phrase "Mind the Gap" to put on signs—and now these are everywhere. When approaching the Bible, I think we need to adopt this warning as well because the same danger exists for us as modern readers of an ancient text. If we are not careful, then we can misunderstand what God has intended to say.

Four gaps exist between the biblical text and us:

1. **Time**—between 2,000 to 3,500 years!

2. **Language.** English is obviously not the same as Hebrew, Aramaic, or Greek.

3. **Historical/cultural situation**. A twenty-first-century America that exalts the absolute freedom of the individual and has seen the scientific, industrial, and sexual revolutions is a very different cultural situation than the ancient writers encountered.

4. **Literary genre.** As we have seen in our chapter on alleged contradictions, ancients and moderns don't utilize the same literary devices and textual assumptions.

It will take effort and careful study to bridge this gap, but it can be done. Before we explore a path for doing this, we need to be clear on the goal of our interpretation.

WHO CONTROLS THE MEANING OF THE TEXT—READER OR AUTHOR?

Over the past century we have seen a debate raging in academia about where meaning resides—with the author or with the reader? This is where postmodernism—with its suspicion of authority, rejection of absolute reason, and belief that reality is socially and linguistically constructed—comes to bear.[11] It might be tempting to think that such esoteric philosophical conversations don't affect our everyday lives, but that is clearly not the case. Remember, ideas have consequences for people.

Take, for example, current debates occurring in the Supreme Court about various laws and what the United States Constitution—the highest authority in our country—actually means. R. Scott Smith notes that in "our postmodern times, law schools tend to teach that, since we cannot know the meaning of the framers of the Constitution (or of any other law), or that such intent is basically irrelevant, we must interpret the Constitution and find out what it means to us now. This belief finds its expression in the phrase 'the living Constitution,' for it is not a static document but one that continually must be constructed and reconstructed according to how we talk and live today."[12]

Notice how radical this approach really is. The postmodern turn is not merely seeking how to apply in today's society the principle that was originally written and intended in the constitution; it's that the very principle itself has changed! This is what reader response criticism gives us—the audience determines the meaning of the text.

Here is an everyday example of the difference between "authorial intent" and "reader response" theories of texts and meanings. If I write a note to my son to "please take out the trash" and leave it on the kitchen table, then I control the meaning. The thoughts in my mind were communicated using English letters on a written page. Therefore, it is incorrect for him to interpret that phrase as "play more video games today." This is true whether it was written twenty minutes ago, or two hundred years ago.

What does this discussion mean for how we approach the Bible? In their helpful book *Journey into God's Word*, J. Scott Duvall and J. Daniel Hays remind us "our goal is to grasp the meaning of the text God has intended. We do not create meaning out of a text; rather, we seek to find the meaning that is already there."[13] It boils down to a very significant question we all must answer when approaching the Bible—whose voice do I most want (and need) to hear? God's or my own? If God really has spoken, then it is of the utmost importance that we try to discover what he has said because it is his voice that is authoritative and the source of life.

CONTEXT IS KING

God intended for us to understand His Word. One indicator of this is the amount of Scripture we are told to obey or listen to; understanding is a prerequisite for obedience. When it comes to reading the Bible, the reader needs to recognize that without "a context, words become meaningless...the most important principle of biblical interpretation is that context determines meaning."[14] New Testament professor Ben Witherington is fond of telling his students, "A text without a context is just a pretext for whatever you want it to mean."[15] Put negatively, context keeps us from making the text say whatever we want it to say. Positively, context is the right neighborhood for us to discover the meaning of the passage. In the end, by "honoring the context of Scripture, we are saying that we would rather hear what God has to say than put words in his mouth."[16]

You have probably had the experience in a small-group Bible study where someone said, "Here is what this passage means to me." That's the wrong statement to start with. Before we can determine what implications a particular text has for our lives, we must first discover what the text means. Again, it is important for our generation to understand that the meaning of a Bible passage is determined by the *author* (the Holy Spirit through the prophet Jeremiah, for example), not the reader (you or me). As a reader, I no more control the meaning of a passage of Scripture than I control the meaning of my income tax statement delivered by the IRS. (Somehow, I don't think they would be very sympathetic to my interpretation of my tax statement, which is that they owe me money, rather than vice versa.) Stating this principle of biblical interpretation succinctly, *a text cannot mean what it never meant.* So how do we discover what it originally meant? We need to investigate the historical and literary context and this is where the interpretive journey begins.

THE FIVE STEPS OF THE INTERPRETIVE JOURNEY

Now that we have cleared away some of the objections and set the context, I want to suggest a method you can practice that will help you discover what God's Word says, means, and how to apply it to your life. This summary will just scratch the surface, so I would highly recommend that you pick up a copy of *Grasping God's Word* by J. Scott Duvall and J. Daniel Hays (this is their approach) to work through in order to improve your interpretive skills and confidence (cf. 2 Timothy 2:15).

Step 1: Grasp the text in its "town."

What did the text mean to the original audience? During this stage, we are asking the text a lot of questions. Here are just a few of the important ones:

- **Who.** Who is the author? What do you know about his background? Who is the intended audience?

- **What.** What is going on in this passage? What are the facts or details? What is the relationship between the audience and the author? What was going on historically when this was written? Any comparisons or contrasts? Lists? Figures of speech?

- **Where.** Where are the events about which I am reading taking place? Where is the author? Any unique features about the region that will help me interpret the text?

- **When.** When did these events take place? When was this book or letter written?

- **Why.** Why does the author say what he says? Are there any clues in the text? Any situation, occasion, or conflict that has prompted this communication?

- **How.** How does the writer communicate the message of this passage? What emotions are on display here? How was the author's/audience's relationship with God?

We also need to ask what kind of literature we are reading—history, narrative, poetry, prophecy, law, wisdom, gospel, letter—each genre has different rules of interpretation.

Asking and answering these kinds of questions will help you head in the right direction as you seek to understand a passage. In our time-starved society with all of the instantaneous tweets, texts, and alerts we are constantly receiving, sometimes we grow impatient with the observation stage and prematurely rush on to interpretation because we think that is where the real action is! But this is a mistake, because the observation stage is critical for good interpretation. We need to heed the sage advice of lifelong Bible teacher Howard Hendricks:

> Observation will give you the basic building blocks out of which you will construct the meaning of a passage. The answers to your questions will come directly from the observation process. That is why I say, the more time you spend in Observation, the less time you will need to spend in Interpretation, and the more accurate will be your results. The less time you spend in Observation, the more time you will need to spend in Interpretation, and the less accurate your results will be.[17]

Once we understand what the text would have meant to them, then we need to look at the differences between their situation and ours today. This brings us to the next step in our journey.

Step 2: Measure the width of the river to cross.

What are the differences between the biblical audience and us? As we noted above, there is a gap between them and us. We have different cultures, languages, time periods, and historical situations. But there may also be a theological gap as well. Which covenant—old or new—is in effect here? What stage of salvation history was this particular text written in? For example, promises made by Paul to the church at Ephesus will apply to us differently than promises made to the nation of Israel through Moses on Mt. Sinai. Being attentive to the nature of the gap we need to cross will help ensure that we don't misapply the passage.

Step 3: Cross the principlizing bridge.

What is the theological principle in this text? Duvall and Hays offer excellent insight on how to form a theological principle once you have discovered what the text originally meant.

- The principle should be reflected in the text.
- The principle should be timeless and not tied to a specific situation.
- The principle should not be culturally bound.
- The principle should correspond to the teaching of the rest of Scripture.
- The principle should be relevant to both the biblical and the contemporary audience.[18]

Step 4: Consult the biblical map.

How does our theological principle fit with the rest of the Bible? Scripture helps interpret Scripture. When all is said and done, Scripture will not contradict itself because its source is the same—the very Spirit of God.

For example, if we are reading one of Paul's letters, we should ask if our interpretation fits with what we know about the rest of Paul's writings. And if our conclusion fits with the general tenor of the New Testament, then we know that we have arrived at a good interpretation of the passage.

A concentric circles diagram is a common illustration for showing the relationship between the various layers of biblical context. (See diagram 1.)

Diagram 1

GRASPING GOD'S WORD

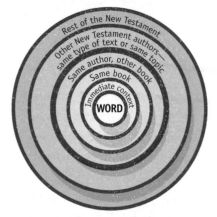

Source: Adapted from J. Scott Duvall and J. Daniel Hays, *Grasping God's Word*, 3rd ed. (Grand Rapids: Zondervan, 2012), 152.

Step 5: Grasp the text in our town.

How should individual Christians today live out the theological principles?[19]
Unfortunately, many of us stop the process at understanding what a text
means. But Christianity is not about acquiring Bible data; it is about our lives
being conformed to the image of Jesus Christ (Galatians 4:19). And this occurs
when we apply the truth discovered in Scripture to our lives.

Once you have completed the first four steps of the interpretive journey,
here are some questions you should ask that will help you discover how to
personally apply God's Word:

• Is there an example for me to follow?

• Is there a sin to avoid?

• Is there a promise to claim?

• Is there a prayer to repeat?

• Is there a verse to memorize?

• Is there a command to obey?

• Is there a condition to meet?

• Is there an error to mark?

• Is there a challenge to face?[20]

While the meaning of a text will never change, the ways to apply the text
are endless. As Hendricks puts it, "There is only one ultimate interpretation of
a passage of Scripture. The text doesn't mean one thing today and something
else tomorrow. Whatever it means, it means forever. But you will never cease
the process of applying that truth to your life."[21]

WHAT IS THE ROLE OF THE HOLY SPIRIT IN HELPING US INTERPRET THE TEXT?

Can an unbeliever grasp the content of the Bible? Yes and no. Yes, if we mean
the text can be understood by employing a sound approach to literature—the
basic grammar, context, and content of a passage. But an unbeliever cannot

fully appreciate and take to heart the truth of the Bible. God's Spirit helps Christians discern the spiritual realities of the text and then apply them to their lives (cf. 1 Corinthians 2:14). Duvall and Hays offer a helpful summary:

> When it comes to biblical interpretation, having the Holy Spirit does not mean that the Spirit is all we need, since he will not make biblical interpretation automatic. He expects us to use our minds, valid interpretive methods, and good study helps. The Spirit does not create new meaning or provide new information, but he does enable us to accept the Bible as God's Word and grasp its meaning. The Spirit will not change the Bible to suit our purposes or match our circumstances, but he will work in our lives as interpreters. He restores us to our senses and helps us grow up spiritually so we can hear his voice in the Scriptures more clearly.[22]

As we conclude this chapter, I encourage you to stand strong in the face of the common objections mentioned above. You can be confident that some interpretations are better than others and that if you follow the method briefly outlined here with a heart that is seeking to honor, glorify, and obey God, you will reliably be able to discover what he has revealed. Paul's challenge to us all is to "do your best to present yourself to God as one approved, a worker who has no need to be ashamed, rightly handling the word of truth" (2 Timothy 2:15).

Three Big Ideas

1. When it comes to interpreting the biblical text, disagreement doesn't settle the matter and that certainly doesn't mean that no one's interpretation is correct. Next, the claim that everything is interpretation is self-refuting. Finally, while we recognize that we all bring our preunderstandings to a text, this does not mean that we are incapable of arriving at an accurate understanding of the meaning intended by the author. While humility and community are important things to emphasize today, a radical postmodern approach to language and reality should be rejected as incoherent, self-refuting, and unlivable in practice.

2. Without "a context, words become meaningless . . . the most important principle of biblical interpretation is that context determines meaning." The historical and literary contexts are keys to unlocking the meaning of the passage—a text cannot mean what it never meant. Finally, authors determine the meaning of the text—not readers. Because we want to take God's Word seriously, we want to hear his voice in the pages of Scripture and not our own.

3. Remember the five steps in the interpretive journey:

   1- Grasp the text in their town—What did the text mean to the original audience?

   2- Measure the width of the river to cross—What are the differences between the biblical audience and us?

   3- Cross the principlizing bridge—What is the theological principle in this text?

   4- Consult the biblical map—How does our theological principle fit with the rest of the Bible?

   5- Grasp the text in our town—How should individual Christians today live out the theological principles? Since all interpretations are not created equal, this is a reliable method for discovering the meaning of the text.

Conversation Tips

- As we noted earlier, if you find yourself on the receiving end of a sound bite or slogan on interpretation, the first thing to do is not allow yourself to be dismissed so easily. Very politely ask a question, "Do you mean that your interpretation should be preferred over mine? If so, I'd like to know why you have chosen your interpretation over mine. You must have a good reason." Wait for a response. The key here is to expose their false confidence that all interpretations are equally good ones. But when people have to defend their slogans, they are usually unable to.

- If you find yourself in a conversation with a Christian—and your heart is right—and they say "this is what this passage means to me," first ask a clarifying question; e.g., "Are you saying that is what you think God through Paul intended in this passage or are you saying that this is how you want to apply the meaning of this passage?" Hopefully, it will be one of these two. If not, you can still engage someone who thinks their reading of the passage determines the meaning with some of our discussion above.

Digging Deeper

- J. Scott Duvall and J. Daniel Hays. *Grasping God's Word: A Hands-on Approach to Reading, Interpreting, and Applying the Bible,* 3rd ed. Grand Rapids: Zondervan, 2012.

- Gordon D. Fee and Douglas Stuart. *How to Read the Bible Book by Book: A Guided Tour.* Grand Rapids: Zondervan, 2002.

WHAT IF A NEW GENERATION TOOK THE BIBLE SERIOUSLY?

C

Therefore, since we have so great a cloud of witnesses surrounding us, let us also lay aside every encumbrance and the sin which so easily entangles us, and let us run with endurance the race that is set before us, fixing our eyes on Jesus, the author and perfecter of faith, who for the joy set before Him endured the cross, despising the shame, and has sat down at the right hand of the throne of God.

Hebrews 12:1–3 (NASB)

If all you know about Eric Liddell is that he chose not to run the 100-meter dash for which he qualified in the 1924 Olympic games because it conflicted with the Sabbath, then you know but one small chapter of the redemptive story that God was writing with his life. After the cheers of the Olympic crowds faded, Eric faithfully served as a missionary in China and would later die in an internment camp there at the age of 43. What the world—and even his family—did not know until sixty-three years after his death, was that Eric had been included in a prisoner exchange deal between Japan and Britain but had given up his place to a pregnant woman.[1]

Those who knew him were not surprised. The inspiring episode made famous by the film *Chariots of Fire* (winner of the 1982 best picture Academy Award) was only a snapshot of the character that flowed from a man who took the Bible seriously: "If I know something to be true, am I prepared to follow it even though it is contrary to what I want. . . . Will I follow if it means being laughed at by friend or foe, or if it means personal financial loss or some kind of hardship?"[2] Knowing the truth and living the truth go together. At his memorial service, Liddell's lifelong friend A. P. Cullen summed up his remarkable life: "He was literally God-controlled, in his thoughts, judgments, actions, words to an extent I have never seen surpassed, and rarely seen equaled. Every morning he rose early to pray and to read the Bible in silence: talking and listening to God, pondering the day ahead and often smiling as if at a private joke."[3] May God raise up thousands of Eric Liddells in this generation!

What we have been doing in this book is academically and intellectually serious; but you will have missed the point of God's Word if it remains *only* academic. For like Eric Liddell, if you really believe that God's Word is true, then you will do something. But what you can't do—if God really has spoken—is go about life as usual.

My prayer for you is that you will search the Scriptures and learn to hear God's voice on the big questions of life. I hope these pages have given you confidence that you can trust the Bible as God's Word. Contrary to what we heard in the Yale freshman address in the introduction, there are authoritative answers to life's biggest questions because God has spoken. And yet, many millennials struggle to accept the Bible as authoritative and to apply it to their lives. (Read appendix 3 to see many of the reasons we don't take the Bible seriously anymore.)

THE TRUE STORY OF THE WORLD

Everyone has a worldview—it's unavoidable. Whether people are aware of it, and whether their worldview adequately explains reality, is another story altogether. Briefly put, a worldview is simply the total set of beliefs that a person has about the biggest questions in life. Worldviews function much like eyeglasses or contact lenses that either bring the world into focus or make things harder to see. Or we could think about a worldview as a mental map or GPS of the way things are. If you have a reliable map, then you will arrive at your intended destination.

In light of this, what are the ultimate questions we all have to answer?

Generally there are four:

1. **questions of origin**—Where did I come from? Do I matter?

2. **meaning**—Why am I here? What is my purpose in life?

3. **morality**—How should I live? What is right and wrong?; and

4. **destiny**—What happens when I die? Is this life all there is?

Here is the way Christianity answers these questions:

- **Origin.** The Bible teaches that humans are the special creation of God and have inherent dignity and worth because we are created in the image of God. Your life is significant because God created you and says it is; you are not an accident.

- **Meaning.** The Bible teaches that you were created for relationship with the triune God and to make something of the world for his glory. Since we live in a fallen world, this task has become significantly more difficult. And we now add the Great Commission (Matthew 28:19–20) to our original cultural commission (Genesis 1–2). We have a mission to accomplish as we bring glory to God.

- **Morality.** The Bible teaches that we are to live our lives according to God's loving, wise, and purposeful design. When we cooperate with reality we flourish but when we go our own way we languish. Moreover, objective right and wrong flow from God's nature and commands to us. We are under God's authority.

- **Destiny.** The Bible teaches that every person lives forever somewhere. Christians will experience the delight and joy of our triune God in a new heaven and a new earth for all eternity. Those who reject the generous love of God in Christ will spend eternity outside of his presence without joy, light, or hope. The biblical term for this awful reality is "hell." We must remind ourselves that this life is not all there is.

KNOWING OUR OWN STORY

Knowing our own story gives us the confidence to live well. As N. T. Wright reminds us, "The whole point of Christianity is that it offers a story which is the story of the whole world. It is public truth."[4] In a very real sense, our task in an increasingly hostile—but spiritually hungry—culture is to remind our world of the true story to which it belongs. The prophet Isaiah could relate to the current situation: "Justice is driven back, and righteousness stands at a distance; truth has stumbled in the streets, honesty cannot enter. Truth is nowhere to be found" (Isaiah 59:14–15 NIV). Given the cultural moment[5] that we inhabit, we should "do all things without grumbling or disputing, that you may be blameless and innocent, children of God without blemish in the midst of a crooked and twisted generation, among whom you shine as lights in the world, holding fast to the word of life" (Philippians 2:14–15). As James, the brother of Jesus, put it, "Be doers of the word, and not hearers only" (James 1:22). There are no insignificant moments because each one of them is an opportunity to speak and live the truth. God is alive and our hope is secure.

It is fitting to close with the words of Paul to his son in the faith, Timothy:

> But as for you, continue in what you have learned and have firmly believed, knowing from whom you learned it and how from childhood you have been acquainted with the sacred writings, which are able to make you wise for salvation through faith in Christ Jesus. All Scripture is breathed out by God and profitable for teaching, for reproof, for correction, and for training in righteousness, that the man of God may be complete, equipped for every good work. (2 Timothy 3:14–17)

The world is in desperate need of a new generation who will take God's Word seriously. Will you answer the call? Will you shine a light into the darkness?

NOTES

Introduction: What You May Not Have Learned in Church about the Bible

1. Bart D. Ehrman, *Jesus, Interrupted: Revealing the Hidden Contradictions in the Bible* (New York: HarperOne, 2010), 19.

2. Richard C. Levin, "The Questions That Matter," *Yale Bulletin & Calendar*, September 14, 2007, italics added; http://opac.yale.edu//opa/arc-ybc/v36 .n2/story5.html.

3. Christian Smith and Patricia Snell, *Souls in Transition: The Religious and Spiritual Lives of Emerging Adults* (Oxford: Oxford University Press, 2009), 293.

4. David Kinnaman, *You Lost Me: Why Young Christians Are Leaving Church— and Rethinking Faith* (Grand Rapids: Baker, 2011), 192.

5. Ibid., 190.

6. Timothy J. Keller, *The Reason for God: Belief in an Age of Skepticism* (New York: Dutton, 2008), xvi–xvii.

7. C. S. Lewis, *Mere Christianity* (New York: Simon & Schuster Inc., 1996), 32.

Chapter 1: Is the Bible Anti-intellectual?

1. Roy McCloughry, "Basic Stott," *Christianity Today*, January 8, 1996, 32.

2. See http://manhattandeclaration.org/#1.

3. Os Guinness, *The Case for Civility: And Why Our Future Depends on It* (New York: HarperOne, 2008), 135–37.

4. For a very helpful treatment of this topic, see D. A. Carson, *The Intolerance of Tolerance* (Grand Rapids: Eerdmans, 2012).

5. Stephen R. Prothero, *God Is Not One: The Eight Rival Religions That Run the World—and Why Their Differences Matter* (New York: HarperOne, 2010), 4.

6. Ross Douthat, "Let's Talk About Faith," *The New York Times*, January 10, 2010; http://www.nytimes.com/2010/01/11/opinion/11douthat.html?_r = 1&.

7. Prothero, *God Is Not One*, 1.

8. I first encountered this illustration in J. P. Moreland and Tim Muehlhoff, *The God Conversation: Using Stories and Illustrations to Explain Your Faith* (Downers Grove, IL: InterVarsity, 2007).

9. Sigmund Freud, *The Future of an Illusion*, trans. James Strachey (New York: Norton, 1989), 38.

10. Sean McDowell and Jonathan Morrow, *Is God Just a Human Invention?: And Seventeen Other Questions Raised by the New Atheists* (Grand Rapids: Kregel, 2010).

11. Paul C. Vitz, *Faith of the Fatherless: The Psychology of Atheism* (Dallas: Spence Pub. Co., 1999), 145.

12. Nancy Pearcey, *Total Truth: Liberating Christianity from Its Cultural Captivity* (Wheaton, IL: Crossway, 2005), 178.

13. To go deeper, you will find this to be a helpful guide: Garrett J. DeWeese and J. P. Moreland, *Philosophy Made Slightly Less Difficult: A Beginner's*

Guide to Life's Big Questions (Downers Grove, IL: InterVarsity, 2005).

14. Greg Koukl, "Religious Stew"; online at http://www.str.org/articles/religious-stew#.

15. Lisa Miller, "Belief Watch: Arguing Against the Atheists, *Newsweek*, October 6, 2008, 16.

16. Steven Pinker, "Less Faith, More Reason," *The Harvard Crimson*, October 27, 2006; http://www.thecrimson.com/article/2006/10/27/less-faith-more-reason-there-is/.

17. Nancy Pearcey, *Saving Leonardo: A Call to Resist the Secular Assault on Mind, Morals, and Meaning* (Nashville: B&H Books, 2010), 35.

18. Gordon R. Lewis, endorsement in Rick Cornish, *5 Minute Theologian: Maximum Truth in Minimum Time* (Colorado Springs: NavPress, 2004), 1.

19. Pearcey, *Saving Leonardo*, 14.

20. John Stott, *Your Mind Matters: The Place of the Mind in the Christian Life* (Downers Grove, IL: InterVarsity, 2006), 18.

21. Dallas Willard, *Renovation of the Heart: Putting on the Character of Christ* (Colorado Springs: NavPress, 2002), 106.

Chapter 2: What Can We Really Know about Jesus?

1. Nancy Pearcey, *Saving Leonardo: A Call to Resist the Secular Assault on Mind, Morals, and Meaning* (Nashville: B&H Books, 2010), 35.

2. For a helpful introduction and overview, see Darrell L. Bock, *Who Is Jesus?: Linking the Historical Jesus with the Christ of Faith* (New York: Howard Books, 2012).

3. As quoted in C. Stephen Evans, *The Historical Christ and the Jesus of Faith: The Incarnational Narrative as History* (Oxford: Oxford University Press, 1996), 170.

4. As quoted in James K. Beilby and Paul Rhodes Eddy, *The Historical Jesus: Five Views* (Downers Grove, IL: InterVarsity, 2009), 22.

5. Ibid., 19.

6. For more on this and the next three sections, see Mark L. Strauss, *Four Portraits, One Jesus* (Grand Rapids: Zondervan, 2007), 351–53.

7. For a devastating critique of this view and why it has been abandoned by scholars today, see Larry W. Hurtado, *Lord Jesus Christ: Devotion to Jesus in Earliest Christianity* (Cambridge, U.K.: Eerdmans, 2003).

8. Darrell L. Bock, *Studying the Historical Jesus: A Guide to Sources and Methods* (Grand Rapids: Baker, 2002), 146.

9. Bock, *Who Is Jesus?*, 8.

10. For a general overview of the rules, see Robert H. Stein, "Criteria for the Gospels' Authenticity," in *Contending with Christianity's Critics: Answering New Atheists & Other Objectors*, eds. Paul Copan and William Lane Craig (Nashville: B&H Publishing Group, 2009). For his more detailed treatment, see Robert H. Stein, *The Synoptic Problem* (Grand Rapids: Baker, 1987).

11. Bock, *Who Is Jesus?*, 18.

12. R. H. Stein, "Synoptic Problem," in *Dictionary of Jesus and the Gospels*, eds.

Joel B. Green and Scot McKnight (Downers Grove, IL: InterVarsity, 1992), 784.

13. They have published their technical work in a 900-page book: *Key Events in the Life of the Historical Jesus*, eds. Darrell L. Bock and Robert L. Webb (repr., Grand Rapids: Eerdmans, 2010).

14. Bock, *Who Is Jesus?*, 212–14.

15. Ibid.

16. Ibid.

17. As quoted in Craig L. Blomberg, "Jesus of Nazareth: How Historians Can Know Him and Why It Matters"; http://thegospelcoalition.org/cci/article/jesus_of_nazareth_how_historians_can_know_him_and_why_it_matters.

18. http://benwitherington.blogspot.com/2007/12/zeitgeist-of-zeitgeist-movie.html.

19. Bart D. Ehrman, "Did Jesus Exist?" *Huffington Post*, The Blog, March 20, 2012, http://www.huffingtonpost.com/bart-d-ehrman/did-jesus-exist_b_1349544.html?ref=religion.

20. Mary Jo Sharp, "Is the Story of Jesus Borrowed from Pagan Myths?" in *In Defense of the Bible: A Comprehensive Apologetics for the Authority of Scripture*, ed. Steven B. Cowan and Terry L. Wilder (Nashville: B&H Academic, 2013), 200.

21. Gregory A. Boyd and Paul R. Eddy, *Lord or Legend?: Wrestling with the Jesus Dilemma* (Grand Rapids: Baker, 2007), 53.

Chapter 3: How Do We Know What the Earliest Christians Believed?

1. Gary Habermas, "The Resurrection of Jesus Time Line: The Convergence of Eyewitnesses and Early Proclamation," in *Contending with Christianity's Critics: Answering New Atheists & Other Objectors*, ed. Paul Copan and William Lane Craig (Nashville: B&H Publishing, 2009), 124.

2. Bart D. Ehrman, *Jesus, Interrupted: Revealing the Hidden Contradictions in the Bible* (New York: HarperOne, 2010), 268.

3. One goal in writing this book is to introduce a new generation of readers to the latest scholarship that supports the historical reliability and accuracy of the biblical text. I have included more endnotes than usual and often will allow you to hear directly from some of the scholars themselves, rather than only summarizing them. In this section, I am relying heavily on the excellent research of Gary Habermas found in his chapter "The Resurrection of Jesus Time Line" (cf. endnote 1 above) cited above and also in Gary R. Habermas, *The Risen Jesus & Future Hope* (Oxford: Rowman & Littlefield Publishers, 2003), 17–25.

4. Ibid., vii.

5. For a great introduction, see Mark L. Strauss, *Four Portraits, One Jesus* (Grand Rapids: Zondervan, 2007).

6. For a more conservative approach to dating the Gospels (with which I agree), see D. A. Carson and Douglas J. Moo, *An Introduction to the New Testament*, 2nd ed. (Grand Rapids: Zondervan, 2005).

7. Richard Bauckham, *Jesus and the Eyewitnesses* (Grand Rapids: Eerdmans, 2006), 265.

8. Habermas, "The Resurrection of Jesus Time Line," 119.

9. See Acts 1:21–22; 2:22–36; 3:13–16; 4:8–10; 5:29–32; 10:39–43; 13:28–31; 17:1–3, 30–31.

10. Bauckham, *Jesus and the Eyewitnesses*, 308.

11. Habermas, "The Resurrection of Jesus Time Line," 124.

12. N. T. Wright, *The Resurrection of the Son of God* (Minneapolis: Fortress, 2003), 710.

13. Bauckham, *Jesus and the Eyewitnesses*, 5.

15. Darrell L. Bock and Daniel B. Wallace, *Dethroning Jesus: Exposing Popular Culture's Quest to Unseat the Biblical Christ* (Nashville: Nelson, 2007), 221.

16. Bauckham, *Jesus and the Eyewitnesses*, 264–71.

17. See Larry W. Hurtado, *How on Earth Did Jesus Become a God?: Historical Questions About Earliest Devotion to Jesus* (Cambridge, U.K.: W. B. Eerdmans, 2005), 83–107.

18. Richard Bauckham, *Jesus and the God of Israel: God Crucified and Other Studies on the New Testament's Christology of Divine Identity* (Grand Rapids: Eerdmans, 2008), 27–28.

19. Gary R. Habermas, *The Historical Jesus* (Joplin, MO: College Press Publishing, 1996), 199.

20. Larry W. Hurtado, *Lord Jesus Christ: Devotion to Jesus in Earliest Christianity* (Cambridge, U.K.: W. B. Eerdmans, 2003), 650. For more on this, see Richard Bauckham, *Jesus and the God of Israel* (Grand Rapids: Eerdmans, 2009); and Robert M. Bowman and J. Ed Komoszewski, *Putting Jesus in His Place: The Case for the Deity of Christ* (Grand Rapids: Kregel, 2007).

Chapter 4: Why Were Some Gospels Banned from the Bible?

1. Charles E. Hill, *Who Chose the Gospels?: Probing the Great Gospel Conspiracy* (Oxford: Oxford University Press, 2010), 231.

2. Bart D. Ehrman, *Lost Scriptures* (Oxford: Oxford University Press, 2003).

4. Hal Taussig, *A New New Testament: A Reinvented Bible for the Twenty-First Century Combining Traditional and Newly Discovered Texts* (Boston: Houghton Mifflin Harcourt, 2013); http://www.amazon.com/New-Testament-Combining-Traditional-Discovered-ebook/dp/B008LQ1B44. Interview with author.

5. These are terms used by Michael Kruger. My point is not that the extrinsic aspect of canon is illegitimate, only that it is not the whole show. Kruger shows the explanatory power of a more three-dimensional approach: "Canon has an ecclesiological dimension, a historical dimension, and an aesthetic/internal dimension. It is when a single aspect of canon is abso-lutized at the expense of the others that distortions inevitably arise. When these three aspects are kept in their proper biblical balance, we can begin to see the controversial issues more clearly. Take, for instance, the never-ending debates over the 'date' of the canon. While some models want to stake their claim on a particular moment in time, the three-dimensional nature of

the self-authenticating model reminds us that it is more appropriate to think of the date of canon in 'stages' rather than in a single airtight category"; in Michael J. Kruger, *Canon Revisited* (Wheaton, IL: Crossway, 2012), 293.

6. This chapter allows me room only to sketch the basic outline, but I refer you to the excellent scholarship being done on the subject of canon by Michael J. Kruger in *The Question of Canon* (Downers Grove, IL: InterVarsity, 2013), 47–78; and in Kruger's *Canon Revisited*.

7. N. T. Wright, *The New Testament and the People of God* (Minneapolis: Fortress, 1992), 217.

8. Kruger, *The Question of Canon*, 59.

9. Ibid., 77.

10. Michael W. Holmes, *The Apostolic Fathers in English*, 3rd ed. (Grand Rapids: Baker, 2006), 61.

11. Other passages include Jeremiah 30:2 and Habakkuk 2:2 in the OT and Luke 1:3 and Jude 3 in the NT.

12. Richard Bauckham, *Jesus and the Eyewitnesses* (Grand Rapids, Eerdmans, 2006), 308.

13. Eckhard J. Schnabel, *Early Christian Mission*, vol. 1 (Downers Grove, IL: InterVarsity, 2004), 913.

14. Kruger, *The Question of Canon*, 153.

15. Ibid., 163.

16. Irenaeus, *Against Heresies* (Veritatis Splendor Publications, 2012). Kindle. 335.

17. Kruger, *The Question of Canon*, 161.

18. Ibid., 162.

19. Philip Schaff (2009-06-08). *Ante-Nicene Fathers*, vol. 2, enhanced version (Early Church Fathers) (Kindle Locations 5580–5582). Christian Classics Ethereal Library. Kindle Edition. Book 3.12.

20. Kruger, *The Question of Canon*, 166–67.

21. Arthur G. Patzia, *The Making of the New Testament: Origin, Collection, Text & Canon*, 2nd ed. (Downers Grove, IL: InterVarsity, 2011), 97.

22. Kruger, *The Question of Canon*, 168.

23. Bruce M. Metzger, *The Canon of the New Testament: Its Origin, Development, and Significance*, Kindle ed. (Oxford: Oxford University Press, 1997), 115.

24. Philip Schaff (2009-06-08). *Ante-Nicene Fathers*. vol. 1, enhanced version (Early Church Fathers) (Kindle Locations 10652–10655). Christian Classics Ethereal Library. Kindle Edition.

25. Philip Schaff (2009-06-08). *Ante-Nicene Fathers*, vol. 1, (Kindle Locations 14474–14475).

26. Patzia, *The Making of the New Testament*, 97.

27. Bruce M. Metzger, *The Canon of the New Testament* (1987; repr., Oxford: Oxford University Press, 1997), 160.

28. Irenaeus, *Against Heresies*, 654.

29. Eusebius, *The History of the Church*, rev. ed. (repr., New York: Penguin, 1990), 69.

30. Kruger, *The Question of Canon*, 186.

31. Philip Schaff (2009-06-08). *Ante-Nicene Fathers*, vol. 1 (Kindle Locations 4629–4630), Romans 4:4.

32. Kruger, *The Question of Canon*, 189–90.

33. Philip Schaff (2009-06-08). *Ante-Nicene Fathers*, vol. 1 (Kindle Locations 2106–2108), Philippians 3:2.

34. Ibid., (Kindle Locations 2316–2321), Christian Classics Ethereal Library, Kindle Edition, Philippians 12:1.

35. Ibid., (Kindle Locations 1287–1292).

36. The reader can profitably consult for further evidence the helpful work of C. E. Hill, *Who Chose the Gospels?* (Oxford, NY: Oxford University Press, 2010).

37. J. Ed Komoszewski, M. James Sawyer, and Daniel B. Wallace, *Reinventing Jesus: How Contemporary Skeptics Miss the Real Jesus and Mislead Popular Culture* (Grand Rapids: Kregel, 2006), 149.

38. This chart uses the four categories of Eusebius and is discussed with commentary in Kruger, *Canon Revisited: Establishing the Origins and Authority of the New Testament Books*, 260–87.

39. This section has been adapted from my article in *The Apologetics Study Bible for Students*, ed. Sean McDowell (Nashville: B&H Publishing Group, 2010).

40. This is a phrase my New Testament professor Darrell Bock was fond of saying.

41. Kruger, *The Question of Canon*, 210. For a podcast interview that I did with Dr. Kruger for Think Christianly, see http://www.thinkchristianly.org/interview-with-michael-kruger-on-the-canon-of-scripture-podcast/.

Chapter 5: Did the Biblical Writers Lie about Their Identity?

1. Terry L. Wilder, "Does the Bible Contain Forgeries?" in *In Defense of the Bible: A Comprehensive Apologetics for the Authority of Scripture*, ed. Steven B. Cowan and Terry L. Wilder (Nashville: B&H Academic, 2013), 181.

2. Bart D. Ehrman, *Jesus, Interrupted: Revealing the Hidden Contradictions in the Bible* (New York: HarperOne, 2010), 112.

3. Ibid., 136.

4. D. A. Carson, "Pseudonymity and Pseudepigraphy," *Dictionary of New Testament Background*, ed. Stanley E. Porter and Craig A. Evans (Downers Grove, IL: InterVarsity, 2000), 857.

5. Arthur G. Patzia and Anthony J. Petrotta, *Pocket Dictionary of Biblical Studies* (Downers Grove, IL: InterVarsity, 2002), 14.

6. Ibid.

7. Carson, "Pseudonymity and Pseudepigraphy," 861.

8. Michael J. Kruger, *The Question of Canon: Challenging the Status Quo in the New Testament Debate* (Downers Grove, IL: InterVarsity Press, 2013), 118, 207. *Nomina Sacra* were shorthand literary devices for the names of God and Christ.

9. As quoted in Paul R. Eddy and Gregory A. Boyd, *The Jesus Legend: A Case for the Historical Reliability of the Synoptic Jesus Tradition* (Grand

Rapids: Baker, 2007), 248–49. "Halaka," according to *The Eerdmans Bible Dictionary*, "came to mean the legal body of rules and regulations established and passed down by the scribes and rabbis as they interpreted and applied the law of Moses"; see Allen C. Myers, *The Eerdmans Bible Dictionary* (Grand Rapids: Eerdmans, 1987).

10. Mark D. Roberts, "Did Jesus Speak Greek?" July 2010; http://www.beliefnet.com/columnists/markdroberts/2010/07/did-jesus-speak-greek.html.

11. D. A. Carson and Douglas J. Moo, *An Introduction to the New Testament*, 2nd ed. (Grand Rapids: Zondervan, 2005), 240.

12. This is based on Papias' quote that "Matthew collected the oracles (*ta logia*) in the Hebrew language." See Eddy and Boyd, *The Jesus Legend*, 249–50.

13. Ehrman, *Jesus, Interrupted*, 115.

14. Eckhard J. Schnabel, "Paul, Timothy, and Titus: The Assumption of a Pseudonymous Author and of Pseudonymous Recipients in the Light of Literary, Theological, and Historical Evidence," *Do Historical Matters Matter to Faith? : A Critical Appraisal of Modern and Postmodern Approaches to Scripture*, ed. James K. Hoffmeier and Dennis R. Magary (Wheaton, IL: Crossway, 2012), 400.

15. Vitrvius Pollio, *The Ten Books on Architecture*, book seven, introduction, para. 1, 3; http://www.gutenberg.org/files/20239/20239-h/29239-h .htm#Page_195.

16. Carson, "Pseudonymity and Pseudepigraphy," 860.

17. Ibid., 860–61.

18. Ibid., 862.

19. Carson, *An Introduction to the New Testament*, 532–53.

20. Schnabel, "Paul, Timothy, and Titus," 402.

21. Carson, "Pseudonymity and Pseudepigraphy," 861.

22. For a full treatment of the other issues at stake, see Carson, *An Introduction to the New Testament*, 554–87; and Schnabel, "Paul, Timothy, and Titus."

23. Schnabel, "Paul, Timothy, and Titus," 387.

24. Ibid., 388.

25. Ibid., 391.

26. Terry L. Wilder, "Pseudonymity and the New Testament," in *Interpreting the New Testament: Essays on Methods and Issues*, ed. David Alan Black and David S. Dockery (Nashville: Broadman & Holman, 2001), 326.

27. Ehrman, *Jesus, Interrupted*, 112.

28. Richard Bauckham, *Jesus and the Eyewitnesses* (Grand Rapids: Eerdmans, 2006), 302.

29. Ibid., 302–303.

30. Ibid., 303.

31. Michael J. Kruger, *Canon Revisited: Establishing the Origins and Authority of the New Testament Books* (Wheaton, IL: Crossway, 2012), 242.

32. As quoted in Jeremy Howard, ed. *The Holman Apologetics Commentary on the Bible: The Gospels and Acts* (Nashville: B&H Publishing Group, 2013), 8.

33. Ibid.

34. Ibid.

35. Darrell L. Bock, *Jesus According to Scripture* (Grand Rapids: Baker, 2002), 29.

36. Grant R. Osborne, *Matthew*, ed. Clinton E. Arnold, Zondervan Exegetical Commentary Series on the New Testament (Grand Rapids: Zondervan, 2010), 34.

37. Bock, *Jesus According to Scripture*, 33.

38. Eusebius, *The History of the Church*, rev. ed. (repr., New York: Penguin, 1990), 69.

39. Bock, *Jesus According to Scripture*, 33.

40. Ibid., 37–38.

41. Howard, *The Holman Apologetics Commentary on the Bible: The Gospels and Acts*, 9.

42. Craig Blomberg, *The Historical Reliability of John's Gospel: Issues & Commentary* (Downers Grove, IL: InterVarsity, 2002), 25.

43. Bock, *Jesus According to Scripture*, 42–43.

44. For a more thorough survey of the internal and external evidence, see Andreas J. Köstenberger, *Encountering John: The Gospel in Historical, Literary, and Theological Perspective*, Encountering Biblical Studies (Grand Rapids: Baker Academic, 1999), 22–25. And Carson, *An Introduction to the New Testament*, 229–54.

Chapter 6: Has the Biblical Text Been Corrupted over the Centuries?

1. Stanley E. Porter, *How We Got the New Testament: Text, Transmission, Translation*, Acadia Studies in Bible and Theology (Grand Rapids: Baker, 2013), 24.

2. Bart D. Ehrman, *Misquoting Jesus: The Story Behind Who Changed the Bible and Why* (New York: HarperSanFrancisco, 2005), 7.

3. http://en.wikipedia.org/wiki/Chinese_whispers; accessed December 19, 2013.

4. J. Ed Komoszewski, M. James Sawyer, and Daniel B. Wallace, *Reinventing Jesus: How Contemporary Skeptics Miss the Real Jesus and Mislead Popular Culture* (Grand Rapids: Kregel, 2006), 82.

5. For numbers and findings in the past decade, see the article by Clay Jones at http://www.equip.org/articles/the-bibliographical-test-updated/#christian-books-2.

6. See http://www.dts.edu/read/wallace-new-testament-manscript-first-century/ on the possibility of a first-century Gospel of Mark papyrus discovery.

7. Paul D. Wegner, *A Student's Guide to Textual Criticism of the Bible* (Downers Grove, IL: InterVarsity, 2006), 256–65; Andreas J. Köstenberger and Michael J. Kruger, *The Heresy of Orthodox* (Wheaton, IL: Crossway, 2010), 210–13; and Darrell L. Bock and Daniel B. Wallace, *Dethroning Jesus: Exposing Popular Culture's Quest to Unseat the Biblical Christ* (Nashville: Nelson, 2007), 43–50.

8. Dan Wallace, live presentation at the Day of Discovery in Dallas, in April 2012.

9. Köstenberger and Kruger, *The Heresy of Orthodoxy*, 211.

10. Ehrman, *Misquoting Jesus*, 98.

11. Ibid., 90.

12. Porter, *How We Got the New Testament*, 79.

13. Ehrman, *Misquoting Jesus*, 55.

14. Bock and Wallace, *Dethroning Jesus*, 55–58.

15. Ibid., 70. Briefly, the three most famous (and largest) disputed sections in the New Testament are 1 John 5:7–8; John 8:1–13; and Mark 16:9–20. If you compare the KJV with a more modern version (like the NIV or NASB) you will notice that an explicit reference to the Trinity has been taken out of 1 John 5:7. Notice how the KJV reads "For there are three that bear record in heaven, the Father, the Word, and the Holy Ghost: and these three are one." In contrast, the NIV and NASB read, "For there are three that testify: the Spirit and the water and the blood; and the three are in agreement." The issue at stake here is whether John explicitly intended to teach the Trinity there. Two brief observations. First, the earliest and best manuscripts don't include the Trinitarian reference, so it is very likely not original. Second, the Trinity is clearly taught elsewhere in the NT (e.g., Matthew 28:19–20 and 2 Corinthians 13:14). Regarding the John 8:1–13 passage, skeptics love bringing this verse up because it is such an emotional story (it is the story of the woman caught in adultery). It is a beloved story, but probably *not* originally part of John's Gospel. Also, it probably happened and so scribes tried to find a place for it (i.e., historical but probably not original). Remember this, however; even if it is not authentic, we have plenty of other occasions where we witness Jesus' compassion (e.g., the woman at the well in John 4). Finally, most Christians typically are not as bothered by the possibility of Mark 16:9–20 not being original because that is where the infamous snake handling passages are located. So even if these are not original, no cardinal teaching is affected. These are all the alleged "skeletons in the closet of the New Testament."

16. Bock and Wallace, *Dethroning Jesus*, 60.

17. Gleason L Archer, *A Survey of Old Testament Introduction*, rev. ed.(Chicago: Moody Press, 2007), 25.

18. Paul D. Wegner, *The Journey from Texts to Translations* (Grand Rapids: Baker, 1999), 165.

19. Bruce K. Waltke, "Old Testament Textual Criticism," in *Foundations for Biblical Interpretation: A Complete Library of Tools and Resources*, ed. David S. Dockery, Kenneth A. Matthews, and Robert B. Sloan (Nashville: Broadman & Holman Publishers, 1994), 157–58.

20. Douglas Stuart, "Inerrancy and Textual Criticism," in *Inerrancy and Common Sense*, ed. Roger R. Nicole and J. Ramsey Michaels (Grand Rapids: Baker, 1980), 115–16.

21. Lee Strobel, *The Case for Christ* (Grand Rapids: Zondervan, 1998), 71.

Chapter 7: Are the Gospels Full of Contradictions?

1. As cited in Stephen J. Nichols and Eric T. Brandt, *Ancient Word, Changing Worlds: The Doctrine of Scripture in a Modern Age* (Wheaton, IL: Crossway, 2009), 94.

2. Bart D. Ehrman, *Jesus, Interrupted: Revealing the Hidden Contradictions in the Bible (and Why We Don't Know About Them)* (New York: HarperOne, 2010), 19.

3. Ibid., 59.

4. Darrell L. Bock, "The Words of Jesus in the Gospels: Live, Jive, or Memorex?," in *Jesus under Fire: Modern Scholarship Reinvents the Historical Jesus*, ed. Michael J. Wilkins and J. P. Moreland (Grand Rapids: Zondervan, 1995), 81.

5. Craig L. Blomberg, "Where Do We Start Studying Jesus?," in *Jesus under Fire: Modern Scholarship Reinvents the Historical Jesus*, ed. Michael J. Wilkins and J. P. Moreland (Grand Rapids: Zondervan, 1995), 34–35.

6. Ben Witherington, *New Testament History* (Grand Rapids: Baker, 2001), 18.

7. Blomberg, "Where Do We Start Studying Jesus?," 32.

8. Richard Bauckham, *Jesus and the Eyewitnesses* (Grand Rapids: Eerdmans, 2006), 93.

9. Mark L. Strauss, *Four Portraits, One Jesus* (Grand Rapids: Zondervan, 2007), 28. See especially Richard A. Burridge, *What Are the Gospels?: A Comparison with Graeco-Roman Biography*, 2nd ed. (Grand Rapids: Eerdmans, 2004). For this section, I am relying heavily on the excellent work of Witherington, *New Testament History: A Narrative Account*, 19–27.

10. Darrell L. Bock, "Precision and Accuracy: Making Distinctions in the Cultural Context That Give Us Pause in Pitting the Gospels against Each Other," in *Do Historical Matters Matter to Faith? A Critical Appraisal of Modern and Postmodern Approaches to Scripture*, ed. James K. Hoffmeier and Dennis R. Magary (Wheaton, IL: Crossway, 2012), 368.

11. Witherington, *New Testament History: A Narrative Account*, 24.

12. Ibid., 17.

13. Strauss, *Four Portraits, One Jesus*, 385.

14. To see this distinction in action, see the excellent work of Bock, "Precision and Accuracy: Making Distinctions in the Cultural Context That Give Us Pause in Pitting the Gospels against Each Other."

15. Bock, "The Words of Jesus in the Gospels: Live, Jive, or Memorex?," 77.

16. See Jeremy Howard, ed. *The Holman Apologetics Commentary on the Bible: The Gospels and Acts* (Nashville: B&H Publishing, 2013), 389.

17. This section is shaped by the very helpful discussion in Strauss, *Four Portraits, One Jesus*, 388–97. See also Darrell L. Bock, *Jesus According to Scripture: Restoring the Portrait from the Gospels* (Grand Rapids: Baker, 2002).

18. Howard, *The Holman Apologetics Commentary on the Bible: The Gospels and Acts*, 111–12.

19. Blomberg, "Where Do We Start Studying Jesus?," 35.

20. Howard, *The Holman Apologetics Commentary on the Bible: The Gospels and Acts*, 270–71.

21. Ibid., 44.

22. Ibid., 157.

23. Douglas R. Groothuis, *Christian Apologetics: A Comprehensive Case for Biblical Faith* (Downers Grove, IL: InterVarsity, 2011), 454.

24. J. Warner Wallace, *Cold-Case Christianity: A Homicide Detective Investigates the Claims of the Gospels* (Colorado Springs: David C. Cook, 2013), 132.

25. Blomberg, "Where Do We Start Studying Jesus?," 35.

Chapter 8: Is the Bible Unscientific?

1. John C. Lennox, *Seven Days That Divide the World: The Beginning According to Genesis and Science* (Grand Rapids: Zondervan, 2011), 28–29.

2. Richard Dawkins, *The God Delusion* (Boston: Houghton Mifflin Co., 2008), 187.

3. *The Apologetics Study Bible*, ed. J. P. Moreland, Paul Copan, and Ted Cabal (Nashville: B&H Publishing, 2007), 96.

4. David Hume, "Of Miracles," as cited in *In Defense of Miracles: A Comprehensive Case for God's Action in History*, ed. R. Douglas Geivett and Gary R. Habermas (Downers Grove, IL: InterVarsity, 1997), 33.

5. C. S. Lewis, *Miracles* (New York: Macmillan, 1947), 105.

6. Paul W. Barnett, "Is the New Testament Historically Reliable?," in *In Defense of the Bible: A Comprehensive Apologetics for the Authority of Scripture*, ed. Steven B. Cowan and Terry L. Wilder (Nashville: B&H Academic, 2013), 246–50. See also Graham H. Twelftree, *Jesus the Miracle Worker: A Historical & Theological Study* (Downers Grove, IL: InterVarsity Press, 1999).

7. Sean McDowell, "Did the Apostles Really Die as Martyrs for Their Faith?" *Biola Magazine*, fall 2013.

8. Craig S. Keener, *Miracles: The Credibility of the New Testament Accounts*, vol. 1 (Grand Rapids: Baker, 2011), 557–58.

9. See N. T. Wright, *The Resurrection of the Son of God* (Minneapolis: Fortress Press, 2003); and Michael R. Licona, *The Resurrection of Jesus: A New Historiographical Approach* (Downers Grove, IL: InterVarsity, 2010).

10. See our discussion in Sean McDowell and Jonathan Morrow, *Is God Just a Human Invention?: And Seventeen Other Questions Raised by the New Atheists* (Grand Rapids: Kregel, 2010), 44–56. For a more technical treatment, see John Earman, *Hume's Abject Failure: The Argument against Miracles* (Oxford: Oxford University Press, 2000).

11. William Lane Craig, "God Is Not Dead Yet," *Christianity Today*, July 3, 2008.

12. For an accessible introduction to these arguments, see McDowell and Morrow, *Is God Just a Human Invention?* For an intermediate treatment, see Paul Copan and Paul K. Moser, *The Rationality of Theism* (London: Routledge, 2003); and for an advanced presentation of these arguments, see William Lane Craig and J. P. Moreland, *The Blackwell Companion to Natural Theology* (Malden, MA: Wiley-Blackwell, 2009).

13. Antony Flew and Roy Abraham Varghese, *There Is a God: How the World's Most Notorious Atheist Changed His Mind* (San Francisco: HarperOne, 2007), 88.

14. As quoted in William Lane Craig, *Reasonable Faith: Christian Truth and Apologetics*, 3rd ed. (Wheaton, IL: Crossway, 2008), 238.

15. Paul R. Eddy and Gregory A. Boyd, *The Jesus Legend: A Case for the Historical Reliability of the Synoptic Jesus Tradition* (Grand Rapids, MI: Baker Academic, 2007), 90.

16. Alvin Plantinga, *Where the Conflict Really Lies: Science, Religion, and Naturalism* (New York: Oxford University Press, 2011), 349–50.

17. Lewis, *Miracles*, 110.

18. Stephen T. Davis, "God's Actions," in *In Defense of Miracles: A Comprehensive Case for God's Action in History*, ed. R. Douglas Geivett and Gary R. Habermas (Downers Grove, IL: InterVarsity, 1997), 165.

19. C. John Collins, "Can God's Actions Be Detected Scientifically?," in *The Apologetics Study Bible: Real Questions, Straight Answers, Stronger Faith*, ed. Ted Cabal, J. P. Moreland, and Paul Copan (Nashville: Holman Bible Publishers, 2007), 1003.

20. Ibid.

21. Ibid.

22. John C. Lennox, "Not the God of the Gaps, But the Whole Show," *Christian Post*, August 20, 2012; http://www.christianpost.com/news/the-god-particle-not-the-god-of-the-gaps-but-the-whole-show-80307.

23. This was distilled from the "Report of the Creation Study Committee" of the Presbyterian Church in America (PCA) after they carefully studied this topic in 2000 (cf. http://www.pcahistory.org/creation/report.html#d; and its summary by the organization Reasons to Believe (http://www.reasons .org/articles/four-views-of-the-biblical-creation-account). I think this is an informative, fair—and thankfully brief—summary of the positions. When I teach on this topic, I have found the accompanying chart helpful to students in laying out some of the options available that do not embrace Darwinian evolution or theistic evolution of the kind that assumes neo-Darwinism and just says God did it that way. I don't share these interpretations to endorse a particular view, but I do find that many Christians are unaware of the variety of views held by faithful, inerrancy-affirming, and evangelical scholars. I have added the "major proponents" and "Further Reading" sections and created this table. For the latest viewpoints, see J. Daryl Charles, *Reading Genesis 1–2: An Evangelical Conversation* (Peabody: Hendrickson, 2013).

24. Johnny V. Miller and John M. Soden, *In the Beginning . . . We Misunderstood: Interpreting Genesis 1 in Its Original Context* (Grand Rapids: Kregel, 2012), 138.

25. John Lennox, "Challenges from Science," in *Beyond Opinion: Living the Faith We Defend*, ed. Ravi Zacharias (Nashville: Nelson, 2007), 111.

26. Lennox, *Seven Days That Divide the World*, 15–38.

27. See, for example, Stephen C. Meyer, *Signature in the Cell: DNA and the Evidence for Intelligent Design* (New York: HarperOne, 2009). And also *Darwin's Doubt: The Explosive Origin of Animal Life and the Case for Intelligent Design* (New York: HarperOne, 2013). For more see, http://www. faithandevolution.org/.

28. *The Genesis Debate: Three Views on the Days of Creation*, ed. David G. Hagopian (Mission Viejo, CA: Crux Press, 2001), 18.

Chapter 9: Is the Bible Sexist, Racist, Homophobic, and Genocidal?

1. Timothy J. Keller, *The Reason for God: Belief in an Age of Skepticism* (New York: Dutton, 2008), 108.

2. Richard Dawkins, *The God Delusion* (Boston: Houghton Mifflin, 2008), 31.

3. See Sean McDowell and Jonathan Morrow, *Is God Just a Human Invention?: And Seventeen Other Questions Raised by the New Atheists* (Grand Rapids: Kregel, 2010), 148–55; 172–84; 185–94; 224–36; and Jonathan Morrow, *Think Christianly: Looking at the Intersection of Faith and Culture* (Grand Rapids: Zondervan, 2011), 161–71; 174–83; 216–26.

4. Sam Harris, *Letter to a Christian Nation* (New York: Knopf, 2007), 14.

5. Christopher J. H. Wright, *Old Testament Ethics for the People of God* (Downers Grove, IL: InterVarsity, 2004), 333.

6. *The Apologetics Study Bible for Students*, ed. Sean McDowell (Nashville: B&H Publishing Group, 2010), 1322.

7. For an excellent summary of Wilberforce, see Eric Metaxas, *Seven Men: And the Secret of Their Greatness* (Nashville: Nelson, 2013), 31–56.

8. The ethics of war for Christians are debated. But here are two very helpful treatments: J. Daryl Charles, *Between Pacifism and Jihad: Just War and Christian Tradition* (Downers Grove, IL: InterVarsity, 2005); and Scott B. Rae, *Moral Choices: An Introduction to Ethics*, 3rd ed. (Grand Rapids: Zondervan, 2009), 302–28.

9. Christopher J. H. Wright, *The God I Don't Understand: Reflections on Tough Questions of Faith* (Grand Rapids: Zondervan, 2008), 90.

10. Clay Jones, "We Don't Hate Sin So We Don't Understand What Happened to the Canaanites," *Philosophia Christi* 11, no. 1 (2009): 61.

11. Wright, *The God I Don't Understand*, 92.

12. Ibid.

13. Ibid., 88.

14. Ibid.

15. Paul Copan, *Is God a Moral Monster? Making Sense of the Old Testament God* (Grand Rapids: Baker, 2010), 74.

16. Lisa Miller, "Gay Marriage: Our Mutual Joy," *Newsweek*, December 15, 2008, 19–30.

17. I relied on the helpful discussions in Joe Dallas, *The Gay Gospel? How Pro-Gay Advocates Misread the Bible* (Eugene, OR: Harvest House, 2007), 159–216; Dennis P. Hollinger, *The Meaning of Sex: Christian Ethics and the Moral Life* (Grand Rapids: Baker, 2009), 171–97; and Paul Copan, *When God Goes to Starbucks: A Guide to Everyday Apologetics* (Grand Rapids: Baker, 2008), 77–118. See also Thomas E. Schmidt, *Straight & Narrow?: Compassion and Clarity in the Homosexuality Debate* (Downers Grove, IL: InterVarsity, 1995); and the most thorough biblical study of homosexuality, Robert A. J. Gagnon, *The Bible and Homosexual Practice: Texts and Hermeneutics* (Nashville: Abingdon, 2001).

18. Mark Mittelberg, *The Questions Christians Hope No One Will Ask* (Carol Stream, IL: Tyndale, 2010), 216.

19. Ibid.

20. Alan Shlemon, "Are Homosexuals Born That Way?" Stand to Reason Blog, February 23, 2012; http://str.typepad.com/weblog/2012/02/are-homosexuals-born-that-way.html#_edn2. The APA research can be found at http://www.apa.org/helpcenter/sexual-orientation.aspx#sthash.HEv0FkH8.dpuf.

21. See, for example, Stanton L. Jones and Mark A. Yarhouse, *Ex-Gays?: A Longitudinal Study of Religiously Mediated Change in Sexual Orientation* (Downers Grove, Ill.: InterVarsity, 2007).

22. Alan Shlemon, "Can Gay People Change?" March 7, 2012; http://www.thinkchristianly.org/can-gay-people-change-is-it-psychologically-harmful-to-make-them-try/.

23. Mittelberg, *The Questions Christians Hope No One Will Ask*, 216–17.

24. For an honest look at this struggle, see Wesley Hill, *Washed and Waiting: Reflections on Christian Faithfulness and Homosexuality* (Grand Rapids: Zondervan, 2010).

25. Copan, *Is God a Moral Monster?*, 111.

26. Bruce A. Ware, "Male and Female Complementarity and the Image of God," in *Biblical Foundations for Manhood and Womanhood*, ed. Wayne Grudem (Wheaton, IL: Crossway, 2002), 79.

27. Copan, *Is God a Moral Monster? Making Sense of the Old Testament God*, 101.

28. http://www.preachingtoday.com/illustrations/2010/may/1051010.html.

29. Rodney Stark, *The Rise of Christianity: A Sociologist Reconsiders History* (Princeton, NJ: Princeton University Press, 1996), 102.

30. Alvin J. Schmidt, *How Christianity Changed the World* (Grand Rapids: Zondervan, 2004), 100.

31. Ibid.

32. Ibid., 102.

33. Since the early church, there have been clear examples of power plays, male chauvinism, and bad theology used to subjugate and diminish women throughout church history. Again, these are not consistent with New Testament theology or more importantly the example and teachings of the founder of Christianity, Jesus of Nazareth.

34. Stark, *The Rise of Christianity*, 100.

35. D. M. Scholer, "Women," in *Dictionary of Jesus and the Gospels*, ed. Joel B. Green, Scot McKnight, and I. Howard Marshall (Downers Grove, IL: InterVarsity, 1992), 886.

Chapter 10: What Do Christians Believe about the Bible?

1. Erik Thoennes, *Life's Biggest Questions* (Wheaton, IL: Crossway, 2011), 41–42.

2. Ibid., 30.

3. Bruce Demarest, "General Revelation," in *Evangelical Dictionary of Theology*, ed. Walter A. Elwell (Grand Rapids: Baker, 2001), 1019–21.

4. John R. W. Stott, *Understanding the Bible* (Grand Rapids: Zondervan, 1999), 159. For a possible way this might have been accomplished according to God's foreknowledge and while retaining the freedom of the human authors, see William Lane Craig, " 'Men Moved by the Holy Spirit Spoke from God' 2 Peter 1:21: A Middle Knowledge Perspective on Biblical Inspiration"; http://www.reasonablefaith.org/men-moved-by-the-holy-spirit-spoke-from-god#ixzz2pAcBG6oI. He summarizes, "It seems to me that the traditional doctrine of the plenary, verbal, confluent inspiration of Scripture is a coherent doctrine, given divine middle knowledge. Because

God knew the relevant counterfactuals of creaturely freedom, He was able to decree a world containing just those circumstances and persons such that the authors of Scripture would freely compose their respective writings, which God intended to be His gracious Word to us. In the providence of God, the Bible is thus both the Word of God and the word of man."

5. Ibid., 158.

6. Millard J. Erickson, *Introducing Christian Doctrine*, 2nd ed. (Grand Rapids: Baker, 2001), 72.

7. See Douglas K. Blount, "What Does It Mean to Say That the Bible Is True," in *In Defense of the Bible: A Comprehensive Apologetic for the Authority of Scripture*, ed. Steven B. Cowan and Terry L. Wilder (Nashville: B&H Publishing, 2013), 55–56.

8. David S. Dockery, *Christian Scripture: An Evangelical Perspective on Inspiration, Authority, and Interpretation* (Nashville: Broadman & Holman, 1995), 64.

9. Dr. Blount's work is very helpful and I am relying on it for the basic outline of my discussion of inerrancy. See ibid., 55–60.

10. Gregory Koukl, *Tactics: A Game Plan for Discussing Your Christian Convictions* (Grand Rapids: Zondervan, 2009), 44.

11. Stott, *Understanding the Bible*, 158.

12. *Inerrancy*, ed. Norman L. Geisler (Grand Rapids: Zondervan, 1980), 500.

13. I think some aspects of "speech act theory" might help us with our categories in biblical discussions (with appropriate qualifications). I was first exposed to this as a possibility through classes and email correspondence with Dr. Garry DeWeese of Talbot School of Theology. Michael Kruger has applied them to the canonical context: "These three definitions of canon can be further illuminated by modern discussions in speech-act philosophy. Speaking (and therefore divine speaking) can take three different forms: (1) locution (making coherent and meaningful sounds or, in the case of writing, letters); (2) illocution (what the words are actually doing; e.g., promising, warning, commanding, declaring, etc.); and (3) perlocution (the effect of these words on the listener; e.g., encouraging, challenging, persuading). Any speaking act can include some or all of these attributes. These three types of speech-acts generally correspond to the three definitions of canon outlined in the self-authenticating model. The ontological definition of canon refers to the actual writing of these books in redemptive history and thus refers to a locutionary act. The functional definition refers to what the canonical books do as authoritative documents and thus refers to an illocutionary act. And the exclusive definition refers to the reception and impact of these books on the church and thus envisions a perlocutionary act." From Michael J. Kruger, *Canon Revisited: Establishing the Origins and Authority of the New Testament Books* (Wheaton, IL: Crossway, 2012), 119–20. I think they can be applied in the context of inspiration (locution), inerrancy (illocution), and infallibility (perlocution). But more work is needed here and it is beyond the scope of this book to dive any further. I must leave it to the motivated reader to do some more digging (and of course any errors in applying these categories remain my own and should not be applied to Dr. Garry DeWeese).

14. I appreciate the insights of Erik Thoennes on the clarity of Scripture in Thoennes, *Life's Biggest Questions: What the Bible Says About the Things That Matter Most*, 44.

15. Ibid., 45.

Chapter 11: Which Interpretation of the Bible Is Correct?

1. James Packer, "Hermeneutics and Biblical Authority"; www.biblicalstudies .org.uk/ article_herm_packer.html.

2. After six years as the equipping pastor at Fellowship Bible Church, Murfreesboro, Tennessee, I joined the staff of the Impact 360 Institute, where I teach and interact with college students at a fully accredited nine-month residential gap-year program for eighteen- to twenty-year-olds. (Learn more at www.impact360institute.org.)

3. Three resources I would recommend for high school and college students are Jonathan Morrow, *Welcome to College: A Christ-Follower's Guide for the Journey* (Grand Rapids: Kregel, 2008); Paul Copan, *True for You, but Not for Me: Overcoming Objections to Christian Faith*, rev. ed. (Minneapolis: Bethany House, 2009); and *The Apologetics Study Bible for Students*, ed. Sean McDowell (Nashville: B&H Publishing, 2010).

4. Paul Copan, *That's Just Your Interpretation: Responding to Skeptics Who Challenge Your Faith* (Grand Rapids: Baker, 2001), 31.

5. Copan, *True for You, but Not for Me*, 32. Copan's insights are very helpful and I have summarized some of them for you in this section.

6. J. P. Moreland, "Truth, Contemporary Philosophy, and the Postmodern Turn," *Journal of the Evangelical Theological Society* 48, no. 1 (2005): 81–82.

7. William Dembski, "The Fallacy of Contextualism," in *Unapologetic Apologetics: Meeting the Challenges of Theological Studies*, ed. William A. Dembski and Jay Wesley Richards (Downers Grove, IL: InterVarsity, 2001), 46.

8. Christian Smith, *The Bible Made Impossible: Why Biblicism Is Not a Truly Evangelical Reading of Scripture* (Grand Rapids: Brazos, 2012), 26.

9. See the (successful in my view) critiques of Smith's work by Robert H. Gundry, "Smithereens!," *Books & Culture*, September/October 2011; and Kevin DeYoung "Christian Smith Makes the Bible Impossible," The Gospel Coalition blog, August 2, 2011, at http://thegospelcoalition.org/blogs/kevin-deyoung/2011/08/02/christian-smith-makes-the-bible-impossible/. Also see DeYoung's follow-up blog entitled "Those Tricksy Biblicists," September 1, 2011, at http://thegospelcoalition.org/blogs/kevindeyoung/2011/09/01/those-tricksy-biblicists/.

10. Erik Thoennes, *Life's Biggest Questions: What the Bible Says About the Things That Matter Most* (Wheaton, IL: Crossway, 2011), 44.

11. While there are finer points that can and need to be addressed, the heart of the matter is that when people talk of language games and communities, they are universalizing these claims. In other words, they think their interpretations are global (for everyone) and not just local (for individuals or cultures). And if they can make claims that can be understood and argued about, then maybe language refers to something after all—namely, facts in our world that we must all make sense of and account for. They smuggle in the belief that

their interpretation of reality is superior, and this is self-refuting in nature.

12. R. Scott Smith, *Truth & the New Kind of Christian: The Emerging Effects of Postmodernism in the Church* (Wheaton, IL: Crossway, 2005), 83.

13. J. Scott Duvall and J. Daniel Hays, *Grasping God's Word: A Hands-on Approach to Reading, Interpreting, and Applying the Bible*, 3rd ed. (Grand Rapids: Zondervan, 2012), 41.

14. Ibid., 149.

15. Ben Witherington, *The Living Word of God: Rethinking the Theology of the Bible* (Waco, TX: Baylor University Press, 2007), 70.

16. Duvall and Hays, *Grasping God's Word*, 150.

17. Howard G. Hendricks and William D. Hendricks, *Living by the Book: The Art and Science of Reading the Bible* (Chicago: Moody, 2007), 39.

18. Duvall and Hays, *Grasping God's Word*, 45.

19. Ibid., 47.

20. Hendricks and Hendricks, *Living by the Book*, 308.

21. Ibid., 293.

22. Duvall and Hays, *Grasping God's Word*, 232.

Conclusion: What If a New Generation Took the Bible Seriously?

1. Eric Metaxas, *Seven Men: And the Secret of Their Greatness* (Nashville: Nelson, 2013), 86.

2. Ibid., 80.

3. Ibid., 85–86.

4. N. T. Wright, *The New Testament and the People of God* (Minneapolis: Fortress Press, 1992).

5. For more on how to engage our cultural moments, see Jonathan Morrow, *Think Christianly: Looking at the Intersection of Faith and Culture* (Grand Rapids: Zondervan, 2011).

Appendix 1: A Noncircular Argument for the Bible as God's Word

1. William Lane Craig, *Reasonable Faith: Christian Truth and Apologetics*, 3rd ed. (Wheaton, IL: Crossway, 2008), 29–62.

2. Steven B. Cowan, Five Views on Apologetics (Grand Rapids: Zondervan, 2000), 28.

3. In this case, while it is not rationally necessary, perhaps it becomes psychologically necessary to respond. In other words, you are still rational because God's testimony to you as you read his Word is sufficient. But since his is now not the only voice you hear concerning the Bible, then in order to experience confidence in the Bible as God's Word, it may become necessary from time to time to respond to objections. In the presence of defeaters (like those raised and responded to in this book) we need to be able to know that there are some reasonable answers out there. If you are the kind of person who tends to fixate on things, then it may be psychologically helpful for you to review the reasons you can trust Scripture or the responses against common objections so that you can experience confidence. But while this is psychologically helpful, it is not rationally necessary for you to always

do so. Remember, just because it is possible you could be mistaken in
your belief that the Bible is the Word of God, it does not follow that you
are mistaken.

4. For more on this point and how it relates to the discussion concerning
knowledge, see Alvin Plantinga, *Warranted Christian Belief* (Oxford: Oxford
University Press, 2000). Because of space constraints, I can't say more
here. But if it is reasonable to believe that God exists, then the account
of how I know the Bible is true is perfectly rational and would require an
argument against it to defeat it. See also C. Stephen Evans, *The Historical
Christ and the Jesus of Faith: The Incarnational Narrative as History*
(Oxford: Oxford University Press, 1996), 268–69. To explore the evidence
for God, see Sean McDowell and Jonathan Morrow, *Is God Just a Human
Invention?: And Seventeen Other Questions Raised by the New Atheists*
(Grand Rapids, MI: Kregel Publications, 2010).

5. This is a point made and defended in Craig, *Reasonable Faith*, 57.

6. I am glad to see more people making use of this argument. See especially
Gary R. Habermas, "Jesus and the Inspiration of Scripture," *Areopagus
Journal* 2, no. 1 (2002); and Steven B. Cowan, "Is the Bible the Word
of God?," in *In Defense of the Bible: A Comprehensive Apologetic for the
Authority of Scripture*, ed. Steven B. Cowan and Terry L. Wilder (B&H, 2013).

7. Books have been written on each of these topics. My goal here is simply to
present the argument as a whole and summarize the reasons for it.

8. "When presenting the evidence for the Resurrection, let's stick to the
topic of Jesus' resurrection. This means that we do not digress into a side
discussion on the reliability of the Bible. While we hold that the Bible is
trustworthy and inspired, we cannot expect the skeptical nonbeliever with
whom we are dialoguing to embrace this view. So, in order to avoid a
discussion that may divert us off of our most important topic, we would
like to suggest that we adopt a 'minimal facts approach.' From Gary R.
Habermas and Michael R. Licona, *The Case for the Resurrection of Jesus*
(Grand Rapids: Kregel Publications, 2004), 44. For more on this approach,
see Habermas and Licona, 44–45. For a more exhaustive treatment of
the evidence, see Michael R. Licona, *The Resurrection of Jesus: A New
Historiographical Approach* (Downers Grove, IL: InterVarsity, 2010).

9. N. T. Wright, *The Resurrection of the Son of God* (Minneapolis: Fortress
Press, 2003), 710.

10. I owe this and the next two insights to John R. W. Stott, *Understanding the
Bible*, exp. ed. (Grand Rapids: Zondervan, 1999), chap. 6.

11. Habermas, "Jesus and the Inspiration of Scripture," 15.

12. This section was adapted from my work in McDowell and Morrow, *Is God
Just a Human Invention*, 266–70.

Appendix 2: Archaeology and the Historical Reliability of the Bible

1. Joseph M. Holden and Norman Geisler, *The Popular Handbook of
Archaeology and the Bible* (Eugene, OR: Harvest House, 2013), 202.

2. Ibid., 200.

3. Mark L. Strauss, *Four Portraits, One Jesus: An Introduction to Jesus and the*

Gospels (Grand Rapids: Zondervan, 2007), 386. See also Colin J. Hemer, *The Book of Acts in the Setting of Hellenistic History* (Tübingen: Mohr, 1989).

4. For a list of these eighty-four facts documented by historian Colin Hemer, see Norman L. Geisler and Frank Turek, *I Don't Have Enough Faith to Be an Atheist* (Wheaton, IL: Crossway, 2004), 256–59.

5. Holden and Geisler, *The Popular Handbook of Archaeology and the Bible*, 291.

6. Ibid., 292.

7. Ibid., 200.

8. Ibid., 255–56.

9. Ibid., 345–47.

10. Walter C. Kaiser and Duane A. Garrett, eds., *Archaeological Study Bible* (Grand Rapids: Zondervan, 2005), 1115.

11. Holden and Geisler, *The Popular Handbook of Archaeology and the Bible*, 363.

12. Ibid., 348–50.

13. John McRay, "*Archaeology and the Bible: How Archaeological Findings Have Enhanced the Credibility of the Bible*," in *Evidence for God: 50 Arguments for Faith from the Bible, History, Philosophy, and Science*, ed. William A. Dembski and Michael R. Licona (Grand Rapids: Baker, 2010), 225.

14. Holden and Geisler, *The Popular Handbook of Archaeology and the Bible*, 310.

15. Ibid., 360.

16. Ibid., 363.

17. Ibid., 293.

Appendix 3: Why a New Generation Doesn't Take the Bible Seriously

1. Thom S. Rainer and Jess W. Rainer, *The Millennials: Connecting to America's Largest Generation* (Nashville: B&H Books), 244.

2. David Kinnaman, *You Lost Me: Why Young Christians Are Leaving Church . . . And Rethinking Faith* (Grand Rapids: Baker Books, 2011), 52.

3. Rainer and Rainer, *The Millennials*, 244.

4. "Religion Among the Millennials," February 17, 2010, Pew Research Religion & Public Life Project. The project findings also noted, "Less than half of young evangelicals interpret the Bible literally (47%), compared with 61% of evangelicals 30 and older." From http://www.pewforum.org/uploadedFiles/Topics/Demographics/Age/millennials-report.pdf.

5. Sean McDowell and I have responded to their challenges to belief in God in our book *Is God Just a Human Invention?* (Grand Rapids: Kregel, 2010).

6. So categorized in a 2009 survey by the research unit of LifeWay Christian Resources and cited in John Blake, CNN, June 9, 2010; http://articles.cnn.com/2010/LIVING/personal/06/03/spiritual.but.not.religious/index.html.

7. Rainer and Rainer, *The Millennials*, 242.

8. Ibid., 244.

9. Bart D. Ehrman, *Misquoting Jesus: The Story About Who Changed the Bible and Why* (New York: HarperOne, 2006), 98.

10. The main force driving this is marketing. But it's easy to see how this can be abused if the people setting the algorithms deem certain questions unworthy of being asked or certain worldviews unworthy of being investigated.

11. Eric Schmidt, former CEO of Google, has said, "It will be very hard for people to watch or consume something that has not in some sense been tailored for them." See Holman W. Jenkins, "Google and the Search for the Future," *Wall Street Journal*, August 14, 2010.

12. See Neil Gross and Solon Simmons, "How Religious Are America's College and University Professors?" February 6, 2007, Social Science Research Council; http://religion.ssrc.org/reforum/Gross_Simmons.pdf (accessed February 27, 2012).

ACKNOWLEDGMENTS

This book has been several years in the making, and I am excited to now publish it to our readers. May reading it give you confidence that God really has spoken.

As always, there are so many people to thank. First and foremost, I want to thank my wonderful wife, Mandi. Without her support, love, sacrifice, and encouragement, this would not have been possible. I would also like to thank my children Austin, Sarah, Beth, and Madison for their patience and encouragement as Dad had to take extra time to write. Next, I would like to thank all of my professors who have shaped my perspective on these issues—specifically Garry DeWeese, J. P. Moreland, and Darrell Bock.

I would also like to thank so many friends who have helped, encouraged, and supported me along the way. Special thanks to Jay Watts, Mark Schmahl, Cole Huffman, and Rex Johnson for reading earlier versions of the manuscript.

Lastly, I would like to thank the talented team at Moody Publishers for giving me this opportunity and bringing this book to fruition.

To God be the glory.

APPENDIX 1
A NONCIRCULAR ARGUMENT
FOR THE BIBLE AS GOD'S WORD

Everything changed during my junior year of high school; that is when I became a follower of Jesus Christ. I vividly remember staying up late in my room reading the Bible and trying to discover the truth about life—after all, these were God's words! As I read page after page, the words were food to my soul. I didn't have the categories for this at the time, but I simply recognized God's familiar voice as I read the Bible.

It wasn't until college when I took the course Bible as Literature that I began to encounter challenges and doubts about the Bible being God's Word (by the way, these challenges in seedling form are the questions I wanted to address in this book). But over time and through careful study, I found reasonable and satisfying answers to my questions.

Two crucial questions emerged during my study. First, How do I know that the Bible is the Word of God? And second, How do I help others come to see that the Bible is the Word of God (who don't already accept its authority)?

How Do I Know the Bible Is True?

I think a distinction made by Christian philosopher William Lane Craig between *knowing* and *showing* provides a helpful way forward.[1] Here is the distinction stated:

> Reason in the form of rational arguments and evidence plays an essential role in our showing Christianity to be true, whereas reason in this form plays a contingent and secondary role in our personally knowing Christianity to be true. The proper ground of our knowing Christianity to be true is the inner work of the Holy Spirit in our individual selves; and in our showing Christianity to be true, it is his role to open the hearts of unbelievers to assent and respond to the reasons we present.[2]

The Bible teaches that a believer knows Christianity is true on the basis of the internal witness of the Holy Spirit (Romans 8:16; Galatians 4:6; 1 John 3:24; 4:13). When a person trusts in Jesus Christ for his or her salvation, God sends his Holy Spirit to permanently live within each of us (John 14:16–17, 20; 1 Corinthians 1:21; Ephesians 1:13–14). God's Spirit then testifies to our spirit that we are his children. In other words, God lets us know directly—without spoken or written words—that we belong to him, that Jesus Christ has forgiven our sins, and that we have been reconciled to God.

I think this kind of approach also explains why our belief in the Bible as the Word of God is properly basic. A properly basic belief is one that is not based on other beliefs—it's the ground floor or foundation. For example, take my belief that there is a tree in front of me. This belief is not based on any other beliefs because I am just directly aware of the tree in front of me and in this sense it is properly basic. I can't get underneath or behind this belief to a better explanation. If my cognitive faculties (my thinking equipment) are functioning properly, then in the appropriate circumstances (namely, a tree being front of me), I will naturally form that belief. No further explanation is needed.

The source of justification in the case of the Bible is testimony—the very testimony of God. And it is being directly aware of this testimony that provides the appropriate circumstances for my properly basic belief that the Bible is the Word of God to be formed. It's important to point out that while my properly basic belief that the Bible is the Word of God is indeed rational, it is also defeasible. Let's unpack this some more. By rational, I simply mean that it is intellectually *permissible* for you to believe something (e.g., that Alexander the Great existed or that you really do see a tree in front of you). In other words, you have *adequate* reasons to believe. To be *defeasible* simply means it is possible for this belief to be defeated or shown to be false.

However, just because it is possible that you could be mistaken about your belief, it does not follow that you are mistaken (the skeptic does not carry the day because of the mere possibility of error).[3] All of this is perfectly rational—if God exists.[4]

How Do I Show the Bible Is True?

If the discussion above is accurate, then an individual doesn't have to have additional arguments and evidence in order to be rational in her belief that the Bible is God's Word. But perhaps our Muslim friends could argue the same way concerning the Q'uran. How do we decide between the two? At this point I think it is important to provide an argument that is publicly accessible and not circular. For example, we want to avoid arguments like the following: "The Bible is the Word of God because Jesus Christ (who was God) said it was and we know that Jesus Christ said it was because the Bible, God's Word, says so."

Regarding the publicly accessible argument, the good news is that believers and unbelievers share the common ground of the laws of logic and the facts of experience (and this would include historical evidence or testimony).[5] Here is an example of a way to argue (inductively) that the Bible is the Word of God from the authority of Jesus of Nazareth.[6]

The Publicly Accessible Argument Summarized

1. Jesus of Nazareth claimed to be God.
2. God authenticated the claims of Jesus of Nazareth by raising him from the dead.
3. Jesus of Nazareth taught the divine inspiration of Scripture (i.e., he endorsed the Old Testament and made provision for the New Testament).
4. Therefore, since Jesus of Nazareth is divine, then his endorsements of the Old and New Testaments carry the very authority of God.

The Publicly Accessible Argument Defended and Explained[7]

1. Jesus of Nazareth claimed to be God.

A. In Jesus' words and actions we clearly see his radical claims to the kind of authority that God alone possess. (It is also important to highlight that those around him clearly understood the message because of how they responded to these radical claims.)

(1) Jesus' authority to announce the inauguration of the kingdom of God (Mark 1:14–15).

(2) Jesus' authority over disease, demons, and nature is demonstrated in his miracles (Matthew 11:2–5; Luke 11:20; Mark 4:39–41).

(3) Jesus' authority to speak for God in his teaching (Matthew 7:28–29).

(4) Jesus' authority over the Law and the Sabbath (Mark 2:27–28; 10:1–12).

(5) Jesus' authority to forgive sins (Mark 2:1–12).

(6) Jesus' authority over the final judgment (Luke 12:8–9; Psalm 9:8; Isaiah 2:4).

B. In Jesus' use of divine titles we see his radical self-understanding.

(1) Jesus as the Messiah (Zechariah 9:9; Mark 15:26)

(2) Jesus as the Son of God (Matthew 11:27 (cf. Mark 12:1–9; Isaiah 5:1–7)

(3) Jesus as the Son of Man (Daniel 7:13–14; Mark 14:61–62)

2. God authenticated the radical claims of Jesus of Nazareth by raising him from the dead.

A. By adopting a "minimal facts" approach, we can then make a historical case for resurrection that does not rely on accepting the Bible as the Word of God (thus avoiding the charge of circular reasoning). There are at least five facts that must be accounted for by anyone who investigates the historical evidence for the resurrection of Jesus.[8]

(1) Jesus died by Roman crucifixion.

(2) Jesus' disciples claimed that he rose and appeared to them.

(3) The Christian persecutor Saul was radically changed to chief proclaimer of the Christian faith.

(4) The skeptic James, brother of Jesus, was suddenly changed and became a leader in the Christian movement.

(5) Jesus' tomb was found empty.

    (a) Jerusalem Factor. The last place to invent the idea that Jesus was raised from the dead is Jerusalem, where it could be most easily disproved by producing the body and where Roman government and Jewish religious leaders wanted to end the movement.

    (b) Enemy Attestation. The Jewish leadership initiated a cover-up by telling the guards to say that the disciples had come in the night and stolen Jesus' body. If there were a body in the tomb, then there would be no need to create a cover story (Matthew 28:11–15).

    (c) The Testimony of Women. In the ancient world the legal testimony of women was not taken seriously if it was even considered at all and yet all four Gospels record the empty tomb being discovered by a group of Jesus' women followers. The Gospel writers would not make up such a "witness list" (the criterion of embarrassment)—yet they include the women.

    d) **Conclusion:** *"We are left with the secure historical conclusion: the tomb was empty. . . . I regard this conclusion as coming in the same category, of historical probability so high as to be virtually certain, as the death of Augustus in AD 14 or the fall of Jerusalem in AD 70."*[9]

B. The preaching by Peter in the earliest days following the public crucifixion of Jesus of Nazareth makes explicit the belief that God authenticated his words and works in the resurrection: "Let all the house of Israel therefore know for certain that God has made him both Lord and Christ, this Jesus whom you crucified" (Acts 2:36; cf. Romans 1:3–4).

3. **Jesus of Nazareth taught the divine inspiration and authority of Scripture.**

A. Jesus clearly recognized the authority of the Old Testament.

(1) Jesus affirmed the permanence, comprehensiveness, and precision of the Old Testament, "Do not think that

I have come to abolish the Law or the Prophets; I have not come to abolish them but to fulfill them. For truly, I say to you, until heaven and earth pass away, not an iota, not a dot, will pass from the Law until all is accomplished" (Matthew 5:17–18).

(2) Jesus affirmed the divine origin and inspiration of even the particular words used in the Old Testament: "As Jesus taught in the temple, he said, 'How can the scribes say that the Christ is the son of David? David himself, in the Holy Spirit, declared, "The Lord said to my Lord, 'Sit at my right hand, until I put your enemies under your feet.'" David himself calls him Lord. So how is he his son?'" (Mark 12:35–37).

(3) Jesus lived under the moral authority of Old Testament Scripture.[10] When he was tempted in the wilderness by Satan, he appealed to the fixed and final Word of God, "The devil said to him, 'If you are the Son of God, command this stone to become bread.' And Jesus answered him, 'It is written, "Man shall not live by bread alone"'" (Luke 4:3–4). This issue is settled because God had already spoken.

(4) Jesus submitted to his God-given mission as revealed in the Old Testament. First, at the age of twelve, Jesus understood that he must be about his father's business— this was part of his messianic mission (Luke 2:49). Later in his ministry, he understood that he "must suffer many things and be rejected by the elders and the chief priests and the scribes and be killed, and after three days rise again" (Mark 8:31). Jesus voluntarily submitted to messianic mission revealed in the Old Testament Scriptures (cf. Luke 24:25–27).

(5) During his public debates with the Jewish leaders of the day, he appealed to the Hebrew Scriptures to settle the matter. On one occasion, he criticized them for neglecting the revealed commandments of God in favor of their invented human traditions (Mark 7:8). On another occasion, Jesus "said to them, 'Is this not the reason you are wrong, because you know neither the Scriptures nor the power of God?'" (Mark 12:24). The not-so-subtle implication is that God had already addressed this one!

B. Jesus provided for the New Testament.

   (1) Jesus appointed and equipped his apostles to be his authoritative witnesses and spokesmen in the world (Luke 6:13; cf. Acts 1:8). The apostles were eyewitnesses of the risen Jesus and the authorized ministers of the New Covenant (2 Corinthians 3:6).

   (2) Jesus promised his apostles the unique inspiration and guidance of the Holy Spirit: "But the Helper, the Holy Spirit, whom the Father will send in my name, he will teach you all things and bring to your remembrance all that I have said to you" (John 14:26). The Holy Spirit would complete what Jesus was not yet able to teach the apostles during his earthly ministry (cf. John 16:12–13).

   (3) The apostles understood that they were speaking and writing with the authority of Jesus himself (cf. Galatians 4:14–15; Ephesians 2:20; Hebrew 2:3–4; 1 Thessalonians 2:13; 1 Peter 1:12; 2 Peter 3:2). Moreover the early church recognized this as well (see our discussion in chapter 4).

4. Therefore, since Jesus of Nazareth is divine, his endorsement of the Old and New Testaments carry the very authority of God. Gary Habermas provides a helpful summary of the publically accessible argument we have been making in this appendix, "Using both traditional and critical paths to determine that Jesus firmly taught inspiration, we may reassert . . . that if God raised Jesus from the dead, then the most likely reason was to confirm the truthfulness of Jesus' teachings. If we are correct in this, then the inspiration of Scripture follows as a verified doctrine, affirmed by God Himself when He raised Jesus from the dead."[11]

What to Do When You Have Doubts about the Bible

Doubt is a natural part of being human because part of what it means to be human is to have limitations. Every one of us, including our skeptical friends, has limitations in energy, time, and even knowledge. We all experience doubts at one time or another simply because we *cannot* know everything about everything. So be encouraged; you are not alone. But in order to live with our doubts in a spiritually healthy and faith-building way, we need to be clear about what doubt is and isn't.

To doubt means to be between two minds or opinions. It is the middle ground between faith and unbelief. There is a big difference between *struggling to believe* in God and *setting oneself against* God. A helpful way to understand faith and doubt is to think about the dashboard in your car. When no warning lights are on, things are working pretty well. But when the check engine light comes on, you know there's a problem. However, this light indicates there could be *several different* problems, but you won't know which problem it is until you go to a mechanic to have your car hooked up to a diagnostic reader. Doubt is like the warning lights on your dashboard. Just as you wouldn't address all the warning lights in the same way (e.g., changing the oil every time the gas light comes on), you also need to recognize that each kind of doubt will require a unique approach.

The most common forms of doubt concerning the Bible originate from intellectual issues, emotional issues, and lack of spiritual growth. Here are some suggestions about how to deal with these.

Regarding *intellectual doubts*, the most important thing you can do is to become very clear and specific concerning what your question or doubt actually is. The longer it remains foggy, the harder it is to address. It's often helpful to dig through your thoughts with others to get at the root intellectual issue or question. Of all the varieties of doubt, intellectual doubt is the one that is best helped by reading and study. You must be persistent. If something is really bothering you, work at finding a *reasonable* answer. Reflect on the evidence discussed in this book and read the books recommended at the end of each chapter.

Sometimes *emotional doubts* look like intellectual ones, but the root cause turns out to be something other than unanswered questions. Sources of emotional doubts can be experiencing disappointment, failure, pain, or loss; having unresolved conflict or wounds from the past that need to be addressed; letting unruly emotions carry us away for no good reason; being spiritually dry and relationally distant; and fearing to truly commit to someone (whether that "someone" be God or another person). Emotions are good and normal but they aren't always right.

In other words, they are an accurate barometer of what is going on inside our hearts, but they don't tell us whether we should or shouldn't be feeling the way we are. Emotions need to be examined. So you may be emotionally drained after a long week or a conflict with a friend, but that shouldn't impact your confidence that the New Testament is reliable or that Jesus was who he claimed to be. What happens is that our emotions get projected onto an intellectual question, and it becomes really easy to confuse the two. Be on the lookout for this.

Finally, we can experience *doubts concerning the Bible due to lack of spiritual growth* or our moral disobedience to a command God has revealed in Scripture. If you are a follower of Jesus, then it is always good to ask yourself if you are growing spiritually. Are you reading your Bible on a regular basis, praying, sharing your faith, and living in community with others? (Not in a legalistic, "God will love me more if . . ." sort of way, but because these are necessary ingredients for spiritual growth.) Also, when we sin and are disobedient to God, our sin creates relational distance from him. God doesn't love us any less and we aren't at risk of losing our salvation, but we may need to ask him to show us if we need to confess anything so that our fellowship with him can be restored. A great prayer to meditate on is Psalm 139:23–24 (NIV): "Search me, O God, and know my heart; test me and know my anxious thoughts. See if there is any offensive way in me, and lead me in the way everlasting."

What I have attempted to show in this book is that even when we ask hard questions of the Bible, there are solid answers. So whatever flavor of doubt you may be currently experiencing, be sure to invite a Christ-following friend or mentor into it (cf. 2 Timothy 2:22). Don't make the well-traveled mistake of isolating from the very people who can help you walk through these difficult times. Remember, if you find yourself with doubts, you're in good company. But having the courage to doubt your doubts and investigate the root of these issues over time will lead to greater confidence as a follower of Jesus. This is what the journey of faith is all about.[12]

APPENDIX 2
ARCHAEOLOGY AND THE HISTORICAL
RELIABILITY OF THE BIBLE

In the summer of 2006 the biblical world came alive for me. Until that time, I had read the Bible and books about the Bible, but then I had the opportunity to travel to Israel and Jordan and experience the Bible firsthand. I walked through the same streets in Jerusalem that Jesus of Nazareth walked two thousand years earlier.

I walked through Hezekiah's eighth-century-BC tunnel (1,750 feet long) and then visited the pool of Siloam right next to it. I stood outside the Garden tomb and walked where Jesus likely gave the Sermon on the Mount. My point in sharing all of this is simple—this is real! The Bible is not a fairy tale that begins with "a long time ago in a land far, far away." Rather it has earthy details in it like, "In the fifteenth year of the reign of Tiberius Caesar, Pontius Pilate being governor of Judea, and Herod being tetrarch of Galilee, and his brother Philip tetrarch of the region of Ituraea and Trachonitis, and Lysanias tetrarch of Abilene, during the high priesthood of Annas and Caiaphas, the word of God came to John the son of Zechariah in the wilderness" (Luke 3:1–2).

Even though archaeology is a relatively young discipline (nineteenth century), it has yielded many important discoveries that have unlocked ancient cultures to us. For our purposes, archaeology serves as a signpost that points to the historical reliability of the Bible. For example, it would be strange if we never found any of the cities mentioned in the Bible. But, as Holden and Geisler point out, "Today, all the major biblical cities and geographical features have been located, including Jerusalem, Jericho, the Sea of Galilee, the Galilee region, the Dead Sea, the Jordan river, Caesarea, Dan, Caesarea Philippi, Beth Shan, Gezer, Hazor, Beersheba, Megiddo, Memphis, Alexandria, Luxor, Thebes, Babylon, Nineveh, Athens, Thessalonica, Corinth, Rome, Ephesus, Philippi, Smyrna, and dozens more."[1] To date, over sixty biblical figures in the Old Testament have been identified.[2] Moreover, Luke has been recognized as a first-rate historian. Mark Strauss notes:

> Particularly striking is Luke's attention to historical detail, providing names of cities and titles of government officials, which are accurate for both time and place. This is especially significant since such names changed frequently. For example, Luke accurately identifies Sergius Paulus as *anthypatos* ("proconsul") of Cyprus (Acts 13:7) and Publius as the *protos* (something like "the first man" = governor) of Melita (Acts 28:7). City officials are *strategoi* in Philippi (Acts 16:20), *politarchi* in Thessalonica (Acts 17:6), and *asiarchai* in Ephesus (Acts 19:31), all historically accurate designations. This would be like someone accurately distinguishing titles like supervisor, councilor, mayor, governor, senator, representative, speaker of the house, vice president, and president. . . . If Luke was so meticulous with these kinds of details in Acts, he was surely also careful in his research and writing about the Jesus tradition.[3]

All told, eighty-four facts have been confirmed in the final sixteen chapters of Acts alone![4]

We need to be careful not to overstate the importance of archaeology— to claim that these discoveries demonstrate the absolute inerrancy of the Bible beyond any doubt. We should also not underreport the archaeological confirmation that does exist. There have been at least two major contributions that archaeology has had relating to the New Testament. First, "the discovery of cities and landmarks described in the New Testament has firmly secured the historical-geographical reliability and setting for the New Testament narratives, which supports the believability of the doctrines that grow out of them."[5] And second, "archaeological data has helped limit the critical theories that dismiss the New Testament as mythological; instead, the data has placed the biblical text squarely within a historical framework."[6] External support for biblical people, places, and events is important and should encourage our faith. However it would be a mistake to assume that something mentioned in the Bible is not historical *unless* it is corroborated by an external source. In other words, the "lack of archaeological data relating to the Bible is not evidence against the historicity of the Bible."[7]

Here are just some of the biblically significant archaeological discoveries:

- **The Tel Dan Stele.** In 1994 a stele (inscribed stone) was discovered that "contains the first extrabiblical mention of David, thus confirming the historicity of the biblical king." The inscription reads "House of David" (cf. 2 Samuel 7:8–17).[8]

- **The Pontius Pilate Inscription.** In 1961 a stone inscription was discovered that dates from AD 26–37 and corroborates references in Matthew 27:2; Mark 15:1–15; Luke 23:1–5; John 18:28–19:16.[9]

- **The Great Isaiah Scroll.** Part of the Dead Sea Scrolls discovery in 1947, this is the earliest complete scroll of Isaiah, which dates to ca. 125–150 BC. This confirmed the accuracy with which ancient scribes copied the Hebrew Scriptures.[10]

- **Pool of Siloam.** In 2005 workers excavating near the Gihon Spring "accidentally unearthed the steps to the Pool of Siloam" that Jesus referred to in John 9:7.[11]

- **Caiaphas the High Priest.** In 1990 an ornate ossuary bearing the Aramaic inscription "Joseph, son of Caiaphas" was discovered. While we can't be 100 percent certain this is authentic, it is probable that it refers to the Caiaphas who was the high priest during the death of Jesus of Nazareth (Matthew 26:3, 57; Luke 3:2; John 11:49; 18:13–14, 24, 28; Acts 4:6).[12]

- **Rolling Stone Tombs.** In Matthew 28:2 the narrative indicates "an angel...descended from heaven" to the tomb of Jesus, "rolled back the stone and sat upon it." John McRay notes that "many tombs from the time of Christ have been discovered in Jerusalem, and some of them still have these rolling stones by their entrances."[13]

- **The Yehohanan Ossuary.** A "first-century AD ossified heel bone with Roman crucifixion nail, belonging to a crucifixion victim identified as Yehohanan ben Hagkol" was discovered that fits descriptions of Jesus' crucifixion in Matthew 27; Mark 15; Luke 23; and John 19.[14]

- **The John Rylands Papyrus.** The earliest known manuscript fragment of the New Testament (ca. AD 117–135), it contains a portion of John 18 in Greek.

- **Tyrannus Inscription.** This name was carved into a pillar in Ephesus, which fits with Paul's visit there in Acts 19:9.[15]

- **Pool of Bethesda.** Excavated in the 1800s, the pool mentioned in John 5:2–3 where the sick and lame would wait for the stirring for the waters was discovered.[16]

As exciting as this is, there is much more that still awaits discovery, "Of the nearly 5,500 sites in Israel that are candidates for excavation, only a few hundred have been excavated."[17] The bottom line is that you can be confident that the biblical text is historically reliable.

APPENDIX 3
WHY A NEW GENERATION DOESN'T
TAKE THE BIBLE SERIOUSLY

The Bible claims to have answers to the questions that matter. Moreover, the creator God described in its pages would have the authority to answer such questions because this is his universe after all—*if the Bible is true.* But for a growing number of teenagers and twentysomethings today, that's a pretty big "if." The largest generation in American history is having a hard time taking the Bible seriously. (The "millennial" generation consists of the seventy-eight million people born between 1980 and 2000.)

Danielle, from Colorado Springs, candidly offers a common millennial perspective on the Bible, "I think the Bible has a lot to offer. . . . But I don't think that we can say that it is some kind of magical book that has all truth in it. I have read some parts of it before, but it's really not something I'm super interested in."[1]

In David Kinnaman's provocative book *You Lost Me: Why Young Christians Are Leaving Church . . . And Rethinking Faith,* he summarizes the Barna Group's research this way:

> The Bible's influence on this next generation is up in the air . . . when we examine the generation as a whole, we see challenges. Young people are skeptical about the reliability of the original biblical manuscripts; they tend to read the Bible through a lens of pluralism . . . and they seem less likely than previous generations to believe the Scriptures have a claim on human obedience.[2]

Thom Rainer's research found that only one-fourth of millennials "agrees strongly that the Bible is the written Word of God and is totally accurate in all that it teaches."[3] And the Pew Forum on Religion & Public Life's report on Religion Among the Millennials indicates that self-describing evangelical Christians of this generation are *less likely* to see the Bible as the literal word of God than their parents' generation.[4]

The implications of this research are clear. The Bible may be special and have sentimental value, but it is no longer considered unique, authoritative, and true. Why is this happening? Why the loss of confidence in the reliability, authority, and relevance of the Bible?

Our Culture's Perfect Storm

A perfect storm arises when a rare combination of adverse and unpredictable meteorological factors converge. Individually, each factor can be dangerous. But when they happen at the same time and in the same location, the effects are often devastating. When it comes to a new generation's confidence in the Bible as God's Word, I think we are facing a perfect storm. There was a time when "The Bible says . . . " carried significant authority in decision-making or personal conversation; that's no longer the case. I want to suggest three key factors that taken by themselves tend to erode confidence in the Bible, but could be catastrophic if they converge in a given culture at a particular moment in history.

1. The Growing Secularization of American Culture

A fundamental shift has occurred in the way we approach life today; we have moved from a *thinking* culture to a *feeling* culture. Our culture has largely divorced the spiritual from the rational. This is the essence of secularism. According to the secular mindset, belief in God is regarded as nonsense and the rational equivalent of fairy tales for grown-ups. If the secularist were to draft a list of first principles, the belief that "you can't know something unless you prove it scientifically" would top the list. Today, the New Atheism attacks Christianity as ridiculous, irrational, false, and dangerous.[5]

Unfortunately, spirituality is now largely understood as being experiential, emotional, and private. It is not publicly accessible and therefore not able to be critiqued by argument or investigated rationally. The word *faith* has become the nebulous placeholder for this attitude. Once this move has been made, the *individual* becomes the sole arbiter of this private truth.

Every civilization has longed for a sense of the divine or transcendent, and ours is no different. But today, a new sociological category has emerged—*spiritual but not religious*. (Interestingly, 72 percent of eighteen to twenty-nine-year-olds identify themselves in this way.)[6] In the wake of the New Atheism, a New Spirituality comes along and tries to salvage the transcendent, even though the rational has been discarded. In contrast to this trend, Christianity stands apart because it unifies the rational *and* the experiential by grounding personal religious experience in knowable history and objective truth.

2. The Strong Anti-Institutional Attitude among Those under Age Thirty-Five.

In *The Millennials: Connecting to America's Largest Generation*, Thom and Jess Rainer reveal that 70 percent of this generation has an anti-institutional view of the church.[7] Here are the reasons they cited. First, they have "witnessed the seemingly never-ending moral failure of pastors and priests." This has disgusted all of us, but it has really turned off the millennials. With our twenty-four-hour news cycle, these stories fill slow news days, providing constant reminders of the church's fallen leaders. Second, "they perceive most churches . . . as inwardly focused, not serving either the world or their communities." This is an activist generation not content with just talking about problems—they want to do something about them.

That is why organizations like Charity Water (whose volunteers dig wells for people in developing countries lacking clean drinking water) are so popular among millennials. Finally, and "probably more than any other factor, they perceive the churches and their leaders to be negative and argumentative."[8] The institutional church is perceived to be judgmental, against everything, and exclusive. This generation is inclusive and values authenticity and dialogue. The last thing the average millennial wants is a corrupt, hypocritical institution that is inwardly focused and often negative telling them what the spiritual life is all about or should be.

To these three sobering observations, I would add a fourth underlying issue regarding the church being perceived as an institution. An insti-tutional mindset limits personal freedom and autonomy. And since our culture's highest value is personal freedom, there is a growing aversion to anything traditional because it has come to be associated with insti-tutions that try to tell you what to do, what to believe, and how to live.

This is where Christianity enters the picture. The Bible—the icon and sourcebook of institutional Christianity—is often perceived to just be a long list of rules that limit freedom, discourage freethinking, and make people feel guilty. Whether this is completely accurate is beside the point, because most millennials have embraced this perception of Christianity and the Bible, and this assumption is operating in the background when the questions regarding the Bible and authority are raised.

3. *The Sophisticated Attacks on the Bible's Origin, Credibility, and Reliability.*

Anti-Science, repressive to women, culturally outdated, morally repulsive, historically inaccurate . . . the reliability and credibility of the Bible is increasingly under attack. But the challenges are now more sophis-ticated than ever and coming on multiple fronts: traditional media, new media, and the classroom. First, consider the traditional media: includes TV, movies, books, and magazines (the final two both in print and online). Whether it's *The Daily Show* (with sardonic host Jon Stewart) or the latest issue of *Time*, the Bible is rarely portrayed in a positive light. The shows and articles are either an outright mockery of biblical teachings or an opportunity to suggest that "the hidden truth" has been kept from all of us for two thousand years! And, there is no shortage of TV specials cropping up every Christmas and Easter to feed our culture's insatiable appetite for a good conspiracy theory.

Challenges come from the publishing world as well. We have cited throughout one key example. Bart Ehrman's *Misquoting Jesus: The Story Behind Who Changed the Bible and Why* (a book on textual criticism!) became a *New York Times* bestseller. As noted in chapter 6, one of his controversial claims is, "We could go on nearly forever talking about specific places in which the texts of the New Testament came to be changed, either accidentally or intentionally. . . . The examples are not just in the hundreds but in the thousands . . . "[9] Unfortunately, Ehrman offers a rather alarmist portrait of New Testament studies. Moreover, he is a capable writer who employs powerful rhetoric that resonates with our "feeling culture." His *modus operandi* is to popularize discussions that have been known about in scholarship for decades and then serve them up for a generally skeptical, increasingly secular, anti-institutional, and biblically illiterate culture.

Second, the new media have become a cultural game-changer. This generation has unprecedented access to a mind-blowing amount of information. The new reality is that young people are far more likely to consult the Internet than their pastor when it comes to questions about the Bible and Christianity. However, there are a couple of inherent concerns to be highlighted about the online world. First, skeptical videos and blog posts that challenge the very foundations of historic Christianity can go viral on Facebook and YouTube reaching millions in just days. One implication of this is that a thirteen-year-old may now need to process emotionally powerful challenges to what her family and church believes, now sent to her ("shared") by a peer on her Facebook page. Sadly, most have not been informed that credible responses exist or trained how to engage these questions with wise discernment.

Another challenge that the online medium presents is personalization.[10] One of the misperceptions about the Internet is that it naturally presents the opportunity to hear other points of view. This is simply false. For example, when you do a Google search for "reliability of the Bible" you are not accessing the same "objective" Internet everyone else is. Times have changed in that the old gatekeepers of information used to be humans who limited access to traditional media outlets (e.g., ABC, NBC, CBS, the *New York Times*, etc.). But the new gatekeepers of today are invisible algorithms that literally edit your web experience in real time. Here's why this matters. If you tend to search more skeptical or liberal sites, the algorithm "learns" this about you and then begins to sort your relevance of search results based on your tendencies. This means other credible viewpoints/evidence are very unlikely to be engaged because they will show up at the bottom of your relevance list while sites skeptical of the Bible will show up first. Every web user now has a unique filter bubble.[11] The problem is that they don't see what has been edited out of their news feed or search.

This new reality can be overcome, but not without awareness and intentionality. All information is not created equal and every source on the web is not necessarily an authority that has earned the right to be heard.

The final challenge to the Bible comes from the classroom. A study conducted by Harvard University and George Mason University professors found that 52 percent of college professors regard the Bible as "an ancient book of fables, legends, history, and moral precepts." This number increased to 73 percent when professors at elite universities were surveyed. Moreover, the percentage of atheist and agnostic professors in America is three times greater than that of the general population (with numbers higher in fields such as biology and psychology).[12]

There are certainly exceptions, but by and large college is not "Christian friendly" and students are not being presented with unbiased information and then allowed to draw their own conclusions. This doesn't mean Christians should avoid challenging environments (far from it!), but we do need to proceed with eyes wide open.

Preparing Teens and Twentysomethings for the Ongoing Challenges

To sum up, it is highly unlikely that teenagers and twentysomethings living through the digital revolution can come of age in a perfect storm like this *without* encountering tough challenges and questions about the Bible.

Is the church ready to engage these factors? Are youth groups talking about any of this? Are parents aware of these objections and able to provide thoughtful answers? Is the next generation being prepared for the questions they will face?

ABOUT THE AUTHOR

Jonathan Morrow is the director of creative strategies for Impact 360 Institute (impact360institute.org), where he teaches college students in their gap year program and high school students in their summer immersion experience. He is the founder of Think Christianly (think-christianly.org) and serves as adjunct faculty with Union University.

Jonathan is the author of several books, including *Welcome to College: A Christ-follower's Guide for the Journey* and *Think Christianly: Looking at the Intersection of Faith and Culture*. He is also the coauthor with Sean McDowell of *Is God Just a Human Invention? And Seventeen Other Questions Raised by the New Atheists*. He has contributed several articles to the *Apologetics Study Bible for Students* and has written for *Leadership Journal Online* of *Christianity Today*.

He has received the MDiv and an MA in philosophy of religion and ethics from Talbot School of Theology of Biola University. After serving as the equipping pastor for six years at Fellowship Bible Church in Murfreesboro, Tennessee, Jonathan completed a DMin. in engaging mind and culture from Talbot School of Theology.

Jonathan speaks nationally on issues of worldview, apologetics, and culture and is passionate about seeing a new generation of Christ-followers understand what they believe, why they believe it, and why it matters in life. His books have been featured on shows like *Family Life Today*, *Stand to Reason*, *Breakpoint*, *WAY-FM*, the *Janet Mefferd Show*, and *Apologetics 315*. He and his wife, Mandi, have three children. You can follow him on twitter @JonathanMorrow and visit him online at thinkchristianly.org.

Note about the Author

Jonathan Morrow (D.Min.) serves as Director of Creative Strategies for Impact 360 Institute in Pine Mountain, GA where he teaches students in the worldview and leadership experiences described below.

KNOW. BE. LIVE.

E verything at Impact 360 Institute flows from the core belief that all Christians should know why they believe, be transformed, and live God's true story together. Know. Be. Live. is the foundation of the 2-week summer Immersion experience for High School students, the 9-month academic Gap Year experience for 18-20 year olds, the residential Masters experience for graduate students, and online equipping resources.

Equipping Christ-centered Influencers

Impact 360 Institute
Speaker Series

Impact 360 Gap Year
Experience

Impact 360 Immersion
Experience

Impact 360 Masters
Experience

FIND OUT MORE INFORMATION
ON OUR WEBSITE:

impact360institute.org